Live Long,
Finish Strong

Live Long, Finish Strong

The Divine Secret to Living Healthy, Happy, and Healed

Gloria Copeland

FaithWords

New York Boston Nashville

FaithWords
Hachette Book Group
237 Park Avenue
New York, NY 10017

www.faithwords.com

Unless otherwise noted, Scripture quotations are from the King James Version of the Holy Bible; Scripture quotations noted AMP are from *The Amplified Bible*, Old Testament. Copyright © 1965, 1987, by the Zondervan Corporation. Used by permission. All rights reserved; and from *The Amplified Bible*, New Testament. Copyright © 1954, 1958, 1987, by The Lockman Foundation. Used by permission; Scripture quotations noted NASB are from the New American Standard Bible®. Copyright © 1960, 1962, 1963, 1968, 1971, 1972, 1973, 1975, 1977, 1995 by The Lockman Foundation. Used by permission; Scripture quotations noted NIV are from the New International Version®. Copyright © 1973, 1978, 1984 by International Bible Society. Used by permission of Zondervan Publishing House. All rights reserved; Scripture quotations noted NKJV are from the New King James Version. Copyright © 1982 by Thomas Nelson, Inc. Used by permission. All rights reserved; Scripture quotations noted NLT are from the *Holy Bible*, New Living Translation, copyright © 1996. Used by permission of Tyndale House Publishers, Inc., Wheaton, Illinois 60189. All rights reserved; Scripture quotations noted TLB are from *The Living Bible*, copyright © 1971. Used by permission of Tyndale House Publishers, Inc., Wheaton, Illinois 60189. All rights reserved.

Printed in the United States of America

Originally published in hardcover by FaithWords.

First Trade Edition: May 2011
10 9 8 7 6 5 4 3 2 1

FaithWords is a division of Hachette Book Group, Inc.
The FaithWords name and logo are trademarks of Hachette Book Group, Inc.

The publisher is not responsible for websites (or their content) that are not owned by the publisher.

The Library of Congress has cataloged the hardcover edition as follows:
Copeland, Gloria.
    Live long, finish strong : the divine secret to living healthy, happy, and healed / Gloria Copeland. —1st ed.
        p. cm.
    ISBN 978-0-446-55928-7
    1. Christian life. 2. Aging—Religious aspects—Christianity. 3. Older Christians—Religious life. I. Title.
    BV4501.3.C6697 2010
    248.8'5—dc22

                                                        2009024806

ISBN 978-0-446-55927-0 (pbk.)

To Kenneth

Thank you for teaching me and living out this long and wonderful life with me.

Thank You, Jesus, for teaching us the absolute authority of the Word of God.

Jesus is Lord!

Contents

Acknowledgments

Thank you, Keith Moore, for your teaching on longevity. (I recommend Pastor Keith Moore's teaching on long life. You can find him and Moore Life Ministries on the Web.)

Thank you, Gina Lynnes, for helping me get this message on long and strong life into book form.

Thank you, Leah Lee, for all the editorial help and wisdom you have imparted.

Jesus is Lord!

Live Long,
Finish Strong

CHAPTER I

How Old Is Old?

How would you respond if a divine messenger showed up at your house today and promised you a long and blessed life? What would you say if a prophet, a minister, or an angel of God looked you squarely in the eye and said:

Your days will be long on the earth. Your days will be strong on the earth. If the Lord tarries His coming, you will live in length of days and strength of days.

Some years ago, that's exactly what happened to my husband, Kenneth. A dear friend of ours, an established minister who was visiting our home, spoke those words to him by the Spirit of God. Because we've learned some things about how to receive God's promises by faith, we knew just how to respond.

We said, "We receive it! We believe it!" We rejoiced!

That's a message anyone would like to receive. It's a powerful and encouraging message.

Best of all, you don't have to wait for a prophet or for some special message to come to you because this message is already confirmed in the Bible. It's God's promise to you. In recent years, I've spent many hours studying what the Word of God has to say about longevity and have seen for myself that the promise of a long, strong life isn't reserved for just a few special people. It's not meant for a select number of people who are divinely ordained to live to a ripe old age.

The promise of a long and blessed life belongs to every obedient child of God.

If you are a believer, it belongs to you.

God doesn't have to send an angel or a prophet to deliver that promise to you. All you have to do is open your Bible to find a multitude of verses that tell you God wants you to live a long, long time. As you read them, they will say to you much the same thing the Lord said to Kenneth:

It's My will for your days to be long upon the earth. It's My desire for your days to be strong upon the earth. If Jesus tarries His coming, My plan is for you to live in length of days and strength of days.

How you respond to that message will make all the difference. If you shake your head in disbelief and only wish it were true, it won't have much effect. If you respond in faith and say, "I receive it! I believe it!" it can revolutionize your life.

But, as most of us have discovered at some time in our lives, that kind of faith response isn't always automatic. It must be cultivated and developed on purpose.

How do we do that? By studying and meditating on what God has to say about this issue. For as Romans 10:17 tells us, "Faith cometh by hearing, and hearing by the word of God."

The pages you are about to read are full of that Word. They are packed with scriptural promises that will help you build your faith for longevity. They are sprinkled with inspiring examples, both from the Bible and from the lives of ordinary people who lived long after the Bible was written, that will encourage you to reexamine your answer to the question: *How old is old?*

Even more important, you'll discover some vital scriptural secrets that can help you extend your years decades beyond what you may have thought possible. You'll learn how, by living God's way, you can live such a strong, satisfying life that you won't want to leave this earth until you are old—really, really old. And not just *old* according to the world's way of thinking, but *old* according to God's way of thinking. *Bible old!*

How Old Is "Bible Old"?

Bible old is much older than most of us think it is. It's older than medical science says it is. And it's far older than the way it used to be portrayed in the movies a generation ago.

That realization hit me a few years ago while I was watching an old John Wayne western that included a scene where a white-haired, bun-wearing old lady was celebrating her birthday. To me, the woman looked at least eighty years old. Imagine my shock when they announced she was sixty!

Whoa! I thought with great gratitude. *We've come a long way since that movie was made. Sixty looks a lot better these days.*

According to recent statistics, sixty doesn't just *look* better these days, it *is* better. In 1960, the year I graduated from high school, the average life expectancy in this nation was only 69.7 years.[1] These days, the average life expectancy has increased to 77.8 years.[2] So, even from a natural perspective, old today is at least seven years older than it was forty years ago.

If we answer the question *How old is old?* with those statistics, we might conclude that seventy-eight qualifies as old in our generation. Many Christians believe even the Bible backs up that idea.

But are they right?

The devil would certainly like for us to think so. He's worked overtime to convince believers that when they celebrate their seventieth or eightieth birthday, they should start preparing to check out of earth and into heaven. But he has had to twist the Scriptures to sell us that deceptive bill of goods, because nowhere in the Bible do we find the average life span of God's obedient people to be a mere seven or eight decades.

In fact, from a biblical perspective, eighty isn't old at all. A number of famous saints, including Abraham and Moses, were just starting to fulfill the call of God on their lives at that age. In God's eyes, an octogenarian is just a "spring chicken."

If you doubt it, study the first few chapters of Genesis. There we see that God designed Adam's and Eve's natural bodies to live not just seventy or eighty years, but *forever*! Even after they sinned and death entered the picture, their life spans were astonishing—as were their children's, and their grandchildren's, and their great-grandchildren's. Consider this:

- According to Genesis 5, Adam lived 930 years.

- His son Seth lived 912 years.

- His grandson Enos lived 905 years.

- His great-grandson Cainan lived 910 years.

- His great-great-grandson Mahalalel lived 895 years. (He died a little younger than the others. Maybe he had some bad habits!)

- Mahalalel's son Jared lived 962 years.

- Jared's son Enoch never died at all. He walked so closely with God that he was caught up to heaven at the tender age of 365.

- Enoch's son Methuselah won the old age award by living 969 years.

- Excluding Enoch, those people had an average earth life span of more than 926 years.

They lived almost a millennium. Think of it! For us today, that's like living from 1009 to 2009. In 1009, the Vikings were still roaming around, raiding villages. The world was in the throes of the Middle Ages. Can you imagine living from then until now?

That puts the concept of biblical longevity in a whole new light!

Living Long in Dangerous Times

"But Gloria, that was before the Great Flood," someone might say. "Conditions on the earth were much better back then. It was easier to live a long time."

Not really. According to the Bible, the years before the Flood were the most violent years this earth has ever seen. Genesis 6 says during that era, as men began to multiply on the face of the earth,

> God saw that the wickedness of man was great in the earth, and that every imagination of the thoughts of his heart was only evil continually. And it repented the LORD that he had made man on the earth, and it grieved him at his heart. And the LORD said, I will destroy man whom I have created from the face of the earth; both man, and beast, and the creeping thing, and the fowls of the air; for it repenteth me that I have made them. . . . The earth also was corrupt before God, and the earth was filled with violence. And God looked upon the earth, and, behold, it was corrupt; for all flesh had corrupted his way upon the earth. And God said unto Noah, The end of all flesh is come before me; for the earth is filled with violence through them; and, behold, I will destroy them with the earth. Make thee an ark. (VERSES 5–7, 11–14)

We think we live in dangerous times today, but the years just before the Flood beat anything we've ever seen. People were so wicked, they didn't have any good thoughts. They were plotting evil all the time. Even so, God, in His great mercy and patience, put up

with them as long as He could. Jewish sages tell us that one reason Methuselah lived so long was because his name meant "When
he dies, judgment will come."[3] That's exactly what happened. The
Flood came the year Methuselah died.

What a wonderful testimony to God's mercy! It endures a long,
long time.

God is so merciful, He refused to send the Flood until the last
possible moment. He waited until there was only one God-fearing
family left on the earth that He could depend on. He postponed
judgment until just one man, Noah, stood between the annihilation
of the human race and future generations.

I'm telling you, Noah lived in a dangerous era!

That ought to encourage us today because we're living again in
a time where violence is rampant in the world. Wickedness is again
increasing. As a result, a certain amount of judgment is going to
come. Many people who are committed to sin and refuse to repent
and honor God will die early. They'll fall prey to disease or catastrophe. Romans 6:23 says the wages of sin is death, and for those who
work hard at sinning, payday comes too early. But we, as believers,
are like Noah. We've found grace in the eyes of the Lord (Genesis
6:8), and we have been forgiven and cleansed of sin by our faith in
the blood of Jesus. We have an ark—a covenant with God—through
His Word, that will protect us from suffering the effects of sin that
are coming on the world.

Of course, for us to enjoy that protection and the long life that
comes with it, we must build our ark by faith in God's promises and
stay there by obeying His Word. We're not going to live long just
because we're born again, although that certainly helps. The new
nature we received when we were saved will empower us to know
and do what's right. But to receive the full benefits of our salvation,
we must walk with the Lord and obey His commandments.

If we ignore the instructions in the Bible, our consciences, and
the promptings of our spirits and give ourselves over to the evils of
the world—born again or not—we'll get caught up in those evils

after a while. If we put our eyes and ears in places they don't belong, we'll be pulled off into sin. If we feed on television programs and movies full of adultery and fornication, we could end up wandering away from the ark of God's protection and living like sinners, even though in our hearts we don't want to.

No one thinks that will happen to them. Most Christians, when they're first tempted to compromise their standards, say to themselves, *Hey, I know I shouldn't watch this stuff. I shouldn't go to those places or associate with those people, but I'm a Christian. It's not going to affect me.*

We'll look at that in more depth later, but I'll warn you right now, that's what every Christian thought who ever fell prey to adultery or some other sin that wrecked his life. He didn't think he could ever do such a thing. But because he looked at, listened to, and thought about things he knew were evil, he eventually did them. He let that ugly stuff stir up the lusts of his flesh, and then he shocked himself and everyone else by acting on it.

Don't let that happen to you. If you haven't already, make a quality decision today to sell out to God and get your spiritual house clean. Get rid of sin, straighten up your life, and set your mind on the Lord. Feed on the Word of God until that's the biggest thing in your life. Put God first and love Him with all your heart, soul, and might.

If you'll do that, He will keep you in perfect peace no matter what's happening in the world. Isaiah 26:3 says, "Thou wilt keep him in perfect peace, whose mind is stayed on thee: because he trusteth in thee." He'll keep you in the center of His plan for your life if you will listen and obey. And in dangerous times like these, that's the safest place on earth to be.

Ask Noah. He can confirm it. When the Flood came, there was only one safe place on the planet, and God made sure Noah and his family were in it. As a result, they were protected from the violence around them and the judgment of sin. In a day when everyone else was dying, they not only survived, they went on to live a long, long time.

Post-Flood Longevity Heroes

Even before the rain began to fall, Noah had already attained what we could consider an impossibly old age. He was six hundred years old the "day all the fountains of the great deep were broken up, and the windows of heaven were opened" (Genesis 7:11 NKJV).

Six hundred years is a long time to live. Considering the conditions Noah faced during those years, and the strenuous labor involved in building the ark, it would have been no surprise had Noah died a few years after the Flood. But he didn't. The Bible tells us that "Noah lived after the flood three hundred and fifty years. And all the days of Noah were nine hundred and fifty years: and he died" (Genesis 9:28–29).

Some of Noah's descendants weren't quite as hardy as he was, however. His son Shem, for example, lived only six hundred years. His grandson Arphaxad passed on at the early age of 438, and his great-grandson Salah died at 433 (Genesis 11:10–15). As you can see, people's faith for longevity was beginning to slip by then, and creation scientists believe conditions on the earth after the Flood were not what they had been before the Flood.

Even so, God's people continued to enjoy such extended lives that patriarchs born centuries apart lived at the same time. According to Jewish historians, Noah's father (Lamech), for instance, knew Adam. And Noah, who was born 1,056 years after the time of Creation, knew Abraham, who was born 1,948 years after Creation. In fact, Abraham was fifty-eight years old when Noah died.[4]

Talk about good examples of longevity! These people lived so many years that the oral tradition about what happened at Creation was passed down from Adam through only seven people until the time it was written down by Moses, who received it on Mount Sinai directly from God.

Job, too, who is believed to have lived during the same era Abraham did, enjoyed a life span that would shock us today. Although Job's friends are famous for criticizing and speaking wrong things about him, one thing they said of him came true: "Thou shalt come to thy grave in a full age, like as a shock of corn cometh in in his season" (Job 5:26).

Job's longevity is especially impressive because, as everyone knows, he had to survive some dangerous times. The devil came after him with a vengeance. He put Job through a terrible time of troubles that lasted somewhere between nine months and a year.

During that time, Job's wife told him to curse God and die. In so doing, she sided with the devil. That's just what the devil wanted. Satan told God that if Job suffered loss, Job would curse God to His face. (Wives, we don't want to follow Mrs. Job's example. When our husbands are having a hard time, we don't want to join up with the devil and discourage them further. We want to join with God and encourage them.)

Thank heaven, Job didn't heed his wife's advice! When trouble came, he stayed with the program. He refused to dishonor God, and he refused to give up and die.

As a result, he not only made it through, but "the LORD turned the captivity of Job, when he prayed for his friends: also the LORD gave Job twice as much as he had before....After this lived Job an hundred and forty years, and saw his sons, and his sons' sons, even four generations. So Job died, being old and full of days" (Job 42:10, 16–17).

The Bible doesn't tell us how old Job was before his trouble started, but historians estimate he was at least sixty years old. That means Job lived to be about two hundred...and the last 140 years turned out to be even more enjoyable for him than the early part of his life. He ended up richer than ever (which is remarkable since he started out as the richest man in the East). He had a whole houseful of beautiful children and lived to see his great-great-grandchildren.

Not bad for a man most people refer to as "poor old Job."

Back to the Garden of God's Goodness

What does all that have to do with us?

We're descendants of these people!

Every one of us can trace our ancestry back to Noah. We're of the same species. We come from this same family of people who lived two hundred, four hundred, five hundred, six hundred, and even nine hundred–plus years.

So when the devil tries to convince us that seventy or eighty is old, we ought to laugh in his face. "No, Methuselah was old," we should say. "Noah was old. I won't be old for a long, long time!"

"But what if God's will for those people is different from His will for us?" you might ask. "Can we really be sure God wants all of us to live long lives?"

Yes, we can, because, as I've already mentioned, God has spelled out His will in His written Word. He has revealed to us, through the Bible, that from the very beginning His desire for humankind was not just long life, but *eternal* life.

God never wanted any of His children to die. His plan was for them to live in His goodness and blessing forever. He wanted things to be well with them. He wanted them to enjoy a life without stress or strain in an environment full of everything good. His plan was and still is the *Blessing Plan*.

The account of Creation in Genesis 1 tells us exactly what that good environment included. It says:

- God created light and saw that it was good.

- He divided the land from the waters and saw that it was good.

- He made the earth bring forth plant life and animal life and marine life and saw that it was good.

- He created humankind, blessed them, gave them dominion, and when He was finished, God stepped back, looked one more time at everything He had made, "and, behold, it was very good." (Genesis 1:31)

> He put Adam and Eve in a garden of that goodness and gave them
> one command. He said, "Of the tree of the knowledge of good and
> evil, thou shalt not eat of it: for in the day that thou eatest thereof
> thou shalt surely die." (Genesis 2:17)

Some claim death is natural. They say it's just a part of God's
good creation and we should embrace it. But the Bible presents a different picture. It tells us that death was not a part of God's original
design. It was not included in His perfect will. In fact, He specifically commanded Adam and Eve *not* to open the door to it.

But Adam and Eve disobeyed. They bowed the knee to Satan
by succumbing to his temptation. Through their sin, they intro-
duced death—the foul offspring of the devil—into God's beautiful
world.

Had the story ended there, there would be no reason for this book.
We would all be helpless victims just waiting for death to overtake
us. But thank God, the story doesn't end there. Before Satan could
slither out of the Garden of Eden after the Fall, God warned him
that death's days were numbered. He foretold the coming of Jesus
and said to the devil:

> Because thou hast done this, thou art cursed above all cattle, and
> above every beast of the field; upon thy belly shalt thou go, and dust
> shalt thou eat all the days of thy life: And I will put enmity between
> thee and the woman, and between thy seed and her seed; it shall
> bruise thy head, and thou shalt bruise his heel. (GENESIS 3:14–15)

As we all know, Jesus came to earth and fulfilled that promise
two thousand years ago. Through His life, death, and resurrection,
He defeated Satan and paid the price for the sin of all humankind.
He was made "sin for us, who knew no sin; that we might be made the
righteousness of God in him" (2 Corinthians 5:21).

Through Jesus, God has set every believer back into the garden
of His goodness. He has made available to us exceedingly great and

precious promises that are divinely designed to help us escape the corruption that is in the world through sin (2 Peter 1:4). Many of those promises offer us long, strong, and blessed lives. They teach us how we can live to a ripe old age.

Again and again, God makes His will and His ways clear to us through Scriptures like these:

- You must serve only the LORD your God. If you do, I will bless you with food and water, and I will keep you healthy. There will be no miscarriages or infertility among your people, and *I will give you long, full lives.* (Exodus 23:25–26 NLT, italics added)

- Know therefore this day, and consider it in thine heart, that the LORD he is God in heaven above, and upon the earth beneath: there is none else. Thou shalt keep therefore his statutes, and his commandments, which I command thee this day, that it may go well with thee, and with thy children after thee, and *that thou mayest prolong thy days* upon the earth, which the LORD thy God giveth thee, for ever. (Deuteronomy 4:39–40, italics added)

- Fear the LORD thy God, to keep all his statutes and his commandments, which I command thee, thou, and thy son, and thy son's son, all the days of thy life; and that thy days may be prolonged. (Deuteronomy 6:2)

- He that dwelleth in the secret place of the most High shall abide under the shadow of the Almighty. . . . *With long life will I satisfy him,* and show him my salvation. (Psalm 91:1, 16, italics added)

- [Wisdom] is more precious than rubies: and all the things thou canst desire are not to be compared unto her. *Length of days is in her right hand;* and in her left hand riches and honour. (Proverbs 3:15–16, italics added)

❀ Hear, O my son, and receive my sayings; and *the years of thy life shall be many.* I have taught thee in the way of wisdom; I have led thee in right paths. (Proverbs 4:10–11, italics added)

❀ *The fear of the LORD prolongeth days:* but the years of the wicked shall be shortened. (Proverbs 10:27, italics added)

❀ Even to your old age I am he; and even to hoar hairs will I carry you: I have made, and I will bear; even I will carry, and will deliver you. (Isaiah 46:4)

❀ Honour thy father and mother; which is the first commandment with promise; that it may be well with thee, and thou *mayest live long on the earth.* (Ephesians 6:2–3, italics added)

Since the New Testament guarantees all the promises of God in Jesus are "Yes, and in Him Amen" (2 Corinthians 1:20 NKJV), when we read those verses, we should agree with them. We should say, "Yes, Lord! I'll obey those instructions. I receive those promises. I believe I'll have a long, strong enjoyable life."

Years of a Life Worth Living

Notice I didn't say we should just believe for a long life. I said we should expect good years, years we can enjoy, because that's what the Bible offers us. It says if we keep God's commandments in our hearts and obey them, we'll have "length of days and years of a life [worth living] and tranquility [inward and outward and continuing through old age till death]" (Proverbs 3:2 AMP).

Some Christians haven't experienced that kind of inward and outward tranquillity, so they don't want to live a long time. They're not happy. Things aren't going well for them. Their lives are riddled with misery, and heaven looks like the only escape.

But those folks are missing out on God's plan. His plan includes many years of a life *worth living*. He has a divine design for us that will give us not just quantity of life but *quality* of life while we are on the earth. He wants our lives to be satisfying (Psalm 91:16).

It doesn't matter how spiritual you are, it's hard to be satisfied when you don't have the money you need to take care of your children. It's hard to be satisfied when your body is sick, your family is in a mess, and the bill collector is knocking at the door.

Life is just more enjoyable when your needs are met and you have a nice home; when you don't have to crowd six children into a two-bedroom house. It's more fun when you're strong and healthy, when your relatives are all saved and loving one another, when you have peace on the inside as well as on the outside.

Psalm 91 says that's the kind of life God desires for us. It also tells us that to have that kind of life, we must dwell in the secret place of the Most High and abide under the shadow of the Almighty (verse 1).

Exactly what is involved in dwelling and abiding in God?

To abide in God means we stay attached to Him. We take up residence in Him and in His Word. We're not living for God one day and living for the devil the next. We live for God every day. When we do sin or stumble out of His will, we repent and get right back on the path of righteousness.

God can do great things for an abider. He can work wonders for the person who will stick with Him, as Job did, in good times and bad. That kind of person opens the door for God to fulfill the promise in Psalm 91:14: "Because he has set his love upon Me, therefore I will deliver him; I will set him on high, because he knows and understands My name [has a personal knowledge of My mercy, love, and kindness—trusts and relies on Me, knowing I will never forsake him, no never]" (AMP).

Those verses reveal another key to abiding in the secret place of the Most High. They tell us that the abider has faith in God and His Word. He isn't stressed out in fear and worry about what the future will bring. He isn't focusing on what the devil happens to be saying at the moment, or what the economy is doing, or what the doctor's report contains. He is trusting God's promises. He is praying in faith and calling on the Lord with confidence.

God leaves no doubt about how He will respond to that kind of person. He says, "I will answer him; I will be with him in trouble, I will deliver him and honor him. With long life will I satisfy him and show him my salvation" (verses 15–16 AMP).

When God tells us He'll be with us in trouble, that covers a lot of territory. It covers sickness, disease, accidents, storms, lack, poverty, children getting off course, husbands becoming difficult, wives becoming difficult. Without God's help and deliverance, those things can steal the joy from life. They can make us wish for an early entrance to heaven. But God promises the abider that He will deliver him from those things and satisfy him with long life.

The word *satisfy* means "to have enough of, to fill up, to have plenty."[5] To be satisfied is to have your desires fully gratified, to be made content.

If you're not satisfied in life, keep growing in the Lord until the things that dissatisfy you get taken care of and you're fully gratified. You can't be satisfied if your child isn't in the kingdom of God. You can't be satisfied if he is on drugs and headed for hell. It doesn't matter how old you are right now, don't leave this earth with your children unsaved. Stick around; keep praying and believing God for them until they're born again and living for Jesus.

If you're not satisfied in your occupation, you may not have found the job God has for you yet. So keep seeking God. Keep believing and obeying His Word until He maneuvers you into the right position.

"But I've been working this job for twenty years!"

That may be so, but if you're dissatisfied, something is wrong. A self-adjustment needs to be made either on the inside or on the outside. If you don't make that adjustment and instead stay in a place of dissatisfaction, you'll get weary of life on earth. You'll develop a premature longing to go to heaven. You'll be tempted to give up on this life and go on to the next too early.

Don't do that!

Live until your needs are met, your family's needs are met, and you're satisfied. Live until nothing of vital importance to you is lacking in your life. Live until you're at peace.

The Hebrew word for peace, *shalom*, means "nothing missing, nothing broken."[6] It means fullness and wholeness in every area of life. So set your sights on *shalom*. Be determined to stay here on earth until you can look around you and say, "Praise the Lord! There is nothing missing and nothing broken. I am full and whole—spirit, soul, and body."

Finish your life in victory as a testimony to other people. Buy up all the time you can here on earth so you can give maximum glory to God.

After all, you have an opportunity to serve Him during your life on earth that you'll never have again. Here you have a choice between good and evil. You can decide to either obey God and give Him honor or yield to the devil and give him honor. In heaven, you won't have that choice—there's only good. In heaven, there's no devil to resist.

Remember, we can't win faith battles for Jesus on the other side of the grave. The good fight of faith takes place here on earth. What's more, we have what it takes to win. We have the power to tell the devil, "No, you're not getting me. I'll not leave this life depressed and dissatisfied. I'll not be unfaithful to God. I'll not walk in darkness just because people around me walk in darkness. I'm going to obey the Lord. I'm going to give God glory in this body for a long, long time!"

So, let's do it. Let's live in victory over the devil, year…after year…after year. Let's get our hearts set on living for God until we're old.

Really old.

Bible old.

Then, when we're fully satisfied, we can leave here and go to heaven.

Or, better yet, maybe we can live until Jesus comes to catch us away. Wouldn't that be fun? We might be in church...or out shopping...or cooking dinner, when all of a sudden, we hear God's trumpet and, in an instant, we're gone! We might just leave the potatoes boiling on the stove, shoot skyward to meet Jesus in the air, and take all our loved ones with us.

What a way to go!

Start Eating from the Tree of Life

"Gloria, do you really believe it's possible to enjoy the kind of longevity our scriptural ancestors did? Do you truly think you'll get 'Bible old'?"

I'm not expecting to give Methuselah any competition, but I have my sights set a lot higher than I once did. After I read and studied what the Bible has to say about it, my perspective on aging has changed in a dramatic way. Eighty years old is looking much younger to me these days.

At the writing of this book I'm in my sixties and can say I feel better now than I did at forty. In fact, I feel more full of life with every passing year. Do you know why? It's because I partake of the tree of life every day.

If you've read the first few chapters of Genesis, you know about that tree. God planted it in the middle of the Garden of Eden. According to Genesis 3:22, if Adam and Eve had eaten of that tree, it would have been a source of everlasting life for them.

They didn't do it...but we can. Because we have access to the Word of God, we have the opportunity to eat every day from the spiritual tree of life described in Proverbs 3:13–18, which says:

> Happy is the man who finds wisdom,
> And the man who gains understanding;
> For her proceeds are better
> than the profits of silver,

And her gain than fine gold.
She is more precious than rubies,
And all the things you may desire
    cannot compare with her.
Length of days is in her right hand,
In her left hand riches and honor.
Her ways are ways of pleasantness,
And all her paths are peace.
She is a tree of life to those who take hold of her,
And happy are all who retain her. (NKJV, italics added)

Though the literal, physical Garden of Eden is long gone, you and I can partake of the tree of life today by attending to the wisdom of God. We can open our Bibles and learn how He thinks and how He does things.

God's written Word is full of His wisdom. As we partake of it—heed, believe, and obey it—that wisdom becomes a wellspring of life to us. It renews our youth like the eagle's (Psalm 103:5). It makes our lives a joy.

If we, as believers, aren't enjoying life, we aren't doing it right. Jesus said, "I came that they may have and enjoy life, and have it in abundance (to the full, till it overflows)" (John 10:10 AMP).

Through the years, I've discovered the more I find out about the Word and the wisdom of God, the more I partake of that tree of life, and the more joyful my life becomes. It gets better every year!

In 1967, when Ken and I first started putting the Word first, our lives weren't nearly as much fun as they are now. We had the joy of the Lord in our hearts, but our circumstances were not enjoyable. We were broke, in debt, making about one hundred dollars a month, and had no natural way to change the situation.

All we knew to do was follow God's pattern in the Garden of Eden and center upon the tree of life. So we did. We fed on the Word every day. We kept that Word in our eyes and ears almost all the time because we knew it was the key to success, prosperity, health, and every other good thing God has to offer.

We didn't just read the Word. We determined to believe and obey it.

Now, forty-three years later, I can tell you that life is far more enjoyable than it used to be. God's goodness surrounds us on every side. We still feed on the Word daily. We have tranquillity within and around us. The longer we live, the more blessed we are. We've proven for ourselves that God's Words "are life to those who find them" (Proverbs 4:22 NKJV).

It's a No-Brainer

Of course, Ken and I could have chosen to live another way. No one forced us to put God's Word first. We could have ignored it. We could have left our Bibles lying unopened on the coffee table and spent all our time watching television, instead of partaking of the tree of life.

God always gives people that choice. He says to everyone what He said to the people of Israel through the words of Moses in Deuteronomy 30:

> See, I have set before you today life and good, death and evil, in that I command you today to love the LORD your God, to walk in His ways, and to keep His commandments, His statutes, and His judgments, that you may live and multiply; and the LORD your God will bless you in the land which you go to possess. But if your heart turns away so that you do not hear, and are drawn away, and worship other gods and serve them, I announce to you today that you shall surely perish; you shall not prolong your days in the land.... I call heaven and earth as witnesses today against you, that I have set before you life and death, blessing and cursing; therefore choose life, that both you and your descendants may live; that you may love the LORD your God, that you may obey His voice,

and that you may cling to Him, for He is your life and the length of your
days. (VERSES 15–20 NKJV)

Moses got straight to the point. To paraphrase, he said, "If you
choose to follow God and His ways, you'll live long and be blessed.
If you don't, your lives will be short and miserable."

You'd think that choice would be a no-brainer. Given the option
of life and blessing or death and disaster, who in his right mind would
choose the latter?

Amazing as it may seem, countless people do.

That's not God's will for them, however. He doesn't want anyone to choose death. He wants us all to choose life. He said it again
and again, "Oh, that they had such a heart in them that they would
fear Me and always keep all My commandments, that it might be
well with them and with their children forever!" (Deuteronomy 5:29
NKJV). Still, because God created us with free wills, the decision is
ours. We can do what we want.

If we're not happy with our lives, we can go for more of the Word
of God. If we have sickness in our bodies or can't pay our bills, we
can open the Bible and renew our minds with God's wisdom. We
can start thinking more the way He thinks so we can act as He acts
and enjoy a greater level of satisfaction and blessing.

If we want to live long, strong lives, we can start partaking of the
tree of life...or choose not to.

God has already done His part. He has made His wisdom available to all of us. He has written down in black and white the Word
that will set us free and prolong our days on the earth.

God's Word will correct and teach us. It will strengthen us.
But if we don't give it any attention or partake of a continual, fresh
supply by getting it into our hearts and expressing it through our
actions, we'll miss out on the wonderful, long lives God has planned
for us.

Don't make that mistake. Choose to center your life around the
Word of God so you can enjoy many years of a life worth living and

grow old—real old! Bible old!—before you depart this earth and go on to heaven.

Choose life!

Start by Choosing Jesus

"But I'm not absolutely sure that I'll be going to heaven when I die," you might say. "I haven't always been a perfect person. I've done some things that were wrong. How can I be sure that heaven is my eternal destination?"

It's simple. All you have to do is put your trust in Jesus. Receive Him as your Savior and the Lord of your life.

Choosing Jesus is the first step in choosing God's wisdom because it's impossible for any of us to obey God's Word without Him. We might desire to obey it, but we can't. Romans 7:18–20 describes the dilemma this way: "To will is present with me; but how to perform that which is good I find not. For the good that I would I do not: but the evil which I would not, that I do. Now if I do that I would not, it is no more I that do it, but sin that dwelleth in me."

Before we're born again, our fallen nature keeps us enslaved to sin. When we receive Jesus' saving grace, however, we are spiritually re-created. We receive a new nature—the very nature of God Himself. Suddenly, we have the inward power to live a life entirely different from the life we lived before. We have the ability to understand and obey the Word of God.

If you've never been born again, don't wait another moment. Pray this prayer from your heart by faith right now:

Lord Jesus, I believe that You are the Son of God who became a man and came to earth to save humankind. I believe You lived a perfect life and died to pay the penalty for my sins. I believe You were crucified, rose again, and are now seated at God's right hand as King of kings and Lord of lords.

I receive You today as the Savior and the Lord of my life. I receive the cleansing power of Your shed blood that frees me from the bondage of sin and the renewing power of the Holy Spirit that makes me a new creation in Christ.

Heavenly Father, thank You for giving me new life. Thank You that I'm born again. Fill me now to overflowing with Your Holy Spirit. From this day forward, begin revealing to me Your perfect will. Teach me through Your Word how to walk and talk with You. Show me how I can give You glory and live a long, strong life in Your service. In Jesus' name I pray. Amen.

Points to Remember

- The promise of a long and blessed life belongs to every child of God. The Bible assures us of it.

- Many of God's Old Testament people lived from two hundred to nine hundred–plus years, and we are their descendants.

- God's will for us is to enjoy length of days and years of life worth living. If we're not enjoying life, we're not doing it right.

- Adam and Eve would have lived forever if they had eaten of the tree of life. As believers we can eat of that tree every day by spending time in the Word of God.

- When we choose Jesus as our Lord and Savior and abide in His Word, we are choosing life.

Scripture

I have set before you life and death, blessing and cursing; therefore choose life, that both you and your descendants may live. (Deuteronomy 30:19 NKJV)

CONFESSION

I receive today God's promise of a long and blessed life. I make a choice to put God's Word first in my life, to spend time in it, obey it, and receive the years of a life worth living and the satisfaction it promises me. I will live in victory over the devil and give God glory on the earth for a long, long time. I choose life!

CHAPTER 2

Set Your Sights on
120 (or More!)

To aim for the kind of long, strong life God promises us in the Bible, the first thing we must do is straighten out our thinking.

How do we do that? By adjusting our thoughts and actions to agree with God's Word and by aligning our expectations with the written revelation of His perfect will.

In a sense, we must do much the same thing my husband, Ken, does when he gets a new hunting rifle. He takes it out right away for target practice so he can check the sights. He knows that a rifle is designed to shoot where it's aimed, and the sights determine the accuracy of that aim. If the sights are off, he won't be able to shoot straight. He'll miss the mark every time.

When it comes to longevity, most believers miss the mark because they don't have their spiritual sights properly aligned. Their expectations are askew due to wrong teachings and religious traditions. As a result, many Christians die younger than God intended for one simple reason: they are convinced it's the right thing to do.

I know that's true because sometimes when I go to churches to teach about long life, I ask at the beginning of the service how many people have been taught that a life span of seventy or eighty years is what the Bible promises us. Many times the majority of the congregation raise their hands.

No wonder so many Christians start getting old and feeble around that age! They think that's what God's Word says they should do. And since the Bible says that "as [a man] thinks in his heart, so is he" (Proverbs 23:7 NKJV), if they think seventy or eighty is the age to die, their bodies will most likely accommodate them. They'll start winding down and giving out. The devil will oblige them, too. He'll attack them with sickness and, instead of fighting it by faith, they'll assume illness is a natural part of old age and give in to it.

We saw that happen to Kenneth's mother, Vinita. Although she was a strong Christian, a woman of faith, and a mighty prayer warrior, she was completely convinced that the Bible promised her only seventy years of life. Because she didn't know any better, she embraced that idea. She believed it, and seventy years became her goal. She pressed her entire life until she made it. But then she quit and went to heaven only seven years later.

Always be sure that what you believe is scriptural, because what you believe and speak is what you get. Jesus said in Matthew 9:29, "According to your faith be it unto you." Vinita Copeland proved that to be true.

In the early years of her life, her seventy-year faith served her well. It helped her fight off the devil's attempts to kill her when she was just a young girl. Since she was a strong person of prayer even at a very early age, he was eager to get her out of the way.

In 1926, when she was fifteen years old, her appendix ruptured while she was on her high school basketball court in Lubbock, Texas. They rushed her to the hospital where a surgeon operated on her. When he saw how bad her condition was, he was so sure she wouldn't survive that he didn't even sew up her incision. He used cadaver clips to close it up, assuming she'd die soon, so it wouldn't matter.

But that stubborn, praying teenager refused to let her life slip away.

She kept on living until, under pressure from her father, the doctor sewed her back up. Her internal organs had been so damaged, however, that the medical experts agreed she couldn't live more than ten years. They also said she could never have children.

Of course, Vinita proved them wrong on both counts. She did live much longer than ten years. Also, after praying nine years for a child, she gave birth to her little darling, Kenneth. She almost died having him, but she made it through. A few years later, she had a miscarriage that almost killed her, so she decided not to have any more children.

Every few years, when she'd go to the doctor, she'd be told again that she wouldn't live another ten years. But she just refused to die. She resisted the devil, amazed the physicians, and kept right on living.

Why? Because she believed the Bible promised her seventy years and, bless God, she had her sights set on seeing the birthday when that promise would be fulfilled.

When the day came, she called our house and started hollering, "I made it! I made it!"

"What did you make, Momma?" Ken asked.

"I made seventy! I got my seventy years!"

Not long after that, her body started failing. We all prayed for her and she was able to live on for a while, but it was impossible to keep her going long because she had spent years with her sights set on seventy. She never expected to live long past that. She died at about seventy-seven years old.

An Extraordinary Infusion of Youthful Vitality

"What's wrong with that?" somebody might ask. "She lived longer than the doctors said she would. She lived a fruitful life and went to heaven."

Yes, she did. Psalm 91:16 says, "With long life will I satisfy him, and show him my salvation." But I'm convinced that if she had aligned her sights with the Scriptures and set them on living until she was satisfied, she could still be with us today. If she were, she'd still be praying sinners into the kingdom of God. She'd still be ministering to people and doing what God had spent so many years training her to do.

When you think of it, God had invested a lot in Vinita. He worked with her for years, teaching her to pray heaven and earth together. She was good at it! Ken is living proof. He says he tried his best to go to hell, but his mother wouldn't let him go. After years of praying for him, she prevailed. He came to the Lord and was born again at the age of twenty-six.

She didn't stop with Ken either. She was determined to see all her kinfolk saved, so she spent countless hours praying for her sister, both her brothers, all their children, and a number of other distant relatives. She even prayed into the kingdom all her husband's family members who weren't saved.

She prayed for me, too, after Ken and I married. I wasn't saved at the time, and I came from a family that didn't know much about the reality of the things of God, so nobody else was praying for me. Since I wasn't a believer, I'm sure she wouldn't have chosen me for a daughter-in-law, but as soon as she found out Ken and I were married, she went after me in prayer. I guess I was an easier prayer project than Ken because I gave my life to the Lord quickly, even before he did. I wasn't accustomed to being prayed for.

Once we both were born again, Vinita hardly knew what to do for a while. She told Ken, "I've had the driest three months spiritually that I've ever had." When he asked her why, she said, "You got saved and I haven't had anything to pray about!"

Do you know how she solved the problem? She made up her mind to pray Ken's entire high school football team into the kingdom of God. She knew everyone on that team and had kept up with them over the years because they had regular team reunions and stayed in touch with one another. So Vinita went after them in prayer, one by one.

Thank God for all the powerful prayers she prayed during her seventy-seven years! But think how much more she would have been able to do for the Lord had she gone on to live another twenty... thirty... even forty years. Can you imagine how much a well-seasoned, well-trained prayer warrior could accomplish in that amount of time?

God might even have had a whole new phase of ministry for her. He might have planned for her to begin a new work at eighty that would have made her even more of a blessing on the earth than she'd already been.

If you think such a thing is impossible, think again. It's not only possible, it happened to several people in the Bible. Look at Moses, for instance. God invested years training and preparing him. Forty years being educated in the house of Pharaoh, and another forty years tending sheep on the back side of the desert—that's what it took to get Moses ready for the most important assignment of his life.

When Moses received that assignment, he was eighty years old. Can you imagine that? At an age when most modern-day believers are thinking their most productive years for God are behind them, Moses was preparing to lead the Jewish people out of Egyptian captivity. At eighty, he was assigned the job of receiving the Torah (the first five books of the Bible) from God on Mount Sinai and leading the Israelites through the wilderness into the promised land.

One Jewish commentary I read said when Moses received that assignment, he received an extraordinary infusion of youthful energy and vitality. God so invigorated him when he was assigned this new, divine mission that his health and strength remained undiminished for the rest of his long life.[1] He lived to be 120 years old (Deuteronomy 34:7).

That puts a whole new light on the solution to the problem of aging, doesn't it? If we find ourselves slowing down at seventy or eighty, what we may need is a new assignment from God. Maybe we need to move into our new ministry and let God rejuvenate us!

According to the Bible, that kind of rejuvenation isn't just for people like Moses who have a unique call of God on their lives. It belongs to all His obedient people. It's one of the benefits of our salvation.

🦅 Psalm 103 says, "Bless the LORD, O my soul, and forget not all his benefits: who forgiveth all thine iniquities; who healeth all thy diseases; who redeemeth thy life from destruction; who crowneth thee with lovingkindness and tender mercies; who satisfieth thy mouth with good things; *so that thy youth is renewed like the eagle's.*" (verses 2–5, italics added)

🦅 Psalm 92 says, "Those that be planted in the house of the LORD shall flourish in the courts of our God. *They shall still bring forth fruit in old age; they shall be fat and flourishing.*" (verses 13–14, italics added)

🦅 Isaiah 40 says, "*They that wait upon the LORD shall renew their strength;* they shall mount up with wings as eagles; they shall run, and not be weary; and they shall walk, and not faint." (verse 31, italics added)

The first time Ken and I woke up to the importance of God's promises of youth renewal was when Vinita was in the hospital slipping toward heaven. Ken was sitting by her bedside praying for her healing, and the Lord spoke to his heart and said, *She doesn't need healing.*

Ken said, "You could have fooled me. The doctors have been telling us she won't live more than a week."

As he considered what the Lord had said to him, however, he realized that Vinita had already been healed of several illnesses in the previous few days. She'd had pneumonia and some other difficulties, but after prayer, those things disappeared.

"Lord, if she's not sick, then what's wrong with her? Why is she dying?" he asked.

"Her body parts are worn out," the Lord answered. "My Word says in the 103rd Psalm that one of the benefits of being a believer is the renewing of your youth like the eagle's. What she needs is for her youth to be renewed. She should have been believing for that every day of her life."

One reason Vinita's body wore out was because she expected to die at seventy. She'd always felt she had to make the most of the time she had, so she prayed day and night. She didn't sleep and get the rest she needed. No one can do that without suffering physical consequences. God created our bodies to rest fifty-two days a year and sleep at night. Every seventh day, they're supposed to get a day off. Ken's mother slept so little during her life that, according to Ken's dad, she hardly wrinkled the sheets.

She hadn't partaken of the youth-renewing benefits of salvation over the years. She didn't realize they belonged to her, so she hadn't believed for them, confessed them, and opened the door for them to manifest in her life. The great minister and author F. F. Bosworth said, "Faith begins where the will of God is known."[2]

We can learn something from her experience. We should start cultivating our faith for rejuvenation before we reach her age. So that's what we've done. These days, we release our faith during our mealtime prayers and say, "Thank You, Lord, for renewing our youth and our strength."

Although we began doing that only a few years ago, I recommend that if you have the opportunity, you start earlier than we did. If you're twenty, start saying it today because forty...fifty...sixty is coming. You might as well get a head start.

Mountain Climbing at 120

"But Gloria," someone might say, "I'm not twenty. In fact, I'm past seventy. Old age has already caught up with me; I can feel it. It's too late for me to receive the benefits of those youth-renewing Scriptures."

No, it's not too late. Remember, Moses proved it. Hebrew scholars say he felt much the same way you do now right before he got his new mission at age eighty. Even though he felt his vitality was ebbing and he had grown weaker with age, the merit of his new mission and the power of God restored his youth and he went on to live strong for another forty years.[3]

God can do something similar for you. He may not be through with you yet. You may have been in training for a long time. You may have wisdom and a capacity to bless people that come only after many years of service to the Lord. If so, you're a valuable soldier in the army of God. You ought not be willing to leave this earth until you're sure you've finished the work He has called you to do. You should be determined to complete your mission so that when you stand before Jesus you can hear Him say, "Well done, good and faithful servant."

That's what Ken and I have set our hearts to do. We've been in the ministry for more than forty-three years now, but as far as we're concerned, all that has been training. We believe our best years, our most productive years in God's service, are still ahead of us. We aren't even seriously thinking of retiring. We're re-firing, getting rejuvenated by faith in God's Word, and expecting new assignments from our heavenly Commander in Chief.

We don't want to stand before our Lord someday and hear Him say, "Well...half done...three-quarters done." We want to finish everything He has called us to do. We want to hear, "Well done, good and faithful servant."

Actually, I have my sights set on serving Jesus on the earth at least until I'm 120. (I could change my decision if I finish my course earlier.) Moses is my inspiration. He not only survived to 120, he thrived at that age. And he did it even though he wasn't perfect.

That's right. Even though Moses was a great man of God, he made some mistakes. One of them was especially costly for him. While leading the Israelites through the wilderness, he lost his temper with them because of their complaining and disobeyed the command of God. Instead of speaking to the rock and telling water to come out of it as the Lord told him to, he got angry.

"Listen, you rebels!" he shouted. "Must we bring you water from this rock?" Then Moses raised his hand and struck the rock twice with the staff, and water gushed out. So all the people and their livestock drank their fill. But the LORD said to Moses and Aaron, "Because you did not trust me enough to demonstrate my holiness to the people of Israel, you will not lead them into the land I am giving them!" (NUMBERS 20:10–12 NLT)

Notice God told Moses right then and there that because of that act of disobedience, he would not be allowed to enter the promised land. Since Moses had been able to talk God into extending extra mercy to the Israelites at times, maybe he thought that at the last minute God would give him a reprieve. But that's not what happened. Just as God had said, Moses guided the children of Israel for forty years through the wilderness and then died at the edge of the promised land.

Even so, his death was an astonishing event. Moses didn't die of old age. He didn't die of weakness. He didn't die of sickness or disease. In fact, his body was as strong and healthy as it had been at the beginning of his mission.

He didn't die by accident or calamity. Death didn't sneak up on him and take him by surprise. When the time came, God let Moses know and he called the Israelites together and told them what was about to happen. He said, "I am an hundred and twenty years old this day; I can no more go out and come in: also the LORD hath said unto me, Thou shalt not go over this Jordan" (Deuteronomy 31:2).

When he said he couldn't go out and come in, Moses didn't mean he was physically unable. What he meant was that God had told him he would not be permitted to go with them any farther; therefore, he couldn't go out of the wilderness and into the promised land with the rest of the Israelites. The time had come for him to depart.

And depart is exactly what Moses did. He didn't die a natural death. He died a supernatural death. God caught Moses' spirit away and buried his body where no one could find it. The book of Deuteronomy describes his passing this way:

> Moses went up from the plains of Moab unto the mountain of Nebo, to the top of Pisgah, that is over against Jericho. And the LORD showed him all the land of Gilead, unto Dan, and all Naphtali, and the land of Ephraim, and Manasseh, and all the land of Judah, unto the utmost sea, and the south, and the plain of the valley of Jericho, the city of palm trees, unto Zoar. And the LORD said unto him, This is the land which I sware unto Abraham, unto Isaac, and unto Jacob, saying, I will give it unto thy seed: I have caused thee to see it with thine eyes, but thou shalt not go over thither. So Moses the servant of the LORD died there in the land of Moab, according to the word of the LORD. And he buried him in a valley in the land of Moab, over against Bethpeor: but no man knoweth of his sepulchre unto this day. And Moses was an hundred and twenty years old when he died: his eye was not dim, nor his natural force abated. (DEUTERONOMY 34:1–7)

I think it's amazing that right before Moses died, he climbed up Mount Nebo so he could look out into the distance and see the promised land. I have a friend who climbed Mount Nebo when he was in his thirties, and he said it was a tough climb. Yet there was Moses, at 120 years old, hiking to the top. (Wouldn't it be great to be fit enough to go mountain climbing at that age?) What's more, his eyes were so sharp that once he got there, he was able to see for miles. He didn't even need binoculars.

A few years ago, I saw a picture of a French lady who was the oldest person on earth for a while. She was 126 years old, as I recall. She was so wrinkled up and her eyes were so dim and squinted that I doubt very much if she could have stood on Mount Nebo and seen the promised land. Looking at her gave me an even greater appreciation for Moses. His eyesight wasn't dim at all at 120. He could see for miles and miles.

Considering how healthy and strong Moses was at that time, we might well wonder, *What caused him to die?*

The answer is simple and astounding. Moses died for just one reason—because God told him to. He had finished the assignment he'd been given. He'd completed his divine mission:

> The Lord spake unto Moses that selfsame day, saying, Get thee up into this mountain Abarim, unto mount Nebo, which is in the land of Moab, that is over against Jericho; and behold the land of Canaan, which I give unto the children of Israel for a possession: and die in the mount whither thou goest up, and be gathered unto thy people; as Aaron thy brother died in mount Hor, and was gathered unto his people. (Deuteronomy 32:48–50)

Moses was gathered to his people. The Lord "gathered" him as He gathered Abraham, Isaac, Jacob, and Aaron (Genesis 25:8; 35:29; 49:29, 33; Numbers 20:24, 26; 27:13). They proved to us that no matter how old we are, we don't have to get sick and feeble to die. We don't have to let the devil evict us from our bodies by inflicting some kind of disease or injury upon us. We can just finish our divine assignments and then let God gather us to Himself.

I like that idea, don't you?

Don't Bow Out Early

Before we leave the subject of Moses' supernatural departure, there's one more truth we should learn: though God told Moses to die, it was Moses—not God—who chose the time of his death. Moses made that choice years earlier when he rebelled against God's command in the wilderness.

Many Christians don't understand that fact. They insist that God appoints a time for every person to die. "When it's your time—whether you're young or old—it's your time, and there's nothing you can do about it," they say. Some people even claim the Bible backs up that idea.

In reality, that's not what the Bible says at all. It doesn't tell us

God has selected a time for us to die. It says, "It is appointed unto men *once to die*, but after this the judgment" (Hebrews 9:27, italics added). In other words, the Lord has ordained that we die just one time. We don't circle around through life again and again. We aren't reincarnated multiple times in different forms. We have one life here on earth, and when that life is over, we will face one of two kinds of judgment.

We must all stand before the judgment seat of Christ, "that every one may receive the things done in his body, according to that he hath done, whether it be good or bad" (2 Corinthians 5:10). Those who have not received Jesus as Lord and Savior will stand before the great white throne of God for judgment. That's what God has appointed.

He has not appointed the time of our death, however. For the most part, He has left that up to us. As we've already seen, He said again and again in the Scriptures that if we will hear and obey His Word, we can extend our lives. If we ignore His Word or rebel and disobey it, our days will be shortened. Even our lifestyle habits lengthen or shorten our years.

Who knows how long Moses might have lived had he not disobeyed God in the wilderness? He might have stayed around for another forty years to see the Israelites occupy the promised land. He might have been gathered to his people at 160 instead of 120.

"Wait a minute," someone might argue, "doesn't Ecclesiastes tell us there is a specific time to die?" No, it doesn't. It says: "To every thing there is a season, and a time to every purpose under the heaven: a time to be born, and a time to die; a time to plant, and a time to pluck up that which is planted" (Ecclesiastes 3:1–2).

Although we do find the phrase "a time to die" in that passage, the context makes clear it isn't referring to an appointed day or moment for death. It's referring to the seasons of life. Just as there is a particular season when it's appropriate to plant a crop, and another season when it's appropriate to harvest that crop, there is a season when it's appropriate for us to depart from this earth.

How do we know when it's the right season?

First of all, as we've already seen, the season isn't right until we're satisfied. It's not right until we can say, "I know I've done what God has called me to do. I've finished my assignments on earth. I've had plenty of years on earth and I'm content now. I'm ready to go to heaven." Psalm 91:16 says, "With long life will I satisfy him, and show him my salvation."

That's the way the apostle Paul felt when he sensed it was the season for his departure from earth. He knew, much as Moses did, that his departure was coming and he was ready for it. I think it is enlightening that he called his death a "departure." He even wrote Timothy, his son in the faith, to tell him he was about to leave. He said:

> I am now ready to be offered, and the time of my departure is at hand.
> I have fought a good fight, I have finished my course, I have kept the
> faith: Henceforth there is laid up for me a crown of righteousness,
> which the Lord, the righteous judge, shall give me at that day: and
> not to me only, but unto all them also that love his appearing.
> (2 TIMOTHY 4:6–8)

We would all do well to follow Paul's example. He didn't bow out of life early. He stayed on the earth until he finished his race, though that race included some very difficult times. He was persecuted for the sake of the gospel. He was beaten on three occasions, on five occasions whipped thirty-nine times, imprisoned, and shipwrecked at sea in the course of his ministry (2 Corinthians 11:23–28).

If Paul had wanted an easy escape, he could have chosen to die before all that happened. He could have decided to leave the difficulties of his ministry behind and go on to be with Jesus. Sometimes he wanted to do that. We know he did because the letter he wrote in prison to the Philippians states:

> To me to live is Christ, and to die is gain. But if I live in the flesh,
> this is the fruit of my labour: yet what I shall choose I wot not. For
> I am in a strait betwixt two, having a desire to depart, and to be

with Christ; which is far better: nevertheless to abide in the flesh is
more needful for you. And having this confidence, I know that I shall
abide and continue with you all for your furtherance and joy of faith.
(PHILIPPIANS 1:21–25)

When our lives seem difficult, we ought to adopt the same attitude Paul had. If we're ever tempted to start considering death as
an easy way out of a tough situation, we should remember we're not
here on earth to just please ourselves, but to be a blessing to people.
We're here to fulfill the will of God, to bring others joy and help
them progress in the Lord.

When we start entertaining thoughts about giving up and dying
a premature death, we should consider the effect it will have on the
people around us. When we start feeling overcome by the difficulties of life, we should remember Psalm 91:15 and say, "God is with
me in trouble, and He will deliver me!"

Notice that verse doesn't promise us we won't encounter trouble.
It doesn't tell us we'll cruise through life without any problems. It
says that God will see us through them in victory. Another psalm
says it this way: "Many are the afflictions of the righteous, but the
LORD delivereth him out of them all" (Psalm 34:19).

Remember that verse the next time circumstances start to
overwhelm you. Remember it when the devil starts whispering in
your ear and saying things like "Nobody loves you....Your life
doesn't make any difference....You might as well just give up and
die."

Answer him right back and say out loud, "You listen to me, Satan.
I may be having a rough time right now, but my God will bring me
through in triumph. He'll change things for me and give me a satisfying life. It's not my season to depart yet. I still have work to do for
God. There are people I can bless and encourage and love. In the
name of Jesus, I rebuke you, Satan. Get out!"

I pray that, because you're a believer, you'll never consider sui-
cide. If you are tempted, refuse that temptation. Decide now that

you won't take your life, you'll give it! Give it to God. Give it to others. God will give you victory, if you give Him a place to work!

If you'll make up your mind now to stop living for yourself and start living for the Lord, your life will become so fulfilling, you won't even think of going to heaven too early. You'll wake up every day and say, "This is the day which the LORD hath made; we will rejoice and be glad in it" (Psalm 118:24).

Consider a Face-Lift...at Ninety

Before you can set your sights on Bible longevity, there's one other misunderstanding you must clear up. You must overturn the unscriptural idea (if you have it) that God has promised you only seventy or eighty years. As we've already seen, Kenneth's precious mother made the mistake of believing that and died too early.

Where did she get such an idea? The same place countless other Christians have gotten it—from Psalm 90, which says:

> The days of our years are threescore years and ten (seventy
> years)—or even, if by reason of strength, fourscore years (eighty
> years); yet is their pride [in additional years] only labor and sorrow, for
> it is soon gone, and we fly away. Who knows the power of Your anger?
> [Who worthily connects this brevity of life with Your recognition
> of sin?] And Your wrath, who connects it with the reverent and
> worshipful fear that is due You? So teach us to number our days, that
> we may get us a heart of wisdom. (VERSES 10–12 AMP)

At first glance, those verses do seem to set a limit on longevity. But they also indicate that the lives of the people affected by that limit were cut short by the anger of the Lord. As believers, we know that we are not under the wrath of God. Through the blood of Jesus, we have been delivered from His wrath, set securely in His love, and inherited all His blessings. So, it's clear these verses are not referring to born-again saints who walk in fellowship and obedience to God.

To whom, then, do they refer? A footnote on Psalm 90 found in *The Amplified Bible* explains the answer to that question. It says:

> This psalm is credited to Moses, who is interceding with God to remove the curse which made it necessary for every Israelite over twenty years of age (when they rebelled against God at Kadesh-barnea) to die before reaching the promised land (Num. 14:26-35). Moses says most of them are dying at seventy years of age. This number has often been mistaken as a set span of life for all mankind. It was not intended to refer to anyone except those Israelites under the curse during that particular forty years. Seventy years never has been the average span of life for humanity. When Jacob, the father of the twelve tribes, had reached 130 years (Gen. 47:9), he complained that he had not attained to the years of his immediate ancestors. In fact, Moses himself lived to be 120 years old, Aaron 123, Miriam several years older, and Joshua 110 years of age. Note as well that in the Millennium a person dying at 100 will still be thought a child (ISA. 65:20).[4]

Praise God, the life-span limit in Psalm 90 doesn't apply to us! God set that limit on the rebellious, wilderness-wandering Israelites who refused to go into the promised land. And He did it for a reason. He'd already sentenced them to die in the wilderness. He'd already said to them:

> Because all those men which have seen my glory, and my miracles, which I did in Egypt and in the wilderness, and have tempted me now these ten times, and have not hearkened to my voice; surely they shall not see the land which I sware unto their fathers, neither shall any of them that provoked me see it. (NUMBERS 14:22–23)

God couldn't wait a hundred years for those people to die. He couldn't wait a century or more to lead their children into Canaan. He had a schedule to keep.

Did you know God has a schedule? He has time all mapped out. He knows the exact moment when Jesus is going to catch away the church, and He has known it from the beginning. He's not going to get up one day and say, "Well, I think this will be a good day for the Rapture."

No, He plans His work and He works His plan. He has a plan for everything in Scripture. If He had allowed those Israelites to live out their entire life spans in the wilderness, there's no telling how long they might have delayed things. After all, they had been eating manna, God's perfect food, so we know their diet was healthy. If God hadn't put a limit on them, they might have lived, as Methuselah did, for 969 years.

You and I are born-again children of God. He doesn't have to put that kind of limit on us. We're not like the rebellious wilderness group. We don't have to be limited to seventy or eighty years. We're in Christ Jesus. We've already received our passport to the promised land. We're members of the group appointed to enter into the blessings of God.

Kenneth E. Hagin used to say, "Live seventy or eighty years and if you're not satisfied, live a little longer." He lived to be eighty-six, was satisfied, and departed.

God isn't waiting for us to die so He can accomplish His will on the earth. He wants us to live and be vehicles of that will. He wants us to live long and finish strong for His glory. To do that, however, we'll have to get rid of religious traditions like the seventy- or eighty-year time limit. Even if we learned it in church, we'll have to throw out misinterpreted teaching and replace it with real, biblical truth. Otherwise, we'll die younger than we should.

My friend Jackie, who works at our ministry, saw that happen in her family. Her mother was a good Christian most of her life. She didn't realize she should check out what she hears with the Word of

God before believing it. So when she heard the seventy- or eighty-year myth, she swallowed it hook, line, and sinker. As a result, when she started experiencing some physical problems around the age of seventy, she gave in to them. She said, "I've had my seventy years," and she died. Jackie's mother had a sister, however, who didn't become indoctrinated in the life-span-limit teaching. She went to church every Sunday but somehow escaped that tradition. Over the years, she developed a close relationship with the Lord. Even though she came from the same family and had the same genes her sister did, that woman flew past seventy and has just kept on going. At ninety-eight years old she is doing great. She still lives alone, is able to drive, and has a seventy-year-old boyfriend!

According to Jackie, her aunt has an entirely different attitude from that of Jackie's mother, who died at seventy. Her aunt *expects* to live a long time. She wasn't winding down when she hit seventy. She wasn't thinking about dying at eighty. She had a face-lift at ninety, so she apparently thought she still had some living to do even at that age. I don't know her, but I've been told she looks twenty years younger than she is.

She doesn't have a poor-me, disgruntled attitude either. If anything bad happens, she cries for a few minutes and then never speaks of it again. She just releases the care and goes on with life. She carries no grief, fear, or anger. She is always happy and carefree.

She's the picture of Proverbs 3:2. She has enjoyed length of days and years of life worth living.

Reset Your Expectations

If you've ever thought seventy or eighty is old, I suggest you regroup and give that some more consideration. Reset your expectations. Adjust your sights and go for at least 120 years. I'm not talking about living in a nursing home until you're 120 and barely functional. I'm talking about living life to the fullest for 120 years. (And 120 is not a limit if you are not satisfied!)

Why not? Moses made it to that age with full vitality intact. He made it with his eyes sharp and his mountain-climbing muscles in shape. Why shouldn't we let him be our example?

Also, 120 is the only number given in the Bible that even resembles a God-given life span (and that is debatable). In Genesis 6:3, just before the Flood, the Lord said to Moses, "My Spirit shall not strive with man forever, for he is indeed flesh; yet his days shall be one hundred and twenty years" (NKJV).

Many people take that verse as a longevity limit, but some Hebrew scholars don't see it that way. One Jewish commentary contends that God was speaking there about the timing of the Flood. He was saying that He would wait 120 more years before sending it in order to give humankind ample opportunity to repent before destruction overtook them.[5]

Others interpret the verse to mean that after the Flood the human life span would gradually decrease to a maximum of 120 years.[6] Either way, I believe that's the least we should expect. For many of us, that may be as far as our faith can stretch. It's certainly a great goal.

If we'll set our sights on that goal, our attitude toward aging will begin to change right away. When someone says something to us about forty being "over the hill," we'll think, *No, that's only a third of the way there.* We'll start thinking of sixty as midlife. We'll start developing a live-long-finish-strong attitude.

And as the lively lady who got a face-lift at ninety proved, that kind of attitude can make all the difference.

POINTS TO REMEMBER

❧ Contrary to popular belief, the Bible sets no limit on our life spans. Unlike the Israelites in the wilderness who were given only seventy or eighty years, we can enjoy healthy, productive lives of 120 years or more.

❧ When Moses was eighty years old, he received an extraordinary infusion of youthful energy and vitality to go with it. That kind of rejuvenation is one of the benefits of salvation.

❧ Start now cultivating your faith for long life. Make it a habit at mealtime prayers to say, "Thank You, Lord, for renewing my youth!"

❧ No matter how long we live, we don't have to get sick and feeble to die. We can just finish our divine assignments and let God gather us to Himself.

❧ When we stop living for ourselves and start living for the Lord, our lives will become so fulfilling, we won't even think of going to heaven too early. We'll wake up every day and say, "This is the day the Lord has made; I will rejoice and be glad in it!"

SCRIPTURE

Bless the LORD, O my soul, and forget not all his benefits:...Who satisfieth thy mouth with good things; so that thy youth is renewed like the eagle's. (Psalm 103:2, 5)

CONFESSION

I set my sights today on a healthy, productive life of 120 years or more. I will live every day of that life for the glory of God and finish with joy every assignment He gives me. According to the Word of God, I believe and declare that my youth is renewed like the eagle's, and I receive a new and extraordinary infusion of energy and vitality, so that I can be a blessing to others all the days of my long, strong life.

CHAPTER 3

If They Did It, Why Can't We?

I realize some people might think what I'm suggesting is impossible. They might argue that the very idea of Christians living by faith to the happy, healthy age of 120 and beyond is silly. They could even conclude that I've spent so much time studying the Bible, I've lost touch with reality.

That's okay. People have been accusing Ken and me of that for decades.

A young man who worked for us some years ago said it best. After hearing us preach the first few times, he told his friends, "Those people live in a bubble!" From his perspective, we didn't have any idea what was going on in the world. *Those Copelands just don't know how bad things really are out there*, he thought. *They actually believe everything is going to work out just as the Bible says in every area of life.*

He didn't mean that as a compliment either. After a while, however, he changed his tune. He decided the bubble of God's Word was a good place to be. He also discovered that since God's promises apply to every believer, he had just as much right to believe them as we did.

Years later, when that young man told us what he'd said to his friends in those early days, I started thinking about it. *Are we really living in a bubble?*

Yes, we are! I decided. We live surrounded by God's Word. We dwell day and night in His "circle of blessing." Psalm 25:12–14 says, "Where is the man who fears the Lord? God will teach him how to choose the best. He shall live within God's circle of blessing, and his children shall inherit the earth. Friendship with God is reserved for those who reverence him. With them alone he shares the secrets of his promises" (TLB).

In a way, we are much like the generation of Israelites who grew up in the wilderness. They, too, were surrounded by a kind of spiritual bubble. They didn't have any heathens living ungodly lives around them in the desert. Moses made sure they were hearing God's Word all the time. And every day when the manna fell from heaven for them to eat, they were reminded that God would always take care of them.

I imagine if those Israelites had gotten an opportunity to chat with someone outside their group, they would have been accused of being out of touch with reality, too. When the Israelites said, "God is going to give us the land of Canaan. We're going to whip the giants in it by His power," a worldly-wise person probably would have said to them, "You're out of touch with reality!"

But the fact is, those up-and-coming young Israelites were in touch with the greatest reality of all. They were living by faith in God's unfailing promises. That's why they were able to take the promised land. They had been living in a bubble of faith in God's promise to them.

So today, when someone accuses us of living in a bubble, I don't deny it. I'm quick to admit that for the past forty-two–plus years, Ken and I have surrounded ourselves with God's unfailing promises. In the process, we've discovered they're as reliable now as they were when Israel conquered the giants.

All along the way, however, we've encountered skeptics. They were there when we first stepped out in faith and began to believe, for instance, that no matter what the circumstances, God can keep His promise to meet all our needs according to His riches in glory by Christ Jesus. We were so buried in debt back then it seemed we could never get out. Yet God did what appeared to be impossible. He not only enabled us to pay off our debts and provided for our family's needs, He financed radio and television broadcasts, ministry buildings, staff payrolls, houses, cars, and even airplanes—all without borrowed money.

When we first began to preach that God could do that kind of thing, people thought we were out of touch with reality. "It's totally impractical. It can't be done!" they said.

But they were mistaken.

There were also skeptics around when we first began to believe that even in the midst of this sickness-ridden world, God can keep His healing promises. They thought we were extreme to expect Him to do such a thing. Some thought sickness is a normal, inevitable part of life.

Yet, from the moment we began to stand in faith on His Word that says by the stripes of Jesus we were healed, God has healed us and kept our family well. As our children were growing up, the only times we needed to take them to the doctor were for school shots and stitches. (John had to be stitched up sometimes because he liked to go fast and turn things over!)

I've spent more than four decades watching God do what people say can't be done. So it doesn't matter much to me if some people are doubtful about the possibility of living long and strong. I'm not bothered by those who think aiming for 120 is unrealistic. I'll always believe that kind of long, strong life is possible because the Bible says it is. The Bible also says:

> 🕊 **With God all things are possible. (Matthew 19:26)**

> 🕊 **All things are possible to him that believeth. (Mark 9:23)**

These two verses alone are enough to settle the issue. They're true, no matter what skeptics may say or whether anyone in recent history or modern times had ever lived to be 120 or not—because God said them.

Naturally speaking, however, even centenarians aren't all that scarce these days. There are many documented instances in recent years of people living well beyond one hundred years of age. There's even an authenticated list of the top eleven supercentenarians. At the top of that list is a woman who lived to 122 years of age!

Check it out for yourself. This remarkable list of people includes:

1. Jeanne Calment (France) born February 21, 1875—died August 4, 1997, at 122 years, 164 days

2. Sarah Knauss (U.S.—Pennsylvania) born September 24, 1880—died December 30, 1999, at 119 years, 97 days

3. Lucy Hannah (U.S.—Alabama) born July 16, 1875—died March 21, 1993, at 117 years, 248 days

4. Marie-Louise Meilleur (Canada—Quebec) born August 29, 1880—died April 16, 1998, at 117 years, 230 days

5. Maria Esther de Capovilla (Ecuador) born September 14, 1889—died August 27, 2006, at 116 years, 347 days

6. Tane Ikai (Japan) born January 18, 1879—died July 12, 1995, at 116 years, 175 days

7. Elizabeth Bolden (U.S.—Tennessee) born August 15, 1890—died December 11, 2006, at 116 years, 118 days

8. Maggie Barnes (U.S.—North Carolina) born March 6, 1882—died January 19, 1998, at 115 years, 319 days

9. Christian Mortensen (Denmark) born August 16, 1882—died April 25, 1998, at 115 years, 252 days

10. Charlotte Hughes (UK—England) born August 1, 1877—died March 17, 1993, at 115 years, 228 days

11. Yone Minagawa (Japan) born January 4, 1893—died August 13, 2007, at 114 years, 221 days[1]

That list alone is impressive enough. But there's even more encouraging news. Centenarians are becoming ever more plentiful these days.

A Lesson from Madame Calment

In light of those statistics, you can see that even by natural standards, I'm not as out of touch with reality as the devil might want you to think.

Want even more natural evidence of that fact?

Consider these findings from the New England Centenarian Study conducted by the Boston University School of Medicine:

- Currently, there are an estimated forty thousand centenarians in the United States. That number represents a little more than one centenarian per ten thousand in the population. (Surely as Christians, we can believe to be one of ten thousand!)

- Centenarians are the fastest-growing segment of our population. The second fastest is the age-group over eighty-five.

- Of the seventy-million-strong "baby boomer" generation, approximately three million can expect to become centenarians. (If you're not sure you can be one of ten thousand, surely you can be one of three million!)

- Today's centenarians disprove the perception that "the older you get, the sicker you get." They prove instead that the older you get and the healthier you've been, it is possible to markedly delay or even escape age-associated diseases.

- Eighty-eight percent of centenarians are functionally independent the vast majority of their lives until the average age of ninety-two, and 75 percent are the same at the average age of ninety-five.

- Many centenarians stay mentally alert and active. Thirty percent have experienced no significant changes in their thinking abilities.

❧ Not all centenarians are alike. They vary widely in years of
   education, economic status, religion, ethnicity, and patterns
   of diets.

❧ The characteristics centenarians do have in common include
   a low rate of obesity; substantial smoking history is rare; they
   handle stress better than the majority of people; and many have
   first-degree relatives who also achieve very old age.

❧ The oldest individual officially on record at this time (whose
   longevity established the current standard for a human life span) is
   Madame Jeanne Calment, who died at the age of 122 years.[2]

Think of it! These are just natural statistics. They're drawn from
the general population. They include all kinds of people, most of
whom have little faith or knowledge of what the Bible says about
long, strong life. No doubt, many of them aren't even born again.
Yet, significant numbers of them are living more than one hundred
years.

I don't know about you, but I like to read about these long-lived
folks because they inspire me. They remind me that many people
are living very long lives who don't even have the advantages we
Bible-believing Christians have because of our faith in God and His
Word. As I've sorted through the research that's been done during
the past few years, I've noticed that most of them have discovered at
least one important key to longevity. And more often than not, they
are keys that can be found in the Bible!

Look at the now-famous Madame Jeanne Calment, for example.
To get a sense of how long she lived, consider this: In 1875, the year
she was born, the telephone had not yet been invented, and the out-
law Jesse James was still running wild in the American West. In
1954, when she was seventy-nine years old, Stalin had just passed
from the world scene, Eisenhower was in the White House, and
the Third Republic had just come into power in her native country
of France. In 1995, when she gave her last television interview (two

years before she died), Bill Clinton was president, and the U.S. space shuttle was connecting with the Russian space station.

Talk about witnessing changes in the world! Madame Calment wins the prize. She was healthy and active well into her hundreds. It's said that she was still riding her bicycle around town at one hundred years old, having outlived her husband, her only child, and grandchild.

By the time photographers and reporters arrived in droves to join in the celebration of her 120th birthday in 1995, she had slowed down some. She could no longer hear very well and, after breaking her hip at 115, she was no longer able to walk. Cataracts had robbed her of her vision, and she refused surgery because she thought it was normal not to see at 120. (She didn't know to believe for the kind of sharp eyesight Moses had.)

But even with those difficulties, her good humor was intact. When reporters asked her what kind of future she expected, she didn't miss a beat. "A very short one," she answered.

What wisdom did Madame Calment have to share that might give us insight into her longevity?

"I've had a beautiful life," she said. "I've had good health. I took pleasure when I could. I acted clearly and morally without regret."[3]

As far as I can tell, Madame Calment didn't know the Lord, but even so, she tried to do what was right and avoided the stress of guilt and shame that comes when we do what's wrong. The Bible leaves no question about it; that's a good way to lengthen your days.

Love Everyone . . . and Lay Off the Cigars

Madame Calment isn't the only centenarian who's had some interesting things to say. There are any number of others as well.

There's Mrs. Dias from Florida who lived to be 114, for instance. The article I read about her said that she loved everyone. She would kiss and hug all the people who came to her house to visit her.

As believers, love is our commandment. And we can see from

Mrs. Dias's example, keeping the commandment will help us live long and strong.

Sad to say, Mrs. Dias also rolled and smoked her own cigars. That's not a good idea for those who want to live long. Who knows how long Mrs. Dias might have lived if she'd laid off those cigars!

Be Lively, Read the Bible, and Stop Watching *As the World Turns*

Granny Ellen Cooper was 112 years old at the time I read about her. She had good advice for those who desire to live long and happy lives: "Be lively." (In other words, get with it! Don't just drag around.) "It's just as easy to be lively as it is to sit there and bite other people's heads off and be sour all the time."

Unlike some of the other centenarians I found, Granny Cooper pointed to her relationship with the Lord as a part of her life and longevity. "I've read through the Bible and I've read a lot of Billy Graham's books and articles," she said. "I don't really care much for TV. I used to watch [the daytime soap opera] *As the World Turns*, but I stopped that." (I think that was a very smart choice and almost surely contributed to her long life!)

Granny Cooper also declared that church had been her guidance and main interest in life. "Ever since I can remember, church has been important to me," she said.

In addition to living many years, she also remained in near-perfect health. She had only one hospital stay, and it was due to a hip injury and not an illness. Even at 112, she never complained of so much as a headache.[4]

Not-So-Grumpy Old Men

Although a great percentage of centenarians are women, plenty of men cruise past one hundred full of life and energy as well. Reverend

Lawrence Scott is one of them. Reverend Scott hails from Clinton, Oklahoma. According to an article written about him in a magazine in 1995, Reverend Scott's first wife died after they had raised their eight children, and at age eighty-eight he fell in love with and married a member of his congregation. At the time of the article, they had celebrated their eighteenth anniversary and he had been in ministry for seventy-eight years.

"I just preach the Bible," said Reverend Scott. At the time of his 104th birthday, he had no plans to slow down. He awakened every day around 2:00 a.m. to prepare the sermon for church. "I have to get up early in the morning and write," he said. "It's the best time to hear from God."[5]

All the men who live long don't necessarily have as sterling a reputation as Reverend Scott did. Take the case of Thomas Parr, for example. According to eighteenth-century Bible scholar Adam Clarke's commentary, Mr. Parr, who resided in Glennington, England, several centuries ago, far outlived all seeming biblical age limits.

At the age of eighty-eight, he married his first wife, by whom he had two children. At the age of 102, he fell in love with Catherine Milton, by whom he had an illegitimate child. (That's something you just don't expect from a 102-year-old man!) He repented of his sin in church. And at the age of 120, he married again. It is said that at 130 years of age, he still worked outdoors and was capable of all kinds of farming tasks. He died at the age of 152 in 1635 after seeing the rise and fall of ten kings and queens in England.[6]

A Methodist, a Widow, and a Countess

Adam Clarke's commentary gives us some other amazing examples of longevity as well. It recounts the story of a Mrs. Somerhill of Bristol, England, who in the year 1790, when she was 106 years of age, could still read the smallest print without spectacles. Although she was unable, due to physical weakness, to go to her normal place of worship, she would read the whole service of the church for each day of the year with all the lessons and songs.

Mrs. Somerhill had been a member of the Methodist Society from its beginning. After hearing Mr. John Wesley's sermon when he visited Bristol in 1739, she was "so struck with his clear manner of preaching the doctrine of justification through faith...she followed him on foot to Portsmouth—a journey of 125 miles."[7] (She was obviously a lover of God's Word!)

The last time Mr. Clarke visited her in 1790, he said,

> I was admitted by a very old decrepit woman, then a widow of seventy-five years of age, and the youngest daughter of Mrs. Somerhill. I found the aged woman's faculties strong and vigorous, and her eyesight unimpaired, though she was then confined to her bed, and was hard of hearing. She died rejoicing in God, the following year.[8]

Another long-lived woman described in Clarke's commentary was Agnes Shuner. She lived in Surrey, England, and survived her husband, who died in 1407, by ninety-two years. Mrs. Schooner was 119 when she died in 1499.[9]

According to Mr. Clarke, the Countess of Desmond in Ireland lived even longer. She flew past the age of 119 and at the age of 140, due to financial ruin and poverty, was obliged to travel from Bristol to London to ask for relief from the court. (Quite a trek for a 140-year-old!) After renewing her teeth two or three times, she died in 1612 at the age of 145.[10]

The longest-lived person reported by Adam Clarke was a "foreigner, Peter Toston, a peasant of Temiswar, in Hungary. The remarkable longevity of this man exceeds the age of Isaac at his death by five years; exceeds the age of Abraham at his death by ten years; falls short of the age of Abraham's father, Terah, at his death by twenty years; and exceeds the age of Nahor, Abraham's grandfather, at his death by thirty-seven years. He died in AD 1724 at the extraordinary age of 185!"[11]

She Grabbed Him Where?

One of my favorite centenarians, a feisty little woman from Detroit, Michigan, may not have lived as long as the Countess of Desmond. But I can tell you that what she lacked in years, she made up for in spunk. Her name was Rosia Lee Ellis. When she was 112, a newspaper in Detroit printed an article about her: "A burglar received a painful surprise early Thursday when he tried to rip off 112-year-old Rosa Lee Ellis." He forced his way through her east side Detroit home and tried to steal her money and valuables.

How did Rosa Lee respond to her intruder?

She grabbed him. When he retaliated by throwing her to the floor she reportedly held on to him, putting a most sensitive part of his body in a viselike grip that put her in control of the situation. Although the intruder experienced pain, he escaped without permanent injury.

"It's a good thing she didn't have her gun," her son commented to reporters. "That was the only thing that saved him."

Neighbors agreed and confirmed Rosa Lee's remarkable energy and attitude. They said she rode her motorcycle through the neighborhood until she was in her eighties.

When asked about the incident, Rosa Lee herself said, "I don't harbor any ill will. I don't hate the man. I don't hate anybody." She attributed her positive outlook and longevity to serving God.[12]

Go, Rosa Lee! Hallelujah!

Still Flying High at 101

Another one of my favorite centenarians is John M. Miller from Poughkeepsie, New York. A well-known airplane pilot, he was featured in some of the aviation magazines Ken receives. The last article I found about him was written in 2006 when Mr. Miller was just a couple of months away from his 101st birthday.

Like most centenarians, he was well known for having a good attitude. He wasn't negative. He wasn't a complainer. He was a "can do" kind of guy.

He loved flying since he was a youngster, and over the years he saw amazing change in the aviation industry. Consider this: the Wright brothers' first successful airplane flight at Kitty Hawk took place in 1903, just two years before Mr. Miller was born. In the 1920s, he had the opportunity to get acquainted with the famous aviator Charles Lindbergh.

At over one hundred years of age he said, "I'm still instrument rated and current. I fly all the time....I'm not doing any professional flying now. I'm just flying for fun. On December 17, 2005, I flew...to North Carolina with a friend to celebrate my 100th birthday. I have three motorcycles and four automobiles. I don't drive the motorcycles much now."

One article I read about Mr. Miller recounted a time when, at age ninety-eight, he was flying to the Kitty Hawk anniversary celebration and found himself in a crisis. His radios quit and the lights in the plane went out as he was coming in for a landing. He said it was no big deal, really. He just got his flashlight and did what he had to do to get the plane down safely. The emergency didn't even throw him.

Once he arrived at the anniversary celebration, Mr. Miller demonstrated once again that he is a person who takes difficulties in stride and not a griper or complainer. He walked more than two miles in the freezing rain to see a re-creation of the Wright brothers' first flight, only to find out the flight had been canceled.

His comment?

"Well, at least I got my morning walk!"

Other young whippersnappers shivered around him in the pouring rain and thirty-five-degree weather, complaining about being wet, cold, and inconvenienced. But Mr. Miller, standing beside them in a sport coat and loafers, under an umbrella, didn't join in the whining. "I'm not cold," he said simply.[13] (I've since learned that Mr. Miller recently died at the age of 102.)

Quickened by Divine Life

As I've read about these and other centenarians, one thing I've noticed that most of them have in common is that they have refused to give in to the stress and the pressures of life. They face the same troubles everyone else faces but just don't let those things get to them. Even the doctors who comment on their longevity remark about their resistance to stress and depression.

These two conditions can shorten our lives. So many sicknesses and diseases are stress related. Some people think stress is inevitable. They believe their jobs or their kids or their finances force it upon them. But these centenarians prove it's not the difficulties we face in those areas that stress us out. It's the way we deal with them.

Somehow, these hardy oldsters have learned to live in peace even in the midst of troubling situations. And most of them are just natural people! They're not born-again believers. Even those who are believers don't have the scriptural revelation that many of us have today. So I can't help wondering, *If they can do it, why can't we?* Surely if these people can live peaceful, satisfying lives to one hundred and beyond, we, as Bible-reading, commandment-keeping children of God, should be able to sail through 120.

After all, we have tapped into the supernatural power of God. We, as believers, have the very life of God working in us.

"But His life doesn't affect our natural bodies," someone might argue. "It just affects our spirits."

Not true! According to the Bible, "If the Spirit of him that raised up Jesus from the dead dwells in you, he that raised up Christ from the dead shall also quicken your mortal bodies by his Spirit that dwelleth in you" (Romans 8:11).

Notice that verse doesn't say the Holy Spirit will just give life to our spirits. It says He will give life to our "mortal" bodies. The word *mortal* means "subject to death."[14] So there's no mistaking what the Bible is referring to there. It's not talking about the glorious bodies we'll be receiving when Jesus returns. They won't be subject to death. They'll be eternal.

That verse is talking about the bodies we live in here and now. It's saying that these fleshly tents we inhabit during our temporary lives on earth can be enlivened by the very resurrection power of Jesus. It's telling us that because we have the power of the Holy Spirit abiding within our spirits, we can draw on that power by faith and it will quicken our physical bodies.

I love the word *quicken* used in Romans 8:11. Its meanings include: "to give or restore vigor or activity to; stir up, rouse, or stimulate: to revive; restore life to: to become more active, sensitive, etc.: to become alive; receive life…to manifest signs of life."[15]

The King James Version of the Bible uses that wonderful old word again and again (italics added):

- In Psalm 119:50, David declares to God, "Thy word hath *quickened* me."

- In Psalm 119:93, he says, "I will never forget thy precepts: for with them thou hast *quickened* me."

- Hebrews 4:12 says, "For the word of God is *quick*, and powerful."

- Ephesians 2:4–5 declares that "God, who is rich in mercy, for his great love wherewith he loved us, even when we were dead in sins, hath *quickened* us together with Christ."

Look at that last verse again. It doesn't put our quickening off into the future. It doesn't say that someday, when Jesus returns, we will receive an impartation of divine life. It says we have *already* received it.

Most believers don't realize it, but this is the truth: as believers, we have already received the greater part of our resurrection. We have God's quickening, life-giving power within us right now.

What an advantage we have over those who are struggling along on their own! What divine resources we have to help us live long and strong!

We not only have the divine life of the Holy Spirit within us, we have the Word of God to assure us that His will for us is longevity and to help us build our faith. Doesn't it make sense that we should be able to live longer than people who are just living natural lives? Isn't it realistic to believe that if thousands of normal, even unsaved people are breaking the century mark right now, we should be able to break that mark and head for 120?

Surely if Madame Calment can do it, we can, too!

POINTS TO REMEMBER

❧ Because all things are possible to him who believes, we could live to 120 even if it were naturally impossible. But it's not impossible! There are many documented instances, in recent years, of people living well beyond one hundred years of age. Many of those are nonbelievers who have discovered scriptural keys to longevity, such as:

❧ Do what's right and avoid the stress of guilt.

❧ Love everybody. Don't hate anybody or harbor ill will against them. Hug liberally.

❧ Be lively and pleasant—it's just as easy as sitting there and being sour all the time. Keep a positive attitude and don't complain.

❧ If nonbelievers can live beyond one hundred, how much more can those of us who, as believers, have inside us the quickening, life-giving power of the Holy Spirit!

SCRIPTURE

If the Spirit of Him who raised Jesus from the dead dwells in you, He who raised Christ from the dead will also give life to your mortal bodies through His Spirit who dwells in you. (Romans 8:11 NKJV)

CONFESSION

My physical body is quickened and enlivened by the resurrection power of the Holy Spirit, who dwells within me. I draw on that power now, by faith, believing that it restores and revives every cell of my body. I determine today to cooperate with that resurrection life by trusting in the Word of God. Resisting all negativity and stress, I walk in God's peace, with a positive, joyful attitude, knowing that He cares for me.

CHAPTER 4

Putting the Gold Back in the Golden Years

t's one thing to get inspired about living long and finishing strong. It's another thing to do it.

I want to be crystal clear about that. I'm not suggesting that just raising our expectations and aiming to live to a ripe old age guarantees we'll hit the mark. It doesn't. Setting our sights is only the beginning. Once we've done that, there's something else we must do.

We must dig into our Bibles and find out more about what God has promised us, and what He says about how we should live. Then we must act on what we learn. In other words, we must believe and obey the Word of God.

Although most people don't think of it this way, the Bible is the best longevity book in the world. *Longevity* is defined as "great age, long life, great span of life" and "length of days."[1] And there's no question about it, the Bible gives us the prescription for it, saying again and again that we can enjoy a great span of life and length of days if we'll follow God's plan.

Not only does the Bible tell us how to lengthen our lives, it tells us how to shorten them. It tells us how to die before our time. I'm sure no one would want to do this, but if someone wanted to make sure he died young, he could look in the Bible and learn how. He could find out that by getting tangled up in the darkness of sin, filling his days with meanness, strife, unforgiveness, and all the other things God warns us to avoid, he can end up with an early exit from planet Earth.

But who wants to do that?

I don't! I want to enjoy the fulfillment of Proverbs 3:1–2. No doubt you do, too. So let's look at those verses again in three different translations of the Bible and give them some more thought:

> My son, do not forget my law, but let your heart keep my commands; for length of days and long life and peace they will add to you. (NKJV)

> My son, forget not my law or teaching, but let your heart keep my commandments; for length of days and years of a life [worth living] and tranquility [inward and outward and continuing through old age till death], these shall they add to you. (AMP)

> My child, never forget the things I have taught you. Store my commands in your heart, for they will give you a long and satisfying life. (NLT)

If we believe those Scriptures, we will not expect to spend our latter years stuck in a corner, sitting sad and disabled in a nursing home, waiting in a wheelchair for someone to come visit us. We won't imagine ourselves living out our nineties or one hundreds hobbling around, depending on our children to take care of us. We won't dread old age and think of it as something unpleasant we must suffer through.

No, if we trust God to keep His Word to us, we will obey Him and expect our senior years to be golden! We will rest with joyful assurance in our heavenly Father's faithfulness and ability to see us through old age in strength and health. We will rejoice and look forward to our latter days, knowing our God will take care of us and keep us, just as Proverbs 3:2 says He will: in "tranquility [inward and outward and continuing through old age till death]" (AMP).

I'm telling you, I have my heart set on that. Ken and I have no plans to move in with our kids and be dependent on them in our old age. We love them. We enjoy their company. But we don't want to live in their houses and look to them for help. We don't want to lean on them for physical assistance or financial support. We don't want to have to ask them for money.

We expect God Himself to take care of us all the days of our lives—physically, financially, and mentally. And we believe He will do it! We believe that all the way through our years on the earth, He will enable us to be self-sufficient. We expect to enjoy days of heaven on earth for the rest of our lives.

"Isn't that a little unrealistic?" you might ask.

Not according to the Bible, which assures us we can have such delightful days and tells us how to get them:

> Lay up these my words in your heart and in your soul, and bind them for a sign upon your hand, that they may be as frontlets between your eyes. And ye shall teach them your children, speaking of them when thou sittest in thine house, and when thou walkest by the way, when thou liest down, and when thou risest up. And thou shalt write them upon the door posts of thine house, and upon thy gates: That your days may be multiplied, and the days of your children, in the land which the LORD sware unto your fathers to give them, as the days of heaven upon the earth. (DEUTERONOMY 11:18–21)

When you think about it, that passage echoes the message of Proverbs 3:1–2. It promises us not only long life, or multiplied days, but the highest quality of life—days of heaven on earth.

I don't know why it is, but sometimes even Bible-believing Christians assume there is an expiration date on promises like that. They think such Scriptures won't work for us when we get old. But the truth is, those promises are good for us at any age. The same Scriptures that promise us a happy, healthy, heaven-filled life at forty years old still promise us those things at eighty. The Word of God never changes. It will work for us in our latter years just as it does in our early years.

Consider again what God said in Isaiah 46:

Even to your old age I am He, and even to hair white with age will I carry you. I have made, and I will bear; yes, I will carry and will save you.... [Earnestly] remember the former things, [which I did] of old; for I am God, and there is no one else; I am God and there is none like Me, declaring the end and the result from the beginning, and from ancient times the things that are not yet done, saying, My counsel shall stand, and I will do all My pleasure and purpose.

(VERSES 4, 9–10, AMP)

According to that passage, there is no reason for days of heaven on earth to stop just because we get older. God's Word, His counsel, will stand for us at every age. He will carry us and save us in the golden years of maturity just as He did in our green years when we were still wet behind the ears.

In fact, if we'll continue in His Word, He'll be able to do even more for us in our latter days because as we get older, we grow wiser. We learn more about how to live this life according to God's plan. And the more we learn, the more we know. And the more we know, the more accurately we're able to live.

If we'll stick with the Lord, our lives will be more packed with faith and power with every passing year. We'll develop a history of walking with God that makes us ever more dangerous to the devil. We'll accumulate so many victories that instead of panicking when trouble arises, we'll be like David when he came up against Goliath. He had confidence because he remembered what the Lord had done for him in the past.

He remembered the time when he was out in the fields guarding his father's sheep and a lion attacked the flock. He remembered how God helped him kill that lion.

He recalled the day a bear attacked, and the Lord enabled him to do what few shepherd boys had ever done. He helped David catch it and slay it all by himself (1 Samuel 17:34–35).

Because of those experiences, when David faced a fight with a giant so big he made the whole army of Israel quake with fear, David didn't panic. He just thought about what he'd seen God do in the past. He said, "The LORD that delivered me out of the paw of the lion, and out of the paw of the bear, he will deliver me out of the hand of this Philistine" (1 Samuel 17:37).

The Bible says if we'll stick with the gospel, it will take us "from faith to faith" (Romans 1:17). It will make us like David, empowering us to progress from lion-killing faith to giant-slaying faith as we mature in the Lord. If we keep storing the Word in our hearts and developing our relationships with the Lord, the good fight of faith will get easier, not harder, as we age. If we'll keep abiding in God's Word, the more the years pile up, the more heavenly our days will be!

Have a "Different Spirit"

Two people in the Bible who demonstrated that fact in a striking way were Caleb and Joshua. They trudged around the wilderness with Moses and the rest of the Israelites for forty years, waiting for their promised land dream to be fulfilled. Unlike the rest of their countrymen, Caleb and Joshua didn't doubt the Word of God. They believed from the very beginning that God was able to give them Canaan, just as He said He would. When all those around them were wailing and wanting to return to Egypt because they were too frightened to fight the giants occupying the land, those two stout-hearted Israelites were shouting words of faith, saying:

If the LORD delight in us, then he will bring us into this land, and give it us; a land which floweth with milk and honey. Only rebel not ye against the LORD, neither fear ye the people of the land; for they are bread for us: their defence is departed from them, and the LORD is with us: fear them not. (NUMBERS 14:8–9)

Caleb and Joshua were about forty years of age when they first declared those words. They were young and strong and ready to receive the fulfillment of God's promise. They were confident God would keep His Word.

The rest of the Israelites, however, wanted to stone them for that confidence. They wanted to rid themselves of the likes of Joshua, Caleb, and even Moses, so they could elect another leader and go back the way they came. They decided they'd rather return to Egyptian slavery than trust God and go into the promised land.

As we've already seen, God decreed that rebellious bunch would die in the wilderness as a result of their unbelief. He told them they'd live only forty more years—to the age of seventy or eighty—and be buried in the desert while their children went in to take the land:

All those men which have seen my glory, and my miracles, which I did in Egypt and in the wilderness, and have tempted me now these ten times, and have not hearkened to my voice; surely they shall not see the land which I sware unto their fathers, neither shall any of them that provoked me see it: But my servant Caleb, because he had another spirit with him, and hath followed me fully, him will I bring into the land whereinto he went; and his seed shall possess it. (NUMBERS 14:22–24)

I love what the Lord said there about Caleb, that he had "another spirit with him." Instead of having an unbelieving, complaining spirit as the other Israelites did, Caleb had a spirit of faith. He followed God and fully obeyed His Word.

The same was true of Joshua. Numbers 32:12 says he "wholly followed the LORD." Joshua and Caleb obeyed God. They not only lived longer lives than their countrymen, they lived stronger lives! Their golden years sparkled in every way. Despite their forty extra years in the wilderness, they remained hardy and vibrant. They stayed full of optimism and faith. They never lost sight of their dreams.

As a result, when the opportunity opened up at last for them to step into those dreams at more than eighty years old, Caleb and Joshua were raring to go. They weren't tottering around getting ready for the grave. They weren't looking back at the "good old days" and thinking their best years were behind them. They were looking ahead to a future brimming with joy and divine fulfillment. They were getting ready to have the time of their lives!

Think of how eighty-year-old Joshua must have felt as he received God's marching orders—the divine instructions that would carry him through the next thirty years of his life. Imagine how thrilled he must have been as he listened to this divine description of the golden years that were ahead of him:

> Every place that the sole of your foot shall tread upon, that have I given unto you, as I said unto Moses. From the wilderness and this Lebanon even unto the great river, the river Euphrates, all the land of the Hittites, and unto the great sea toward the going down of the sun, shall be your coast. There shall not any man be able to stand before thee all the days of thy life: as I was with Moses, so I will be with thee: I will not fail thee, nor forsake thee. Be strong and of a good courage: for unto this people shalt thou divide for an inheritance the land, which I sware unto their fathers to give them. Only be thou strong and very courageous, that thou mayest observe to do according to all the law, which Moses my servant commanded thee: turn not from it to the right hand or to the left, that thou mayest prosper whithersoever thou goest. This book of the law shall not depart out of thy mouth; but thou shalt meditate therein day and night, that thou mayest observe to do according to all that is written therein: for then thou shalt make thy way prosperous, and then thou shalt have good success. Have not I commanded thee? Be strong and of a good courage; be not afraid, neither be thou

dismayed: for the Lord thy God is with thee whithersoever thou goest. (Joshua 1:3–9)

It's obvious that God did not intend for Joshua to start winding down at eighty. He didn't mention anything about Joshua being too weak, sickly, or feeble to lead the Israelites into Canaan. He expected Joshua at eighty years old to have the health, strength, and mental clarity to fight and conquer the promised land giants.

When Joshua heard God's plan for his golden years, he knew one thing for sure. There would be no nursing-home days for him. He had too much to do!

Caleb did, too. He had been waiting more than forty years to possess the mountain he'd set his heart on when he and the other Israelite scouts had first spied out the land. Moses had promised him way back then that he and his children could have that mountain as an inheritance. So, when Joshua finally led the march into the land of Canaan, Caleb became an eighty-five-year-old man on a mission. He went to Joshua and said:

> The Lord hath kept me alive, as he said, these forty and five years, even since the Lord spake this word unto Moses, while the children of Israel wandered in the wilderness: and now, lo, I am this day fourscore and five years old. As yet I am as strong this day as I was in the day that Moses sent me: as my strength was then, even so is my strength now, for war, both to go out, and to come in. Now therefore give me this mountain, whereof the Lord spake in that day; for thou heardest in that day how the Anakims were there, and that the cities were great and fenced: if so be the Lord will be with me, then I shall be able to drive them out, as the Lord said. And Joshua blessed him, and gave unto Caleb the son of Jephunneh Hebron for an inheritance. (Joshua 14:10–13)

Those words reveal just what kind of a different spirit Caleb had. He had the kind of spirit that hung on to God's Word for forty-five years by faith, waiting for it to come to pass. After all his faithless friends and relatives died around him in the wilderness and the time came for him to go after his God-given dream, he didn't say, "Well, I'm eighty-five now. I'm too old. I'm too weak to fight the giants living on that mountain."

No. He said, "I can do it! I am as strong as I've ever been. Give me my mountain!"

That's the attitude we must have, too, if we want to live long and finish strong. We must hold on to every word that God has spoken to us and keep believing for it to come to pass, no matter how long it takes. When divine doors of opportunity open for us in our golden years, we must be ready to say, "I can do that because I am in Jesus and He is in me. I have God's Word. I have His strength. I have His life in me, renewing my youth like the eagle's!"

Most people would be afraid life would defeat them if they took that attitude at eighty-five, but Caleb wasn't afraid at all. He was bold and full of faith. He tore out after the giants who had occupied his property with the energy of a forty-five-year-old. Those giants didn't defeat him either. He won the battle. He kicked them off his mountain and spent his golden years basking in a dream come true.

Get a Fresh Word

"Well, I'm happy for Caleb," you might say, "but I just don't have the spirit of faith that he did."

You can get it!

How?

From the Word of God. As we've already seen, "Faith cometh by hearing, and hearing by the word of God" (Romans 10:17).

Notice that verse doesn't just say "Faith comes by hearing." It says faith comes by "hearing and hearing." In other words, faith comes from continually feeding on the Word of God.

That's something we must remember, especially as we age, because after we've been in church and hearing the Word for a few decades, we can be tempted to say, "Oh, I've heard those Scriptures many times. I know them so well that I don't need to hear them anymore." That's a dangerous attitude! We can't ever afford to slack off on the Word.

It doesn't matter how many times we've heard it. We still need to hear it again. It doesn't matter how many years we've meditated on it. We need to keep on meditating on it. God's Word is the bread of life, and if we want to live long and finish strong, we must feed on that bread daily. We can't live on last year's Word. We can't walk in victory if all we have is the Word we remember from a church service or convention we attended last year.

We need the Word every day. We need to keep reading and meditating on it until it comes alive in us and takes over our lives. We must obey what it says and stay in it so that it stays fresh in us and we don't forget to do it.

We don't ever want to neglect and forget the promises of God as we age. On the contrary, we want to rehearse His blessings all the days of our lives. We want to wake up every morning praising the Lord and following the example David gave us in Psalm 103.

I especially like the New Living Translation version of that psalm:

> Praise the LORD, I tell myself,
>> and never forget the good things he does for me.
> He forgives all my sins
>> and heals all my diseases.
> He ransoms me from death
>> and surrounds me with love and tender mercies.
> He fills my life with good things.
>> My youth is renewed like the eagle's! (VERSES 2–5)

Notice that passage tells us we must never forget the benefits and blessings of God. Why is that? Because the blessing we walk in today is the blessing we remember! That's the reason we must open our Bibles every morning and look again at what God has said to us. That's why it's a good idea to listen to the Word when you're in your car, to attend a good Word-preaching church, and to spend time in the Word every day. Doing those things will help you remember and receive all the good things the Lord has made available to you. Your faith will stay active and strong. You will be a doer of the Word and not a hearer only.

It pays to be a student of the Word at every age because the Word is where our lives are. It's where our well-being is. It's what makes our marriages strong. It's the source of our prosperity. Knowing, believing, and obeying the Word of God is what puts the gold in the golden years of our lives.

It was the Word that Caleb hung on to for all those years that kept him young enough to whip a hillside full of giants at eighty-five. The Word did for him (and will do for us) just what Isaiah 40:28–31 says it will do.

We've already looked at that passage once, but let's go over it again in *The Amplified Bible*:

> Have you not known? Have you not heard? The everlasting God, the Lord, the Creator of the ends of the earth, does not faint or grow weary; there is no searching of His understanding. He gives power to the faint and weary, and to him who has no might He increases strength [causing it to multiply and making it to abound]. Even youths shall faint and be weary, and [selected] young men shall feebly stumble and fall exhausted; but those who wait for the Lord [who expect, look for, and hope in Him] shall change and renew their strength and power; they shall lift their wings and mount up [close to God] as eagles [mount up to the sun]; they shall run and not be weary, they shall walk and not faint or become tired.

Still Alive and Kicking at 175

If Caleb and Joshua aren't evidence enough of the youth-renewing power that comes to those who stand in faith on God's Word and wait on Him to fulfill His promises, Abraham proves the point beyond question. He was in his seventies when God first promised him a son, and his barren wife, Sarah, was only a few years younger. Abraham and Sarah had to stand in faith for more than twenty years for God's promise to come to pass, but they did it. As they did, an amazing thing happened.

Their youth was renewed.

It must have been, because Genesis 20 tells us that when Sarah was in her nineties, a heathen king wanted her for himself. Kings aren't usually too excited about ninety-year-old women, so that tells us Sarah must not have looked her age. What's more, later that same year, she gave birth to Isaac, nursed him (how many almost-centenarians can do that?), and lived to see him grow up. She didn't die until she was 127 years old.

Sarah wasn't the only one whose youth was renewed. Abraham fared quite well, too. He not only fathered a son at one hundred years old, but after Sarah died, he remarried. (The Bible isn't specific about how old he was at the time but since he was about ten years older than Sarah, he must have been at least 137.)

Remarrying at 137 is amazing enough, but Abraham didn't stop there. He went on to father five more sons and lived another forty years or so. The Bible indicates in Genesis 25:7–8 that he enjoyed those years, too.

> ⚱ This is the sum of the years of Abraham's life which he lived: one hundred and seventy-five years. Then Abraham breathed his last and died in a good old age, an old man and full of years, and was gathered to his people. (NKJV)

> ⚱ Abraham lived for 175 years, and he died at a ripe old age, joining his ancestors in death. (NLT)

> ⚱ The days of Abraham's life were 175 years. Then Abraham's spirit was released, and he died at a good (ample, full) old age, an old man, satisfied and satiated, and was gathered to his people. (AMP)

Abraham showed us what the golden years can be like for people who trust God and believe His Word. They're good! They're satisfying and satiating! They're ample, full, and ripe!

Genesis 24:1 confirms that picture of Abraham's old age: "Abraham was old, and well stricken in age: and the LORD had blessed Abraham in all things."

Abraham wasn't surprised by that blessing either. He expected his life to end up that way because he was a man who believed God, and God had promised him a blessed and lengthy life. When Abraham was still just a youngster of eighty or ninety years, the Lord had spoken to him and said, "Thou shalt go to thy fathers in peace; thou shalt be buried in a good old age" (Genesis 15:15).

Abraham believed God would keep that promise and, of course, He did. So, all through Abraham's latter years—from his 70s to his 170s—Abraham enjoyed a full, satisfying life. He was loved and respected. He was prosperous. He lived in peace. When anyone gave him trouble, he had the strength and resources to overcome it.

When an army of enemy kings kidnapped his nephew Lot and Lot's family, for example, Abraham gathered three hundred of his trained servants and went after them. He won the battle and got Lot and his family back. People learned not to mess with Abraham. Even though he was pushing one hundred, he could still whip his enemies when necessary.

Can we be like Abraham?

Yes, we can! The Bible calls him the father of our faith. It says we can walk in his footsteps (Romans 4:12). But to do that, we must remember that Abraham not only believed God, he also obeyed Him.

When God told Abraham to leave his homeland and his father's house, he packed up and moved. He left his idol-worshiping culture and kinfolk behind and set out for the land God promised to show him. I'm sure that wasn't an easy command for Abraham to obey, but because God had blessed him and promised to take care of him, he trusted God and followed His command.

When God told Abraham to take his son Isaac, whom he loved, and offer him as a sacrifice, Abraham obeyed:

> By faith Abraham, when he was tried, offered up Isaac: and he
> that had received the promises offered up his only begotten son,
> of whom it was said, That in Isaac shall thy seed be called: accounting
> that God was able to raise him up, even from the dead; from whence
> also he received him in a figure. (HEBREWS 11:17–19)

Of course, God provided a ram to take Isaac's place at the last moment, so Abraham didn't actually have to sacrifice him. But even so, Abraham had every intention of fulfilling God's command. He believed since God had promised that Isaac would be the son through whom Abraham's descendants would come, God would resurrect him. That's faith!

That's the kind of faith in God and obedience that open the door to a life lived long and finished strong!

Keep on Pressing

I must admit, one thing that inspires me about Abraham is the fact that he stayed so active in his golden years. He must have—he had five sons to raise when he was more than 140 years old! So if we're going to follow in his footsteps, we shouldn't envision ourselves sitting around watching soap operas in our latter years. We should see ourselves busy and in motion.

Actually, the very definition of the word *life* conveys a sense of movement. It includes terms such as "quick," "running," and "springing."[2] *Life* is a motion word, so we should stay in motion all the days of our lives!

This is not a book on exercise, but I will say this: God made our bodies to move. He didn't design them to sit around watching television all the time. What's more, He warned us in His Word not to be lazy. He said, "The way of the slothful man is as an hedge of thorns: but the way of the righteous is made plain" (Proverbs 15:19). So if we don't want to have prickly, painful problems in our old age, we'd be wise to keep moving.

If you think you're already too old to start an exercise program, think again. In my research on longevity, I came across a photo of a seventy-two-year-old woman bodybuilder! Her muscles were amazing. (That was quite evident because she was wearing a bikini!)

The accompanying article explained that this lady had started lifting weights in her later years when she realized she lacked the strength to handle everyday tasks such as keeping her cat supplied with kitty litter. She didn't want to call someone for help with those kinds of things, so she joined a bodybuilding class.

Her attitude was probably a lot like Abraham's when he started thinking about remarrying at 137. "Sure, you'll get older. So what?" she said.

That's the kind of perspective we all will have if we really believe that God has promised us length of days and years of a life worth living, all the way through old age. We won't be talking like grumpy old men and women. We won't be a drag on everyone around us, griping and complaining about how terrible it is to get old.

Gripers and complainers probably won't make it to a hundred. The Israelites in the wilderness proved that. So, if we're aiming for 120, we'll be upbeat in our attitude about aging. We'll talk about the faithfulness of God. We'll stay in motion and tell everyone about how God has promised to keep us strong, well, and whole all our days.

As believers, we're supposed to be full of joy and let people know about it. The Bible says so! It tells us, "The voice of rejoicing and salvation is in the tabernacles of the righteous: the right hand of the LORD doeth valiantly" (Psalm 118:15).

We shouldn't have depression, sadness, moaning, and groaning in our houses. There should be a continual celebration of the goodness of God all the way through our golden years.

"But what if I start getting sick as I get older?" you might ask. "What if I get a bad report from the doctor and he says I'll never recover?"

The next few verses of Psalm 118 give us some insight about how to respond to circumstances like that:

> The right hand of the LORD is exalted: the right hand of the LORD doeth valiantly. I shall not die, but live, and declare the works of the LORD....Open to me the gates of righteousness: I will go into them, and I will praise the LORD: this gate of the LORD, into which the righteous shall enter. I will praise thee: for thou hast heard me, and art become my salvation. (VERSES 16–17, 19–21)

One Jewish commentary, the *Tehillim*, says about that passage: "When he reaches a plateau of piety, the righteous man remains unsatisfied and immediately seeks to climb even closer to [God]. It is precisely this intense yearning which infuses the righteous man with the strength to overcome all obstacles in his path."[3]

There's something about pressing toward God, even in difficult times, that gives us supernatural strength to triumph over all attacks of the devil. If you doubt it, look at the life of the apostle Paul. He discovered the key to finishing life in victory. He lived strong until he fulfilled his calling and decided he wanted to depart and be with Jesus.

What was Paul's secret?

In his latter years, despite all the persecutions, beatings, stonings, shipwrecks, and hardships he had suffered, he was still pressing on to know the Lord in a deeper way. He was still reaching out to fulfill God's plan and purpose for his life. "[For my determined purpose is] that I may know Him," he said in his letter to the church at Philippi,

> [that I may progressively become more deeply and intimately acquainted with Him, perceiving and recognizing and understanding the wonders of His Person more strongly and more clearly], and

that I may in that same way come to know the power outflowing
from His resurrection...and that I may so share His sufferings as to
be continually transformed [in spirit into His likeness even] to His
death, [in the hope] that if possible I may attain to the [spiritual and
moral] resurrection [that lifts me] out from among the dead [even
while in the body]. Not that I have now attained [this ideal], or have
already been made perfect, but I press on to lay hold of (grasp) and
make my own, that for which Christ Jesus (the Messiah) has laid
hold of me and made me His own. I do not consider, brethren, that I
have captured and made it my own [yet]; but one thing I do [it is my
one aspiration]: forgetting what lies behind and straining forward to
what lies ahead, I press on toward the goal to win the [supreme and
heavenly] prize to which God in Christ Jesus is calling us upward.
(PHILIPPIANS 3:10–14 AMP)

Most Bible scholars believe Paul was in the last phase of his life
and ministry when he wrote those words. He was in prison, yet he
was still growing and changing. He hadn't become stagnant and set
in his ways. He was still pressing to become more like Jesus. He was
still reaching for life in God.

Reaching for life leads to more life! It keeps us alive and in motion
in our latter years. It gives us the energy we need to finish our course
the way Paul did.

If we'll follow Paul's example and heed the words of Psalm 118,
when symptoms try to manifest in our bodies or we get a negative
report from the doctor, we'll say, "I'll live and not die and declare
the works of the Lord." We'll stand against those reports by faith
in God's Word and declare, "Don't be talking to me about death.
I haven't finished my race yet. Don't be putting any death penalty
on me!"

We'll say, as the Jewish commentary does, "I shall be counted
among the righteous who are considered alive even after death. Certainly I will not be considered dead while I live!"[4]

Stay Sappy and Full of Vitality

I realize the world teaches us that we have to get sick and weak as we grow older, but we can't listen to what the world says. We can't look at unsaved people to see how we're supposed to turn out. We can't even look at Christians who don't know what the Bible says to see how we're supposed to age.

We must look at the Word. It contradicts the worldly picture of aging. It says your senior years should truly be golden. It says you should live long, strong, and healthy until you finish what God has called you to do and you're satisfied. It tells you to keep God's commands and walk with Him, "that it may go well with you and with your children after you, and that you may prolong your days in the land" (Deuteronomy 4:40 NKJV).

Do you know what it means for things to be *well* with you? According to the definition of the primary root of the Hebrew word, it means "to be literally sound; to make beautiful; to be happy, successful, and right; to be accepted, made better; to benefit, make cheerful, be comely, find favor, be glad, be made merry, to please, to show kindness, to make sweet, thoroughly."[5] That's a great description of the golden years of God's people. They are thoroughly sweet years. They are sound, beautiful, successful, happy, cheerful, glad, favorable years. They are years filled with God's kindness toward us.

You may think that sounds like an exaggeration, but it's not. Psalm 92 depicts the latter years of God's obedient people in that very same way:

> The [uncompromisingly] righteous shall flourish like the palm tree [be long-lived, stately, upright, useful, and fruitful]; they shall grow like a cedar in Lebanon [majestic, stable, durable, and incorruptible]. Planted in the house of the Lord, they shall flourish in the courts of our God. [Growing in grace] they shall still bring forth fruit in old age; they shall be full of sap [of spiritual vitality] and [rich in the] verdure [of trust, love, and contentment]. [They are living memorials] to show that the

Lord is upright and faithful to His promises; He is my Rock, and there is no unrighteousness in Him. (VERSES 12–15 AMP)

That means we don't have to spend the last few years of our lives ailing, crippled, and confused. We don't have to scrape by on little Social Security checks that leave us in poverty. We can live out our golden years in such blessing that people will consider us living memorials whose lives testify of the goodness and faithfulness of God. We can be living letters, "known and read of all men" (2 Corinthians 3:2), who reveal God's mighty power and love.

Imagine what an impression we could have on others as we walk down to the town square at 119 years old, dressed sharp, looking good, full of energy, and with a spring in our step, telling people about Jesus. Don't you think people might listen to someone like that? Don't you think when strangers came to town, people would tell them about that group of 120-year-olds who pray, read the Bible every day, lay hands on the sick, and heal them?

Sure they would!

Actually, today we don't have to wait until 120 to be living memorials. We can start much younger. We can be living memorials at sixty, seventy, or eighty if we'll stay full of sap and spiritual vitality.

Of course, to do that, we can't let ourselves start getting depressed when we hit forty. My goodness! On God's timetable of life, a forty-year-old is little more than a child. (I have a real revelation of that because my daughter, Kellie, turned forty a few years ago.) Forty shouldn't bother us. Neither should fifty…sixty…seventy…or eighty. We can keep going as long and strong as we want—all to the glory of God.

"But what about age-related diseases like Alzheimer's?" someone might ask. "Aren't we as vulnerable to those as everyone else?"

No, we're not. Jesus bore our sicknesses and carried our diseases on the cross. He provided healing for us by His stripes. So Alzheimer's is not for us! If it comes knocking at our doors, we should send it packing.

How do we do that? By resisting it with the Word of God. If we begin getting confused or forgetting things, we don't say, "Oh, I guess that's just a part of old age." We start speaking the Word of God. We say, "I refuse to be confused. My mind is at peace through old age. I have a sound mind. I have the mind of Christ. I walk in divine health all the days of my life."

In a later chapter, we'll see more about the healing that belongs to us because of our blood covenant with God, but I will say this: the Bible tells us that as born-again believers we have been set free from every aspect of the curse. It says, "Christ hath redeemed us from the curse of the law, being made a curse for us: for it is written, Cursed is every one that hangeth on a tree" (Galatians 3:13).

According to Deuteronomy 28:20, 28 (NKJV), "confusion" is part of the curse. Therefore, we don't have to put up with it in our youth or in our old age. We can stand on the Word of God by faith and refuse to receive it.

I'm not just talking theory here either. I've had to do it myself. Some years ago, I started having memory problems, and the devil tried to do to me what he tries to do to all of us. He tried to scare me with the threat of Alzheimer's or some other age-related mental confusion. So I went straight to God's Word and began studying and meditating on Scriptures that promise me a sound, healthy mind.

One of my favorites turned out to be Proverbs 10:7: "The memory of the righteous is blessed" (NKJV). I may have taken the interpretation of that verse a little loosely, but it agreed with other Bible promises, and it spoke to my heart. So, whenever I forgot something, I confessed that Scripture. I said, "Praise God, the memory of the righteous is blessed!"

Live Sumptuously and Be a Blessing

The Bible tells us we can remain mentally sharp in our old age. Why, then, do we fear aging and diseases such as Alzheimer's? Because the devil wants us to be afraid. He knows that fear is the counterfeit of faith. Just as faith in God's Word draws to us what we are believing for, fear draws to us what the devil has in store for us. As Job discovered, the thing we greatly fear will come upon us (Job 3:25).

So, don't allow yourself to fear Alzheimer's (or any other "age-related" diseases). We can still triumph because we are born-again, supernatural people. We are filled with the Spirit of God. We have eternal life inside us and the Word of life available to us on the pages of our Bibles to help us renew our youth every day.

Some time ago, I came across a little note from one of our ministry Partners who is living out her golden years in light of those revelations. At ninety-two years old, she experiences no pain and owes no one anything. She is still young at heart, delighting in the abundant care of God.

What a testimony to God's power and goodness! That lady is not only healthy and free of aches and pains, she is prosperous. She has no debts and her needs are met "sumptuously." We should all believe for that kind of provision in our old age. We shouldn't expect it to come through our Social Security checks either. It would truly be a miracle if Social Security would be available when we are 120!

If we'll tithe and give throughout our lives as the Lord leads us, we won't have to depend on Social Security checks. We can be more prosperous in that season than at any other time in our lives, and that monthly check can just be something extra.

Here's why.

God multiplies the financial seed we sow. When we give, He sees to it that in return, it will be given to us again, in "good measure, pressed down, and shaken together, and running over" (Luke 6:38). What's more, Jesus promised in Mark 10:30 that we would receive a return on our giving "now in this time": "He shall receive an hundredfold now in this time, houses, and brethren, and sisters, and mothers, and children, and lands, with persecutions; and in the world to come eternal life."

That means the older we get, the more blessed we will be because we have more seed in the ground that must produce a harvest before we leave here and go to heaven. I've been believing and confessing for years that the hundredfold return Jesus promised is coming to me in this life. I've said again and again that the older I get, the better and more prosperous I am because my harvest is catching up with me.

Ken and I are experiencing that now. We are more blessed in every way and more prosperous than we've ever been in our lives. We are not finished prospering either. We are going to keep increasing until we finish our course and take off for heaven.

I'm not ninety-two yet, but when I am, I expect to be a living memorial to God, just as our sumptuously fed and clothed, daily-meditation-writing Partner is. What a great example she is of a long, strong life! She isn't sitting around thinking and acting old, waiting for someone to come minister to her. She is busy ministering and being a blessing to others.

Things are well with her. Her life is altogether sweet.

Her golden years are gleaming with the faithfulness of God.

POINTS TO REMEMBER

- The Bible is the best longevity book in the world. If we expect to live to a ripe old age, we must dig into it and find out more about what God has promised us, and what He says about how we should live.

- If we believe and obey God's Word, we can rest assured that our senior years will be golden. We can expect them to be as days of heaven on earth.

- If we keep storing the Word in our hearts, our lives will be more packed with faith and power with every passing year.

- It was the Word that Caleb hung on to for forty years that kept him young enough to whip a hillside full of giants at eighty-five. We, too, can enjoy that kind of victory if we will hold on to God's promises and keep believing for them to come to pass, no matter how impossible it looks.

❀ God's Word is the bread of life. To live long and strong, we must feed on it daily. We can't live on last year's Word. We need a fresh Word every day.

SCRIPTURE

Those who wait for the Lord [who expect, look for, and hope in Him] shall change and renew their strength and power; they shall lift their wings and mount up [close to God] as eagles [mount up to the sun]; they shall run and not be weary, they shall walk and not faint or become tired. (Isaiah 40:31 AMP)

CONFESSION

My golden years will sparkle with the goodness of God. Because I believe and obey His Word, I will grow stronger and more victorious as the years go by. The fight of faith will become easier for me as I age. Like Caleb, I will still be defeating giants in my latter years and enjoying the fulfillment of God's promises in my life. Days of heaven on earth are ahead for me!

CHAPTER 5

Protecting Your Fountain of Youth

'm amazed at how often people claim to have discovered the "fountain of youth." Month after month, year after year, magazine covers and book jackets tout the latest and greatest longevity secrets. Scientists come up with genetic keys, and nutritionists proclaim the one...or two...or seven foods that guarantee long, healthy lives to those who eat them. Fitness experts invent exercise plans that promise to keep us young, slim, and agile at any age.

Although good nutrition and exercise really do help, no one has yet come up with a guaranteed life-lengthening, youth-renewing plan that provides people in their eighties, nineties, hundreds, and beyond the strength and vitality of people half their age.

No one, that is, except Moses.

His secret for long, strong life, echoed throughout the Bible, is the only one that really works. He proved it beyond any doubt by staying youthful to the ripe old age of 120. Moses practiced what he preached. Despite his rugged life in the wilderness and his potentially high-stress job of leading a million-plus cantankerous, unbelieving people to the promised land, he tapped into a fountain of youth that kept him young year after year, decade after decade. He found a source of life-renewing power that kept him sharp eyed and physically strong twenty years beyond the century mark.

What was Moses' secret? What was the force that kept him going so strong for so long?

It wasn't a particular gene. It wasn't a certain kind of food. (Although I'm sure manna was perfect.) It wasn't some kind of super-duper exercise program. (Though the Israelites' walking program was exceptional!) It was the living Word of almighty God. It was the Word Moses received on Mount Sinai in the midst of the fire of God's glory, the Word he believed and obeyed (with one rock-striking exception) from the time he was eighty until his mission was finished forty years later. It was the Word of God that prolonged Moses' days. The Word from God was his life. It protected him, preserved him, and kept him going…and going…and going.

That's why, just before he sent the Israelites into the promised land, Moses called them together and said: "Set your hearts unto all the words which I testify among you this day, which ye shall command your children to observe to do, all the words of this law. For it is not a vain thing for you; because *it is your life: and through this thing ye shall prolong your days* in the land" (Deuteronomy 32:46–47, italics added).

The New Living Translation quotes verse 47 this way: "These instructions are not mere words—they are your life! By obeying them you will enjoy a long life."

For the most part, the people Moses spoke to on the border of Canaan grasped the truth of his message. That particular generation of Israelites truly honored God's Word. They believed it and received it as their life. As a result, they experienced victory after victory in the land God gave them. They overcame their enemies and received the inheritance He promised them. The Bible doesn't tell us how long they all lived, but if their leader, Joshua, was any indication, they did all right. He lived to be 110 years old.

Sad to say, most people these days aren't as wise as those Israelites were. They don't treat God's Word as if it is their life. Instead of honoring it and hungering for it, they act as if they're bored with it. They seem to think spending time reading and studying it is a waste of time.

But they are mistaken. God's Word is not a vain thing. It contains the very life of God. When we receive it in faith, when we set our minds on it and fill our eyes and ears with it, it energizes us with divine power. It affects us in a wonderful way—spirit, soul, and body.

I know that's true, not only because the Bible says so, but because I continually experience the reality of it on a regular basis.

Many times, especially when preparing to minister, for example, I get caught up in the Word and I experience such stirring up of my spirit, I am physically affected. I feel it start churning within me. Sometimes my face will actually get hot! It will turn red as if I've been running a race, even though all I've been doing is sitting receiving revelation from the Bible.

Sometimes, when I'm preparing to do a television broadcast, Sher, the lady who applies my TV makeup, will comment on it. "I can tell you've been in the Word," she'll say. "Your face is flushed."

If the Word can affect my physical appearance that much, think what it does for the rest of my body. Think what it's doing for my heart, lungs, liver, and muscles!

"Oh, Gloria," someone might say, "surely you don't believe God's Word affects you the way it affected Moses! He lived in Old Testament times. Believers today are under a different covenant."

That's true, but it's a better covenant, and God's Word is still as alive and full of power as it ever was. Granted, we aren't bound to Old Covenant law anymore. We live, instead, by faith in Jesus. What does the New Testament call Jesus? It calls Him "the Word"!

> In the beginning was the Word, and the Word was with God, and the Word was God. The same was in the beginning with God. All things were made by him; and without him was not any thing made that was made. In him [In whom? In the Word!] was life; and the life was the light of men....And the Word was made flesh, and dwelt among us, (and

we beheld his glory, the glory as of the only begotten of the Father,)
full of grace and truth. (JOHN 1:1–4, 14)

That passage makes it very clear: life is in Jesus, and Jesus is the Word made flesh.

That means it's impossible to separate Jesus from God's Word. He and the Word are one. When we, as born-again believers, open God's written Word, we find Jesus there. We find the quickening power of His Holy Spirit. Don't ever let anyone convince you that God's Word isn't essential to us as New Covenant believers. It is still as powerful and indispensable as ever. If you doubt it, read the New Testament book of Hebrews. It says that God's Word not only created the world in eons past, but it still holds creation together today. Hebrews 1:3 declares that right now Jesus is "upholding all things by the word of his power." He is literally keeping the universe on course with His Word. Don't you think He can keep *you* going long and strong?

What's more, Hebrews 4:12 tells us that the Word affects us as born-again believers in a real and dynamic way. It is life to us just as it was to the people in Moses' day because now, as then:

❧ The word of God is living and powerful, and sharper than any two-edged sword, piercing even to the division of soul and spirit, and of joints and marrow, and is a discerner of the thoughts and intents of the heart. (NKJV)

❧ The Word that God speaks is alive and full of power [making it active, operative, energizing, and effective]; it is sharper than any two-edged sword, penetrating to the dividing line of the breath of life (soul) and [the immortal] spirit, and of joints and marrow [of the deepest parts of our nature], exposing and sifting and analyzing and judging the very thoughts and purposes of the heart. (AMP)

❧ The word of God is full of living power. It is sharper than the sharpest knife, cutting deep into our innermost thoughts and desires. It exposes us for what we really are. (NLT)

It's not surprising that I can sometimes sense the Word affecting my physical body because, according to that verse, the Word impacts more than our souls and spirits. It penetrates all through our cells and organs to the innermost part of our bones. It reaches all the way to our marrow—a place where our blood is made!

That may sound far out, but other Scriptures confirm it. Proverbs 3, for instance, says:

> My son, forget not my law; but let thine heart keep my commandments: for length of days, and long life, and peace, shall they add to thee. Let not mercy and truth forsake thee: bind them about thy neck; write them upon the table of thine heart: So shalt thou find favour and good understanding in the sight of God and man. Trust in the LORD with all thine heart; and lean not unto thine own understanding. In all thy ways acknowledge him, and he shall direct thy paths. Be not wise in thine own eyes: fear the LORD, and depart from evil. It shall be health to thy navel, and marrow to thy bones. (VERSES 1–8)

Look again at that last verse. It says God's Word will be "health to thy navel, and marrow to thy bones." Or, as another translation puts it, "health to your nerves and sinews, and marrow and moistening to your bones" (AMP). God's Word literally gets inside you when you receive it in faith. In a very real way, it "effectually worketh also in you that believe" (1 Thessalonians 2:13) by touching not just your spirit and soul but your body as well. To those who will believe and obey it, the Word becomes a veritable fountain of youth.

Feeding the Real You

"But how is that possible?" you might ask. "How could God's Word affect our bodies in such a literal way? The life in the Word isn't physical, it's spiritual!"

That's true. But it is our spirits that give life to our bodies.

People often forget that. They get so body-oriented (because the body is what's seen and felt) that they start thinking their outer man is more real than their inner man. The truth, however, is just the opposite. Your inner man, your spirit (or what 1 Peter 3:4 calls "the hidden man of the heart"), is the most powerful part of you. It is actually the real you.

Your body, on the other hand, is just your "earth suit." The Bible refers to it as your earthly tent or your mortal clothing (2 Corinthians 5:1–4). It's like a coat that wraps around your spirit. Someday, if Jesus tarries, you'll finish your earthly assignment and you (the spirit) will leave your body and go to heaven. (At least, that's what will happen if you're born again. If you're not born again, you will go somewhere else, a very hot and horrible place where you definitely don't want to be. So if you haven't yet done it, I'd encourage you to make Jesus your Lord right now, and make sure you don't spend eternity in the wrong place!)

Do you know what will happen to your body when your spirit leaves?

It will die. It will become as still and lifeless as a cast-off coat. The mortician will fix it up and make it look as nice as possible. Your friends will probably go to the funeral home and talk about how sad it is to see you there and how "natural" you look. But in reality you won't be there at all. Only your empty earth suit will be left behind. The real person, you the spirit, will be alive and well, celebrating in heaven!

Once you truly understand that your spirit is the real you and that it actually keeps your body alive, it's easy to see how God's Word, which strengthens and gives life to your spirit, can affect your body as well. Suddenly, verses like Proverbs 18:14, which says, "The spirit of a man will sustain [him in] his infirmity," don't seem far-fetched at all. In fact, they make perfect sense because if our spirits sustain our bodies, it's obvious that the stronger our spirits are, the better off our bodies will be. The more vibrant our spiritual health, the more ability we'll have to live long and strong.

It's also obvious that if we allow our spirits to grow weak, we'll go the way of the grave more quickly.

That's why God's Word is so vital to us as believers. It's the Word of God that nourishes our spirits (1 Timothy 4:6). It's the Word that feeds our inner man. Jesus said it this way: "Man shall not live by bread alone, but by every word that proceedeth out of the mouth of God" (Matthew 4:4).

In the same way that natural food becomes the fuel of life to our physical cells, the bread of God's Word, digested by faith, becomes fuel for our inner man. The Word keeps our spiritual engines running. When we believe and obey it, it becomes the quickening spark that renews our lives, day after day.

No wonder in Psalm 119 the psalmist wrote:

⚹ Quicken me according to thy word. (verse 154)

⚹ Revive me and give me life according to Your word. (verse 154 AMP)

⚹ Quicken me according to thy judgments. (verse 156)

⚹ Give me life according to Your ordinances. (verse 156 AMP)

⚹ Consider how I love thy precepts: quicken me, O LORD. (verse 159)

⚹ Give life to me, O Lord, according to Your loving-kindness! (verse 159 AMP)

One man who discovered that the inner quickening of God's Word can affect our outward man in a most powerful way was F. F. Bosworth, the early 1900s author of the wonderful book *Christ the Healer* and a minister who helped multitudes receive healing from God. Mr. Bosworth made a habit of praying and trusting God to quicken not only his spirit but his body with divine life. As a result, he preached into his eighties with such tireless fervor that, according to his son, "It was as if he had...lived two lives."[1] When he died, it was not because of sickness, but because he was satisfied that he had finished his race.

Of course, to receive the kind of supernatural quickening from the Word Mr. Bosworth experienced, we must do more than just look mindlessly at Scriptures. We can't just read a few verses, yawn, close our Bibles, and say, "Ho hum. I've done my spiritual duty for today." That kind of attitude is a sure sign we're not letting the Word get through to us.

If we have that attitude, we can change it simply by reading the Bible with expectancy. We can approach God's written Word believing it's the truth and trusting Him to speak to us through it the very thing we need to hear. When we receive God's Word like that, it doesn't just get into our minds, it goes down into our hearts.

Notice I said our *hearts*, not just our brains. That's important because God's Word is not just a head thing. It's a heart thing, too! It becomes a fountain of life and youth for us only when we let it take root and come alive inside us.

Jesus explained it this way: "If ye abide in me, and my words abide in you, ye shall ask what ye will, and it shall be done unto you" (John 15:7). The word *abide* means "to live, dwell, or take up residence in a place."[2]

How do you know if God's Word is abiding in your heart? The Word that abides in you will talk to you. As you go about your day and encounter various situations, it will speak to you about them. It will tell you what to do and how to live. It will direct your thoughts and actions.

Be Sure to Eat from the Tree of Life

When the Word comes alive in your heart and begins to guide your life, it becomes what Proverbs 3:13–18 calls "a tree of life." Long life is definitely influenced by the Word of God. Although I mentioned that passage earlier, let's read it again:

Happy is the man that findeth wisdom, and the man that getteth understanding. For the merchandise of it is better than the merchandise of silver, and the gain thereof than fine gold. She is more precious than rubies: and all the things thou canst desire are not to be compared unto her. Length of days is in her right hand; and in her left hand riches and honour. Her ways are ways of pleasantness, and all her paths are peace. *She is a tree of life to them that lay hold upon her: and happy is every one that retaineth her.* (ITALICS ADDED)

Think about what the original tree of life, the one God put in the center of the Garden of Eden, offered to Adam and Eve. It made available to them such divine energy and youth-renewing power that if they had partaken of it, they would never have died. We know that's true because after they sinned, God sent them out of the garden to keep them from eating its fruit. He didn't want them to reach out in their fallen state and "take also of the tree of life, and eat, and live for ever" (Genesis 3:22).

In many ways, that tree offered to Adam and Eve the same thing God's Word offers us—eternal, abundant life. There's really just one difference. The Word doesn't promise us that our bodies will never die. It doesn't extend to us the opportunity to live on this earth forever in our natural, unglorified bodies. But then, what Christian in his right mind would want to do that? This earth, in its current state, isn't fit to live in forever. Neither are these fallen, flesh-and-blood earth suits we're wearing.

Think about it. Our physical bodies are a lot of trouble. They have to be washed and combed and tended to every day or they start looking and smelling bad. Most of us women even paint them with makeup trying to make them more presentable.

I don't know about you, but I am not interested in having to fix my hair and put on makeup every day for all eternity. So I'm not looking for a way to keep this earth suit alive forever. But I do want to fulfill the number of my days in it and finish what God has called me to do.

Every believer I know feels the same way. When we've finished our assignments on earth, all of us who belong to Jesus will be eager to blast out of here so we can go to heaven and be with Him. We'll be happy to leave these old bodies behind until resurrection day when we'll receive our glorified bodies. Those bodies will be great! They'll be much more beautiful and low maintenance than the ones we have now. They'll be fit to live in forever.

Although God's Word doesn't promise our temporal earth suits will never die, in every other way, His Word does for us just what the tree of life would have done for Adam and Eve. It gives life to our spirits, quickens our mortal bodies, and puts us back in the Garden of Eden.

Yes, the Garden of Eden!

Look again at the verses we just read. They say God's wisdom makes our lives pleasant and peaceful. Isn't that how you'd describe Adam's and Eve's lives in the garden?

They say God's wisdom makes us happy and rich. It brings us honor and length of days. That sure sounds like a Garden of Eden life to me!

I like what one commentary I read said about that. It said the tree of life was designed to protect that kind of Garden of Eden existence and called it the "tree that preserves life."[3]

When you think about it, that's accurate. The original tree of life was given to preserve Adam's and Eve's lives and keep them good and strong. It was meant to keep them from knowing (or sensing and experiencing) evil. If they had obeyed God and eaten of that tree instead of the one He told them to leave alone, Satan would have had no way into their lives. He could never have done them any harm. They would have been protected from him by their obedience to God. If Adam and Eve had partaken of the tree of life, they could have lived in that Eden-like realm of protection forever.

But they didn't. When the devil tempted them, they fell into sin.

I don't know for sure how long Adam and Eve lived in the Garden of Eden before that happened. The Jewish sages say it took place the first day they were there. That means Adam and Eve didn't obey

God for even one whole day! They got in trouble before sunset and died spiritually without experiencing much of the garden kind of life.

As a result, we were all born sinners—spiritually dead. But the good news is we don't have to remain sinners, because Jesus came to be our Savior. He went to the cross to pay the price for our sin and opened the way for us to be born again. Because He did, those who have received Him as Lord are back in full fellowship with God. We have a Garden of Eden kind of relationship with Him again.

To enjoy all the blessings of that relationship, all we must do is what Adam and Eve should have done. We must partake of the tree of life by receiving, believing, and obeying God's Word. If we'll do that, if we'll lay hold of His wisdom and not let it go, it will preserve us and make our lives on earth peaceful, pleasant, prosperous, and long. It will keep us in the wonderful garden of God's perfect will.

"But how can that be?" someone might ask. "We live on a sin-racked, fallen planet. This is a messed-up place!"

That's true. Yet, even in its fallen state, the earth still responds to the wisdom of God. Proverbs 3:19 gives us the reason: "The LORD by wisdom hath founded the earth; by understanding hath he established the heavens."

Because the natural elements of creation were brought into existence by God's word and by His wisdom, they still cooperate with His word and His wisdom when we apply them. Jesus demonstrated that during His ministry on earth. When the wind and waves got out of hand on the Sea of Galilee and threatened to sink His boat, He spoke to them with the wisdom of God by the Holy Spirit and said, "Peace, be still."

What happened when the elements heard His Word? "The wind ceased, and there was a great calm" (Mark 4:39).

On another occasion, when Jesus had a hungry crowd to feed and only five pieces of bread and two small fish, He didn't do what most of us would do. He didn't wring His hands and say, "Oh, no! We don't have enough food for all these people!" He did the opposite.

He spoke God's blessing over that little dab of food and, "breaking the loaves into pieces, he gave some of the bread and fish to each disciple, and the disciples gave them to the people. They all ate as much as they wanted, and they picked up twelve baskets of leftovers" (Matthew 14:19–20 NLT).

When we follow Jesus' example by partaking of the tree of life and doing things God's way, everything in our lives—even the natural world around us—begins to work better.

When that happens, we become like the man Psalm 1 describes. Because we walk in God's ways and meditate on His Word day and night, we become "like a tree planted by the rivers of water, that bringeth forth his fruit in his season; his leaf also shall not wither; and whatsoever he doeth shall prosper" (verse 3).

Whatever we do prospers!

I've known of Word-believing, Word-obeying farmers whose crops produced greater harvests than those of their unbelieving neighbors. I've known businessmen who lived according to God's wisdom and prospered when others in the same business were failing around them. I've seen fractured, strife-filled homes that were transformed into little heavens on earth when moms and dads took hold of the life-giving tree of God's Word and began to live by it.

Every area of our lives—our spirits, our bodies, our relationships, our finances—everything responds to the wisdom of God! The more we know of that wisdom, the stronger and more blessed those areas become. If we will lay hold of the tree of life and partake of it every day by believing and acting on God's Word, not only will we be able to tap into God's fountain of youth and live longer, stronger lives, but our days will be happier and more fruitful than we ever dreamed they could be.

Find a Church That Serves Good Food

I do want to add a word of warning. Not everyone who goes to church or carries a Bible...not everyone who stands behind a pulpit...is a partaker of the tree of life. I was reminded of this a few years ago during a time of national crisis, when great numbers of people were flocking to churches to find help and comfort. Initially, I thought that was great. But when I turned on the television and watched some of the services they were attending, looked at the drawn faces of the ministers, and listened to their lifeless messages, I changed my mind.

Oh, no! I thought. *Those people need to go to a church that has some life in it. Otherwise, they'll think the gospel doesn't have any power at all!*

You'll have a tough time living long and finishing strong if you go to a church where there's no life. So don't do it. Get into one that preaches the Word with such faith and love that you leave more alive and full of joy than when you arrived. That kind of church is good for you!

A church that sends you out just as sad and discouraged as you were when you came in is not helping you. If you look around you and the whole congregation is depressed and doubtful instead of happy and full of confidence in God, you're in the wrong place. The spiritual food being offered there is hazardous to your health.

That's just common sense. If you went to a restaurant and everyone in it was gagging or being carried out on a stretcher, you wouldn't eat there, would you? You'd automatically know something was amiss.

Apply that same wisdom to your spiritual life. Choose a church where people are spiritually healthy, enjoying themselves, and victorious in life.

I'm not saying you should expect the pastor to have you swinging from the chandeliers every service. But you need a pastor who will help straighten out your thinking and feed you messages so full of the Word that they consistently help you grow. A pastor like that won't just tell you uplifting anecdotes and inspiring stories. He'll teach you the Word. Week after week, he will hand-feed you fruit from the tree of life.

One week he'll give you a meal of healing from the Word. The next week, he'll give you a meal on faith. He'll also teach you to feed on the Word yourself so you can eat at home as well as at church.

That's important because you can't get everything at church. You can't expect to live on just what you receive from God on Sundays. You can't get by just feeding your spirit once a week any more than you can get by feeding your body once a week. Your heart must have the bread of the Word daily to stay strong, and the Word can't get in your heart unless you put it there. It can't go to work in your heart unless you consistently keep it in front of your eyes and in your ears.

That's why it's necessary to spend time in the Word on your own as well as at church. You need the Word talking to you every day. You need God speaking to you through it all the time. The Word needs daily access to your mind, so it can chase out all the unbelief, lies, fear, fables, and traditions of men that have been bombarding your life.

Some people claim they're too busy to spend time in the Word every day. "I work two jobs," they say. "I have a houseful of little children!" But the truth is, no matter how tight your schedule, you can always make time for God's Word. If you do, it will help you prosper so much you won't have to work two jobs. It will help you organize your household in such a way that you have all the time you need.

Most people would have plenty of time for God's Word if they'd just stop watching all that nonsense on TV. The last I heard, Americans spend an average of 151 hours a month watching television.[4] Think of how much of the Word we could feed on in six hours! Even if you're not "average," if you're like most of us, you still watch more TV than you should. If you're not careful, even a little bit of television these days will lead you into darkness because there's so much trash on the air.

Television isn't the only thing that distracts us from the Word. Sometimes we let other things overcrowd our lives. We become like the people Jesus described who allow "the cares and anxieties of the world and distractions of the age, and the pleasure and delight and false glamour and deceitfulness of riches, and the craving and passionate desire for other things creep in and choke and suffocate the Word" (Mark 4:19 AMP).

That's why it's always a good idea to take stock of your schedule on a regular basis. If you don't, other things will encroach on the time you've set aside for the Word.

Remember, the Word is your life, so it must always be your first priority. Above all else, protect your time in the Word.

Be a Thrill Seeker

Really, if you trust the Word of God to do for you what the Bible says it will, if you truly believe it is a tree of life to you, you will never be too busy for it. Think about it. No one in his right mind would ever say, "I've found the fountain of youth, but I'm too busy to drink from it. Somehow I just can't fit that fountain into my schedule."

We'd never say that, would we? We'd all find time for a daily trip to the fountain of youth if we knew for sure we'd found it. The same is true of the Word. We will protect our time in it at all costs if we truly believe it will be to us just what God said it would be—pleasantness, peace, length of days and years of a life worth living, riches, honor, and a tree of life.

"But I've read the Word on and off for years," someone might argue, "and it didn't produce those things for me."

That's probably because you weren't consistent or didn't obey it. The Word doesn't work very well for people who just dabble in it now and then. It produces powerful results only for those who put it in first place, day after day. It works for people who commit them-selves to attend to it and obey it all the time.

I remember when I first discovered that. Ken and I were just learning how to base our lives on the Word and live by faith. Few churches then were teaching these things, so we got as many tapes as we could from Kenneth E. Hagin's ministry and began listening to them every day.

Without going into too much detail, our lives were in sad shape back then. Ken was just beginning to go out and minister, and I was staying at home with the children. We were renting a house that was so run down when we moved into it that I refused to unpack for a while. (I didn't want to believe I really had to live there.) We had old furniture, an old car, and two small children. We were so broke that, for the most part, we had to operate on a cash-only basis because if we overdrew our account we were in serious trouble—not to mention the overdraft fees. (I think a returned check cost two or three dollars in those days!) When I went to the grocery store, I prayed in tongues and believed God that I'd have enough money to pay the bill when I got to the checkout stand.

One day, I was sitting in that dumpy little house, listening to one of Kenneth Hagin's tapes entitled "You Can Have What You Say." He was preaching a message about speaking the Word, and as I typed out the Scripture I began to understand how faith works: that what we continually say is what we believe.

> And Jesus answering saith unto them, Have faith in God. For verily I say unto you, that whosoever shall say unto this mountain, Be thou removed, and be thou cast into the sea; and shall not doubt in his heart, but shall believe that those things which he saith shall come to pass; he shall have whatsoever he saith. Therefore I say unto you, What things soever ye desire, when ye pray, believe that ye receive them, and ye shall have them. (MARK 11:22–24)

We are to believe we receive when we pray and say the desired result from now until it is finished—done. The Lord spoke these words, "In consistency lies the power."

At that moment, I realized it's what we say continually that comes to pass in our lives. It's not just what we say in church, not just what we say when we pray, not just what we say when Christian friends are around, but what we say all the time that will determine what we receive from God.

To keep our words full of faith and in line with God's promises, we must spend time in the Word every day. We must consistently read, study, and meditate on it so it can get into our hearts in abundance, "for out of the abundance of the heart the mouth speaketh" (Matthew 12:34).

That's why it's not enough to just open our Bibles every now and then. It's not enough to go to church on Sunday and then leave our Bibles gathering dust on our nightstands during the week. We must partake of (receive and believe) God's Word continually if we want to enjoy the full blessing it offers.

In consistency lies the power!

Some people think they'd get bored reading the Word every day for years on end, but I can tell you from personal experience that when you believe the Word is true, it is never boring. It is so marvelous and full of life—so full of God Himself!—that you can study it for a lifetime and still receive fresh revelation every time you read it. If you approach the Word with faith and reverence, it will always excite you. It will always bless you.

After more than forty-two years of studying God's Word, I still love to open my Bible every morning and read it again. One of my greatest thrills is discovering something there I haven't seen before...or seeing a familiar truth in a deeper or different light.

Some people seek thrills through alcohol or drugs or some other kind of sinful behavior. They find temporary pleasure in those things, but such thrills don't last long. And, as the Bible says, those behaviors ultimately lead to death. When we get our thrills from God's Word, however, the joy of it lasts and lasts! It stays with us as long as we stay with the Word, and instead of leading downward to death, God's thrills lead upward to more abundant life.

So, if you really want to have a good time, dive into God's Word. Experience the rush that comes from letting God's wisdom energize your heart. You'll be amazed how much fun that can be. You'll discover, as I have, that the Word of God isn't just good for you, it makes you happy. What Proverbs 3:13 says is the absolute truth: "Happy is the man that findeth wisdom, and the man that getteth understanding."

No Excuses

If you don't know how to study the Word, start by getting some CDs or DVDs of your favorite ministers. Check the television listings and find out what faith-building, life-giving Christian broadcasts are available in your area, then tune in to them or record them so you can watch them later. These days there are any number of good, tree-of-life-partaking preachers out there, so get connected with them and let them help you feed on the Word.

That's what Kenneth and I did when we first got started in ministry. Of course, that was back in 1967 so we didn't have CDs or DVDs available to us. And, as I said before, we didn't have too many preachers to choose from either. Most ministers hadn't caught on to the things of faith yet. There wasn't any such label as "Word church" or "faith church" in those days. The primary ministers we knew who could help us were Oral Roberts and Kenneth E. Hagin.

We didn't have Oral Roberts's messages on tape, but Ken learned wonderful things from him when he traveled with him to the healing meetings. (Ken was Oral Roberts's copilot for a while when he was a student at Oral Roberts University.) Kenneth E. Hagin offered seminars four times a year, and we attended every session. We also played his tapes so much that Ken actually sounded like him when he first started preaching. He'd listened and relistened to Kenneth Hagin's messages so many times that he'd picked up his accent and figures of speech!

Once, during those early years, when Ken was asked to preach at a Full Gospel Businessmen's meeting, Kenneth Hagin was scheduled to be one of the speakers, too. During Ken's session, Kenneth Hagin was walking down the hall and a little boy came running up to him in amazement and said, "What are you doing out here? You're in there preaching—but you're out here!"

In a way, the boy was right. Ken was preaching Kenneth Hagin's sermons almost word for word. He didn't even bother to change the title of the messages! (Kenneth Hagin used to tease him about that.)

If Ken and I could find a way to surround ourselves with good Word teaching back then, when it was so scarce, you can certainly do it now that such teaching abounds. Today, there are good Word churches all over the country. There are whole flocks of "faith people" who know how to believe, act on the Word, and receive what it promises.

You and I don't have any excuse for neglecting the Word. We have more easy-to-read-and-understand translations of the Bible than any other generation. We have more access to preaching and teaching than Christians in years past could have imagined.

Personally, I'm making the most of those advantages. I probably have a hundred Bibles in my house. I have the Word coming to me on television, on DVDs, and on CDs. I have cassettes and videos. And I'm constantly attending wonderful meetings where I can hear the Word preached live and in person.

I realize that because I'm a minister, I may have a little more time to spend in the Word than you do, but really, I became a serious student of the Word years before I began to minister. So I say this with confidence: you have more time for the Word than you realize. If you'll ask God to show you how to make the most of what you have, He'll help you buy up time you've been wasting on other things. The Bible will transform your life if you'll obey it.

He might lead you to keep a CD player in your bathroom so you can listen to the Word while you're shaving (men) or putting on your makeup (ladies). He might prompt you to listen to the Word instead of a silly talk-radio program during your drive to work. Those of you who spend time commuting could become spiritual giants.

One thing is sure, you'll be sharper when you get to your destination if you'll do that. The wisdom of God will flow from you, and you'll come up with better ideas and solutions for the people and situations around you. (Of course, they could have those inspired ideas, too, if they'd tune in to the Word.) You'll get the attention of the boss or other people in places of influence. They'll think, *Hey, he's a smart man! She's a smart woman!* You'll be the one who comes to mind when it comes time for promotion, too.

When you finish your workday and get back into your car, all worn-out, you can listen to the Word again on your drive home. As you do, it will minister life to you. It will quicken your body and reenergize you so you won't be tired anymore. Instead of being grouchy when you get home, you can have a nice night relaxing with your family. You'll enjoy it more, and they will, too!

At night, when you lay your head on your pillow, you can spend the last waking moments of the day thinking about some Scripture the Holy Spirit highlighted to you that day. You can drift off to sleep meditating on the Word of God. If you'll do that, you won't toss and turn all night worrying about your problems or feeling anxious about dangers that might lie ahead. You'll fall into a peaceful sleep with ease, and you won't need sleeping pills to help you. Proverbs 3:21–24 assures us of that:

> My son, let not [God's wisdom and His Word] depart from thine eyes: keep sound wisdom and discretion: so shall they be life unto thy soul, and grace to thy neck. *Then shalt thou walk in thy way safely, and thy foot shall not stumble. When thou liest down, thou shalt not be afraid: yea, thou shalt lie down, and thy sleep shall be sweet.* (ITALICS ADDED)

Sleep is vital to our health and strength. A few years ago, I went to a Christian doctor for a physical and he asked me how many hours a night I was sleeping. I told him that on a good night I got about six hours. Do you know what he said? He told me that wasn't enough. He said my body needed at least seven or eight hours of sleep to rejuvenate itself. (Since then I've purposed to get more sleep!)

God knows what we need to live long and finish strong. He knows we need a good, peaceful night's rest for our youth to be renewed the way He intends it to be. That's why He gave us a divine prescription for sweet sleep.

It's a prescription that has no harmful side effects and doesn't cost a penny. It can be addicting, but that's okay because the more you take, the better off you'll be. It's the prescription of the Word.

So go ahead, take in as much of it as you want, as often as you like. Eat from it every day because it is to you a tree of life. It is your heavenly Father's gift to you—His divine fountain of youth.

I learned this habit from Kenneth: as soon as he gets ready to sleep he quotes Psalm 127:2: "It is vain for you to rise up early, to sit up late, to eat the bread of sorrows: for so he giveth his beloved sleep." He says it. He receives it. He goes to sleep!

POINTS TO REMEMBER

※ The Word Moses received on Mount Sinai in the midst of the fire of God's glory was what protected him, preserved him, and prolonged his days.

※ The very life of God is contained in His Word. When we receive it in faith, it energizes us with divine power.

※ The Bible says that the Word penetrates all through our cells and our organs to the innermost part of our bones. It even reaches to the marrow—the primary place where our blood is made.

※ If we allow our spirits to grow weak, we'll get physically sick and frail. That's why God's Word is so vital. It nourishes our spirits and feeds the inner man.

※ The Word is your life, so it must always be your first priority. Above all else, protect your time in the Word, and believe and act on what God says in the Word.

SCRIPTURE

Man shall not live by bread alone, but by every word that proceedeth out of the mouth of God. (Matthew 4:4)

CONFESSION

The Word of God protects me, preserves me, and prolongs my life on earth. As I receive it by faith and obey it, it energizes me with divine power. From this day forward, I will put that Word first in my life. I will keep it before my eyes, in my ears, and in the midst of my heart every day, for it is life and nourishment to my spirit, and health to all my flesh.

CHAPTER 6

One Sure Way to Shorten Your Life

If it weren't for verses like Hebrews 4:12 and Deuteronomy 30:19, I wouldn't need to write this chapter. If God's Word were just a single-edged sword, if it spoke only of life and blessing and mentioned nothing about death and the curse, what I've already told you about the Word being our life would be sufficient. Nothing more, no words of caution or warning, would be needed.

We could all go about our business without giving any thought to the consequences that come from disobeying God's commands. "I'll just obey them when it's convenient," we could say. "When it's not, I'll do things my own way."

The scriptural fact is, that kind of attitude is dangerous. It will cost us more than we want to pay because God's Word *is* a double-edged (not a single-edged) sword. On one side is the life that comes when we obey it, on the other are the deadly consequences we experience when we don't. Moses put it this way: "I have set before you life *and death*, blessing *and cursing*: therefore choose life, that both thou and thy seed may live" (Deuteronomy 30:19, italics added).

Like the Israelites who first heard those words thousands of years ago, we as God's people today have only two options. We can believe God's Word and do what it says, which leads to life; or we can doubt and disobey it, which leads to death. Obedience or disobedience are our only choices.

There is no door No. 3.

Sad to say, many people act as if there were. They live as if they can ignore God's Word and be blessed anyway. They disregard the wisdom of the Bible and imagine they can still have long, strong, satisfying lives.

But they can't. It's impossible. The nation of Israel demonstrated that again and again.

As we've already seen, when the Israelites obeyed God's Word, as they did under the leadership of Joshua, they enjoyed great blessing. They won impossible battles, overcame enormous odds, and achieved one victory after another. They experienced such success in conquering the promised land that at the end of Joshua's life, he made this announcement to them: "Behold, this day I am going the way of all the earth: and ye know in all your hearts and in all your souls, that not one thing hath failed of all the good things which the LORD your God spake concerning you; all are come to pass unto you, and not one thing hath failed thereof" (Joshua 23:14).

Wouldn't you like to have that testimony at the end of your life? Wouldn't you love to be able to say you'd received every blessing God promised you in His Word, and not one had failed to come to pass?

You and I can have that testimony if we'll do what the Bible tells us to do. We can enjoy the same kind of blessing and success those promised land–conquering Israelites did (and even more because we're born again). To do so, however, we must follow their example. We must be obedient. We must choose to live by the Word.

That was the key to their success. They followed the instructions God gave Joshua at the beginning of their journey. They obeyed Him when He said, "This book of the law shall not depart out of thy mouth; but thou shalt meditate therein day and night, that thou mayest observe to do according to all that is written therein: for then thou shalt make thy way prosperous, and then thou shalt have good success" (Joshua 1:8). As a result, they lived long, successful lives; they finished strong. They stayed on the blessing side of God's two-edged sword.

The problem is, they didn't stay there very long. Only one generation of Israelites honored God's Word. The next chose the path of disobedience. When they did, success turned to failure. Joy turned to misery. Victory turned to defeat. In other words, they felt the sting that comes from being on the wrong side of the sword of God's Word.

How could such a thing happen? The Old Testament book of Judges tells us:

> The people served the LORD all the days of Joshua, and all the days of the elders who outlived Joshua, who had seen all the great works of the LORD, which He had done for Israel....Another generation arose after them who did not know the LORD nor the work which He had done for Israel. Then the children of Israel did evil in the sight of the LORD....And the anger of the LORD was hot against Israel. So He delivered them into the hands of plunderers who despoiled them; and He sold them into the hands of their enemies all around, so that they could no longer stand before their enemies. Wherever they went out, the hand of the LORD was against them for calamity, as the LORD had said, and as the LORD had sworn to them. And they were greatly distressed. (JUDGES 2:7, 10–11, 14–15 NKJV)

Think of it! The Israelites went from being greatly blessed to being greatly distressed because of one simple thing: disobedience. They exchanged life for death and blessing for cursing, and, astonishingly, they did it by choice.

That's shocking, isn't it?

You'd think no one in his right mind would ever trade the blessing for the curse. It doesn't make sense. Yet people still do it today. Even born-again believers sometimes choose to yield to the desires of their flesh and disregard the Word of God. In the process, they trade success for failure, make themselves miserable, and cut their lives short. That's a dumb thing to do!

Ken and I determined many years ago to give up that kind of foolishness. We decided when we gave our lives to Jesus that we had already experienced our fill of defeat. We were tired of living cursed lives. We'd been sick, broke, sorry, and sad far too long and were ready for a change. So we determined to find out what the Bible says and do it.

Hear and obey the Word. That was our plan.

It was a simple plan, too. We didn't have to be rocket scientists to follow it. We just had to dig into our Bibles, believe what we read there, and act on it. When we started doing that, our whole lives turned around. In the forty-two years since, we've experienced victory in every situation when we stuck to our plan and obeyed God's Word in faith. As a result, we're well on our way to being able to say, like Joshua: "Not one thing has failed of all the good things the Lord our God has promised us."

Turn Entirely Away from Evil

Ken and I discovered for ourselves that kind of victory doesn't come just because we're Christians. We lived defeated lives for five years after we were born again. Not much happened for us on the outside until we began to exercise faith in God's Word and obey what it says.

We proved God's blessings don't fall on any of us like ripe apples off a tree simply because we're born again. Faith and obedience open the door for God's promises to be fulfilled in our lives, including His promise of a long, strong, satisfying life. That kind of life isn't automatic. God didn't say that all Christians everywhere would experience great longevity. As we've already seen, He was speaking to a specific kind of person when He said:

Because he hath set his love upon me, therefore will I deliver him: I will set him on high, because he hath known my name. He shall call upon me, and I will answer him: I will be with him in trouble; I will deliver him, and honour him. With long life will I satisfy him, and show him my salvation. (PSALM 91:14–16)

According to those verses, God guaranteed long, satisfying lives only to people who love Him.

How do we know if we love Him?

Jesus answered that question for us. He said, "He who has My commandments and keeps them is the one who loves Me" (John 14:21 NASB). That makes it easy for us to judge ourselves, doesn't it? If we love God, we will obey His Word. If we don't love Him, we will live in disobedience…and we won't qualify for His promise of a long, satisfying life.

"Oh, no!" you might say. "I'm in disobedience to God right now, and I know it."

If that's the case, repent. Make a U-turn and go the other way. Whatever you're doing that's wrong—stop it. Otherwise, you may die too young. That's not just my opinion, it's what the Bible tells us. Again and again, it says things like:

> Be not over much wicked, neither be thou foolish: why shouldest thou die before thy time? (Ecclesiastes 7:17)

> He that keepeth the commandment keepeth his own soul; but he that despiseth his [God's] ways shall die. (Proverbs 19:16)

> Strength faileth because of…iniquity, and…bones are consumed. (Psalm 31:10)

> God…will bring down the wicked into the pit of destruction; men of blood and treachery shall not live out half their days. (Psalm 55:23 AMP)

The Bible is quite clear about it. People who live wicked lives will live shorter lives. Wickedness brings death just as righteousness brings life. No wonder Proverbs 3:7 says, "Be not wise in your own eyes; reverently fear and worship the Lord and turn [entirely] away from evil" (AMP).

Turning away from evil is literally a matter of life and death.

Think how much trouble we could avoid if we'd do just that one thing. Imagine how much better everyone's life could be. People would save themselves all kinds of sorrow and calamity. They wouldn't be plagued with so many sicknesses and diseases.

I realize there are some sicknesses that attack our bodies just because we live in a fallen world, but many are a direct result of the sins people commit. Sexually transmitted diseases, for example; or cancer that develops as a result of smoking; drug addiction; and the variety of ailments that accompany overeating—all are the result of one thing: disobedience to the Word of God.

That's why, if you want to stay well and strong, you must turn entirely away from evil. You can't choose to watch "a little" pornography now and then. You have to say with the psalmist, "I will refuse to look at anything vile and vulgar. I hate all crooked dealings; I will have nothing to do with them" (Psalm 101:3 NLT). Granted, that's a challenging commitment to keep in this day and age because vulgar images are everywhere. Even billboards along the highway are often so vile these days, you have to look the other way when you drive by them. You can't let your eyes go there.

You'll come across all kinds of bad things just flipping innocently through the television channels. When you do, you must turn away from them. Close your eyes. Turn off the television. Throw the remote down and run out of the room if you must. Do whatever it takes to close the door to that stuff because it's an evil force, and it will suck you in.

You can't let yourself think thoughts such as *No one will ever know. It won't hurt anything.* A little evil always opens the door to more evil. You put one pornographic picture in front of your eyes, and the first thing you know you'll be looking at another and another. You'll get addicted to it, and eventually you'll start doing sinful things you never thought you would do.

You can't afford to play around with pornography or any other kind of sin. You must turn your back on it completely. If you don't, it will kill you.

First Peter 3:8–12 confirms that:

> All of you be of one mind, having compassion for one another; love as brothers, be tenderhearted, be courteous; not returning evil for evil or reviling for reviling, but on the contrary blessing, knowing that you were called to this, that you may inherit a blessing. For *"He who would love life and see good days, let him refrain his tongue from evil, and his lips from speaking deceit. Let him turn away from evil and do good; let him seek peace and pursue it. For the eyes of the LORD are on the righteous, and His ears are open to their prayers; but the face of the LORD is against those who do evil.* (NKJV, ITALICS ADDED)

According to that passage, turning away from evil doesn't just mean refusing to do things that are contrary to God's Word. It also means refusing to say things contrary to it. Because the tongue is a powerful force—for good or for evil—if we want to live long and finish strong, we remember that the Bible says:

- The tongue of the wise is health. (Proverbs 12:18)

- A wholesome tongue is a tree of life: but perverseness therein is a breach in the spirit. (Proverbs 15:4)

- Death and life are in the power of the tongue: and they that love it shall eat the fruit thereof. (Proverbs 18:21)

- If anyone does not stumble in word, he is a perfect man, able also to bridle the whole body. . . . And the tongue is a fire, a world of iniquity. The tongue is so set among our members that it defiles the whole body, and sets on fire the course of nature; and it is set on fire by hell. (James 3:2, 6 NKJV)

Those are sobering Scriptures. They'll make you think twice next time you're around a bunch of foulmouthed nonbelievers and you're tempted to throw a few curse words into the conversation. You'll be reluctant to start damning things if you realize that, according to the Bible, condemnation will come back on you. God's Word talks about the person who enjoys using that kind of language:

> As he loved cursing, so let it come to him;
> As he did not delight in blessing, so let it be far from him.
> As he clothed himself with cursing as with his garment,
> So let it enter his body like water,
> And like oil into his bones.
> Let it be to him like the garment which covers him,
> And for a belt with which he girds himself continually.
> (PSALM 109:17–19 NKJV)

Maybe you work around people who think cursing is a way of life, and it's easy for you to fall into that with them. But if you ask yourself, *Do I want to wear cursing like a coat? Do I want a curse to cling to me?* you'll probably decide to hold your tongue and start exercising your faith for a better job with a more wholesome environment.

You'll also be wary of saying and doing evil things if you keep in mind that such words and actions will rob you of life and good days, close God's ears to your prayers, and cause His face to be turned against you. I don't know about you, but I want the Lord to hear my prayers all the time. That's a life-and-death issue to me. If I encounter a sudden calamity and need to call on Him for help, I want to be sure His ears are open. I want to know He is paying attention. I want to be strong in faith and not in condemnation because I know I'm not living a wholesome life.

If I'm in a difficult situation, I might not have time to repent of the disobedient things I've been saying or doing. I might need instant access to the throne of God. That's one reason why I decided long ago to live in obedience every day. I've never regretted that decision, because I've discovered that the more I obey Him, the quicker He is to hear and move when I pray.

Why is that? Is it because He is hard nosed and just wants to boss me around?

No, it's because the more I obey Him, the more room I give Him to work in my life. The more I cooperate with Him, the easier it is for Him to move me into a position where He can bless and protect me.

Living in the Danger Zone

Being in that position of divine protection is vital for all who want to live out their full number of days because this planet is a dangerous place. Ever since Adam sinned and gave the devil authority to operate on the earth, there's been a curse hovering over it. That curse includes sickness, calamity, lack, and distress of every kind (Deuteronomy 28).

God never wanted those things to be here. He desired that humankind know only good. That's why He told Adam and Eve not to eat of the Tree of Knowledge of Good and Evil. He wanted to keep them from experiencing darkness and death. But, since He is not a dominator, He gave them a choice—to obey or to disobey Him. As we know, they chose disobedience. They used their free will to sin, to open the door to evil, and to turn the earth into a danger zone.

Had God not extended mercy to us, we would have no refuge of safety, no place to find protection from that danger. But He did have mercy on us! He sent His Son, Jesus, to pay the price for man's disobedience. He made a way for us to take cover under what Psalm 91:1 calls "the shadow of the Almighty." He created a supernatural shelter for us that the same verse refers to as "the secret place of the most High." Anyone is welcome there. Through the blood of Jesus, God has opened it up to all mankind. As we've already seen, however, only the people who love and obey God can truly dwell under His shadow. We can abide (dwell, remain, live) under His shadow. Only those who believe and live by His Word can declare with confidence:

> He who dwells in the secret place of the Most High
> Shall Abide under the shadow of the Almighty.
> I will say of the LORD, "He is my refuge and my fortress;
> My God, in Him I will trust."
> Surely He shall deliver [me] from the snare of the fowler
> And from the perilous pestilence.
> He shall cover [me] with His feathers,
> And under His wings [I] shall take refuge;
> His truth shall be [my] shield and buckler.
> [I] shall not be afraid of the terror by night,
> Nor of the arrow that flies by day,
> Nor of the pestilence that walks in darkness,
> Nor of the destruction that lays waste at noonday.
> A thousand may fall at [my] side,
> And ten thousand at [my] right hand;
> But it shall not come near [me].
> Only with [my] eyes shall [I] look,
> And see the reward of the wicked. (PSALM 91:1–8 NKJV)

According to the last verse, the wicked can't expect to enjoy the same protection from calamity that secret-place dwellers enjoy. On the contrary, the wicked are actually rewarded with such calamities. Exactly who are the "wicked"?

The E. W. Bullinger *Companion Bible* commentary says the wicked are the lawless.[1] They are the people who have not given God's Word any attention. They do things their own way instead of God's way. Such people—even born-again believers who have received Jesus as their Savior and Lord—don't dwell in the secret place of God's protection. They don't abide under the shadow. They wander around outside it; to abide means to remain, to stay. The disobedient live in the danger zone, unprotected from the terrors at night, the arrows that fly during the daytime, and the kinds of massive destruction that can kill ten thousand people at once.

Sometimes I marvel at the fact that thousands of years ago, when Psalm 91 was written, with the exception, perhaps, of natural disasters, no one had really seen this kind of destruction. No one in that time had ever heard of biological warfare or atomic bombs. Who would have dreamed, even a hundred years ago, that men would go into a laboratory and create diseases for the purpose of destroying entire cities? Who would have believed people could be that evil?

Not many generations ago, such a thing would have sounded preposterous. Yet it's happening today. We are living in the day Jesus described when He said, "There will be mighty and violent earthquakes, and in various places famines and pestilences (plagues: malignant and contagious or infectious epidemic diseases which are deadly and devastating); and there will be sights of terror and great signs from heaven" (Luke 21:11 AMP).

Today that verse reads like the headlines of a newspaper. Such natural and man-made catastrophes are possible. We may be shocked by them, but none of these occurrences have taken God by surprise. He foresaw all those things and promised to deliver us from them before they ever came on the scene. He promised He'd protect us from the dangers we face in our day just as surely as He protected the Old Testament saint Daniel from the lions he faced in his day.

As you probably remember, Daniel came out of that deadly situation without a scratch. All who want to live long lives should learn a lesson from him. We should follow his example. When the king threw him in with the lions, Daniel didn't cry and whine and shake with fear. He trusted the Lord. He knew because he had believed and obeyed God's Word, he'd be safe even in a dangerous place.

The Bible doesn't specifically say so, but I believe Daniel slept peacefully with the lions that night. I think he may have dozed off with his feet propped up on one and his head resting on another.

The king, on the other hand, couldn't sleep at all. Early the next morning he hurried to the lions' den to see if Daniel had survived. When he got there, he cried out:

> "Daniel, servant of the living God, has your God, whom you serve continually, been able to deliver you from the lions?"
>
> Then Daniel said to the king, "O king, live forever!
>
> "My God sent His angel and shut the lions' mouths, so that they have not hurt me, because I was found innocent before Him; and also, O king, I have done no wrong before you."
>
> Now the king was exceedingly glad for him, and commanded that they should take Daniel up out of the den. So Daniel was taken up out of the den, and no injury whatever was found on him, because he believed in his God. (DANIEL 6:20–23 NKJV)

There's no question about it, Daniel was on the blessing side of the sword of God's Word. He was in position for God to protect him, and he came through that situation just fine. The men who had accused him of wrongdoing and gotten him into that trouble, however, didn't fare as well. They were on the wrong side of God's sword. What's more, the lions were especially hungry since they had missed their dinner the night before. The king "cast them into the den of lions—them, their children, and their wives; and the lions overpowered them, and broke all their bones in pieces before they ever came to the bottom of the den" (Daniel 6:24 NKJV).

That wasn't the only time in Daniel's day God proved He could keep His secret-place dwellers safe. He worked the same kind of wonder for Daniel's friends Shadrach, Meshach, and Abednego. They, too, lived on the obedience and blessing side of God's Word. So when the king ordered them to worship a golden idol, they refused to do it. From a natural standpoint, that didn't appear to be a wise decision. It made the king so angry he swore to burn them in a fiery furnace. He turned up the heat so high that the king's servants (who obviously weren't living in the secret place of the Most High!) were burned to a crisp when they threw Shadrach, Meshach, and Abednego into it.

What are the odds of coming out of such an inferno alive?

Zero! It's absolutely impossible.

Be sure to remember that the next time someone tells you it's impossible to live to 120 in this dangerous world. When you read articles and hear news reports saying all the natural odds are against you, think about how Shadrach, Meshach, and Abednego defied insurmountable odds. By obeying God and relying on His protective power, they not only survived their stay in the fiery furnace, they emerged without so much as a heat rash. When they walked out of that blaze...

> the princes, prefects, governors, and advisers crowded around them and saw that the fire had not touched them. Not a hair on their heads was singed, and their clothing was not scorched. They didn't even smell of smoke! Then Nebuchadnezzar said, "Praise to the God of Shadrach, Meshach, and Abednego! He sent his angel to rescue his servants who trusted in him. They defied the king's command and were willing to die rather than serve or worship any god except their own God."
> (DANIEL 3:27–28 NLT)

"But that's a Bible story!" somebody might say. "God doesn't protect people today the way He did in Bible days."

Sure He does! He "is the same yesterday, today, and forever" (Hebrews 13:8 NKJV). You can count on it! I read a story in a Louisiana newspaper a few years ago about a man trapped in a burning building who called on the name of the Lord and all of a sudden he found himself outside the fire. He didn't even know how he got there. God supernaturally translated him to a safe place.

I know of another man, Norman Williams, who was in an airplane accident some years ago—one of the worst in aviation history—that took place when two planes collided on a runway in the Canary Islands. The plane he was sitting in burst into flames so hot that he saw people's flesh melting off their bones. But because this man believed the Word of God and believed Psalm 91, he didn't burn up. Instead he shouted the name of Jesus, and the next thing he knew he popped up through a hole in the top of the plane and landed outside, on the wing. When he jumped from the wing to the ground, he broke his ankle, but he did not get burned. (And his ankle healed.)[2]

Both men can vouch for the truth of Isaiah 43:2–3, which says, "When you walk through the fire, you shall not be burned, nor shall the flame scorch you. For I am the LORD your God" (NKJV).

Keep Your Angels on the Job

Of course, today most of us will never be thrown into a lions' den or a fiery furnace, but we face other kinds of threats. We're always being warned about some new virus or disease, for example. "Better get a flu shot or you might die," the experts say.

I know from experience that the most effective vaccine isn't found in medical clinics. It's found in the Bible. Many years ago when our children were small, Ken gathered our family together and gave us a scriptural vaccination. At the time, the Asian flu was going around and people were getting shots to protect themselves from it.

Of course, the children weren't too excited about getting a flu shot until Ken opened his Bible and they realized it wasn't going to come from a needle but from the Word of God. He read healing Scriptures, then we all prayed together and received by faith what God has said about no plague coming near us (Psalm 91:10). Guess what? No one in our household has ever had the flu. We are immunized by the protecting power of God.

Through the years, Ken and I have also enjoyed protection from storms and tornadoes. (Where we live, it's important to have that kind of protection because the weather often gets fierce.) When I was a little girl growing up in Arkansas, we didn't have radar or weather channels on television the way we do now, so whenever an ominous storm cloud gathered, we'd all go down into the storm cellar and wait for it to pass. A little town just north of us had once been almost destroyed by a tornado, so at the first sign of trouble, we headed for the cellar.

Ken and I don't have a storm cellar now. When a dangerous storm threatens, Ken goes out and takes authority over it in Jesus' name. (When he isn't home, I do it myself.) I don't know how many nights he has stood on our porch in his pajamas talking to dangerous clouds: "You're not coming to our house," he says. "I rebuke you and command you to fall apart in Jesus' name. Our house, our yard, and all our property is under the protection of Psalm 91. So get out of here in Jesus' name!"

In the airplane one day we saw a funnel come out of a cloud some distance away. We spoke to it in the name of Jesus, and it just went back up into the cloud.

Once when I was preaching in Florida, a tornado tried to blow us away right in the middle of Healing School. The audacity of the devil is amazing. Why would he ever think he could attack God's people with a tornado while the Word is being preached?

He couldn't, of course. We stood our ground in faith, rebuked the tornado, and it didn't harm anyone. The following day, the newspaper map showed its path through the city stopped right there at the convention center where we were holding our meetings. It never went anywhere else! I still have that newspaper in case you don't believe it!

I don't know exactly what God did with that tornado. Maybe He sent an angel to stuff it back up into the clouds where it belonged. Angels do all kinds of things, you know. We see that in Psalm 91:

> If you make the LORD your refuge,
> > if you make the Most High your shelter,
> no evil will conquer you;
> > no plague will come near your dwelling.
> For he orders his angels
> > to protect you wherever you go.
> They will hold you with their hands
> > to keep you from striking your foot on a stone.
> (VERSES 9–12 NLT)

Angels are a major key to our longevity. They are with us to help us survive the dangers of this world so we can live out the full number of our days. How many angels do we have? As many as we need. There is no angel shortage. You can get some idea of how many angels there are from various Scriptures. I don't know how many exist, but I can tell you there are a lot of them. And if God had a need for more, He could just create a couple of billion more.

I'm sure angels have saved our lives many times when we didn't even know about it. That's their job! They are "all ministering spirits, sent forth to minister for them who shall be heirs of salvation" (Hebrews 1:14). If you are an heir of salvation, if Jesus is your Lord, angels have been assigned to you personally. They go with you everywhere. They protect you. They're strong and big and can help you when you need it. They are an important part of your long life.

Years ago, Ken and I were planning a ministry trip to South Africa during a time when that nation was plagued with violence. People told us we shouldn't go unless we took security people with us. Although Ken and I believe that natural security guards are helpful, we didn't have any at that time. That didn't bother us, however, because we're never without security. Everywhere we go—to the grocery store or overseas—we have angels traveling with us. If we allow them to do their jobs, they make sure we don't even stub our toes against a rock. Now that's what I call security!

Did you notice I said we must let them do their jobs? That's an important point. Many Christians think angels automatically protect us, but they don't. According to Psalm 103:20, they spring into action at the sound of God's commandments. They "[hearken]...unto the voice of his word." Angels don't run around doing good deeds just because they can. They respond primarily to what we say and do. They protect people who obey and speak God's Word. Angels respond to what God says.

That's why God so emphatically warns His children not to disobey His Word and talk fear and doubt the way nonbelievers do. He knows if we do, our angels won't be able to help us. We'll be in the danger zone on our own, subject to the same sicknesses and calamities the rest of the world is experiencing. Those things are out there, and if we put ourselves in the devil's territory by ignoring God's instructions and living in sin or fear, we'll be vulnerable to trouble. We'll miss out on the protection of the secret place, which is part of our inheritance as believers. We'll become partakers of the judgment that comes on sin, and our lives can be damaged and even cut short.

Ephesians talks about that fact:

Be ye therefore followers of God as dear children: and walk in love, as Christ also hath loved us, and hath given himself for us an offering and a sacrifice to God for a sweetsmelling savour. But fornication, and all uncleanness, or covetousness, let it not be once named among you, as becometh saints; neither filthiness, nor foolish talking, nor jesting, which are not convenient: but rather giving of thanks. *For this ye know, that no whoremonger, nor unclean person, nor covetous man, who is an idolater, hath any inheritance in the kingdom of Christ and of God. Let no man deceive you with vain words: for because of these things cometh the wrath of God upon the children of disobedience. Be not ye therefore partakers with them.* For ye were sometimes darkness, but now are ye light in the Lord: walk as children of light. (EPHESIANS 5:1–8, ITALICS ADDED)

It's Dangerous to Ride the Fence

I don't know many Christians who just go all-out for the world's sin. (If they did, I'd have to wonder whether they were really saved.) But I do know that some Christians try to keep one foot in the world and one foot in the kingdom of God. They think they can ride the fence between obedience and disobedience and still enjoy divine protection.

Don't let the devil sell you that idea. It's a lie. You can't live in the light and fool around with the darkness at the same time. You can't live successfully if you're trying to be ruled by both worlds.

Do you know why?

This world's system is in direct opposition to God. It is ruled by the devil, and his way of thinking is crazy, evil, and obnoxious. His ways always lead to defeat. So, if you buddy up with worldly people and let the world's voices tell you how to think, you'll get confused. You'll start thinking as they think, acting as they act, and being as defeated as they are.

The world doesn't know right from wrong. Worldly people think sinful things are just great. "Oh, that doesn't hurt anybody!" they'll say. "God isn't bothered by it." They don't even know—or if they know, they don't care—that the Bible says certain kinds of behavior are an abomination to God.

Some Christians believe they can fellowship with people who act that way and not be influenced by their opinions, but the Bible tells us otherwise: "Do not be deceived: 'Evil company corrupts good habits'" (1 Corinthians 15:33 NKJV). It tells us that to live in obedience and enjoy the protection of God's secret place, we must come out from the sinful lifestyle of the world around us. We must separate ourselves from its ways of thinking and acting.

To put it plainly, that means you can't go back to the bars and parties you frequented before you got born again and expect to live long and finish strong. You can't make a habit of hanging out with sinners and live a victorious life. To grow and prosper in God, you must cut off close fellowship with people who do things you know are displeasing to God. You can witness to them, of course, and love them; but you can't be a part of their crowd without being diminished.

"But Gloria, that means I won't have any friends!"

Even if that were true, it's better to be alone than to be surrounded by people who are dragging you toward an early grave. The fact is, however, you won't be alone. God will bring you some new friends. He'll help you find a group of Christians who will really love you. He'll bring you some believing friends who will help keep you on the highway of holy living and encourage you to be obedient to God.

To me, making that exchange is a no-brainer. I can't imagine why anybody would want to keep one foot in the darkness when he can walk with God by getting both feet in the light. Why party with the world and wake up with a hangover, needing some kind of antidepressant to get you going, when you have the option of waking up full of the joy of the Lord and enjoying His blessings all day long? How much more wonderful is it to have a good family, a faithful wife or husband, obedient children, and a peaceful home with blessing, than to endure the hell of a devilish life, where you're always in strife with your children and wondering if your marriage is going to last?

Anyone with any sense can see that God's way is better. Being blessed is better than not being blessed. Being prosperous is better than being poor. (I know, I've tried it both ways.) Being healthy is better than being sick. Living a long, satisfying life is better than living a short, miserable life.

So, choose life and blessing, not death and cursing. Stay on the good side of the sword of God's Word—the obedience side. Heed the counsel Paul gave the Corinthians:

> Be ye not unequally yoked together with unbelievers: for what fellowship hath righteousness with unrighteousness? and what communion hath light with darkness? And what concord hath Christ with Belial? or what part hath he that believeth with an infidel? And what agreement hath the temple of God with idols? for ye are the temple of the living God; as God hath said, I will dwell in them, and walk in them; and I will be their God, and they shall be my people. Wherefore come out from among them, and be ye separate, saith the Lord, and touch not the unclean thing; and I will receive you, and will be a Father unto you, and ye shall be my sons and daughters, saith the Lord Almighty. Having therefore these promises, dearly beloved, let us cleanse ourselves from all filthiness of the flesh and spirit, perfecting holiness in the fear of God. (2 CORINTHIANS 6:14–7:1)

POINTS TO REMEMBER

- As God's people, we have only two options: we can believe and obey His Word, which leads to life; or we can disobey it, which leads to death.

- The Bible clearly says that people who live wicked lives will live short lives. Wickedness brings death just as righteousness brings life.

- If we want to stay well and strong, we must turn entirely away from evil. We can't afford to play around with any kind of sin.

- The more we obey and cooperate with God, the easier it is for Him to move us into a position where He can bless and protect us.

- Catastrophes are cropping up all around us, but none of them have taken God by surprise. He promised to protect us from them before they ever came on the scene.

SCRIPTURE

He who would love life and see good days, let him refrain his tongue from evil, and his lips from speaking deceit. Let him turn away from evil and do good. (1 Peter 3:10–11 NKJV)

CONFESSION

I love the Lord, therefore I keep His commandments. I turn away from every kind of evil and refuse to entertain any kind of sin. Because I choose to separate myself from the world's wicked ways, I live in the secret place of the Most High, where He protects me from every danger. No matter what happens around me, I am safe. My days will be good and my life will be long because I choose obedience. I choose to walk the path of life!

CHAPTER 7

The Ultimate Guide to Longevity

You have probably heard this: "I don't like all this talk about obeying God's commands. It sounds like legalistic bondage to me."

Those kinds of comments baffle me. I don't see how anybody who is born again could consider obedience to God a form of bondage. If we are truly born again, we love God and we know that He loves us. We have a deep desire to do the things that are pleasing in His sight. When we don't do those things, we're not satisfied and feel at odds, not just with God, but with our own hearts.

Why is that?

When we made Jesus Lord of our lives, God imprinted Himself inside us. He fulfilled the age-old promise recorded in Hebrews 8:10–11:

This is the covenant that I will make with the house of Israel after those days, saith the Lord; I will put my laws into their mind, and write them in their hearts: and I will be to them a God, and they shall be to me a people: and they shall not teach every man his neighbour, and

every man his brother, saying, Know the Lord: for all shall know me,
from the least to the greatest.

For born-again believers who love the Lord, obeying God's instructions isn't a burden—it's a blessing! For us, the Bible isn't just a set of rules we're required to keep. It's a marvelous way of life. It's a divine Guidebook that tells us how to live the way we were born to live—in total victory. God gave it to us because He loves us and wants us to know about all the good things He has in store for us. He wants us to learn how to believe for and walk in His blessings.

People who aren't born again, of course, can't live by that Guidebook or receive those blessings because they are still bound by the sin nature of Adam. They don't have the ability to consistently obey the commands of God. For the most part, they can't even understand the Bible. The revelations that we, as born-again believers, get excited about don't make sense to them. First Corinthians 2:9–14 explains it this way:

> Eye hath not seen, nor ear heard, neither have entered into the heart of man, the things which God hath prepared for them that love him. But God hath revealed them unto us by his Spirit: for the Spirit searcheth all things, yea, the deep things of God. For what man knoweth the things of a man, save the spirit of man which is in him? even so the things of God knoweth no man, but the Spirit of God. Now we have received, not the spirit of the world, but the spirit which is of God; that we might know the things that are freely given to us of God. Which things also we speak, not in the words which man's wisdom teacheth, but which the Holy Ghost teacheth; comparing spiritual things with spiritual. But the natural man receiveth not the things of the Spirit of God: for they are foolishness unto him: neither can he know them, because they are spiritually discerned.

I especially like the way the *Expanded Translation* by Kenneth Wuest phrases that last verse: "The unregenerate man of the highest intellectual attainments does not grant access to the things of the

Spirit of God, for to him they are folly, and he is not able to come to know them because they are investigated in a spiritual realm."[1]

Only the born-again person who has received the righteousness of God and the indwelling Holy Spirit can understand and live the lifestyle of victory revealed in the Bible. Unsaved people just can't do it. Their minds are blinded by the devil's darkness. They are slaves to sin. For them, trying to obey God's commands is impossible and results only in failure and condemnation.

The new birth, however, changes everything. It sets us free from sin. It enables us to fellowship with God and gives us His nature. It's not hard for born-again believers to receive and obey God's commandments. It's easy. It's what we were made to do. We have God's own Spirit dwelling in us to strengthen us, to be our Helper, Intercessor, Standby, and Comforter. We have Bibles to read and good ministers to preach to us. Most important of all, we have the Holy Spirit Himself to remind us of everything God has said (John 14:26).

Instead of complaining the way sinners do and saying, "The Word of God is too high a standard to live up to. Who can do it?" we can joyfully paraphrase Romans 10:8: "The Word is near us, even in our hearts and our mouths!"

Maybe you're born again but haven't yet received the Baptism in the Holy Spirit. If so, I encourage you to do it right away so you can take full advantage of His wonderful help. You need His living inside you to live a victorious Christian life. Ken and I didn't know that when we first became born again, so we struggled along without being filled with the Holy Spirit for a few years. We didn't make much spiritual progress during that time, because we didn't have all the equipment God meant for us to have. We had the Holy Spirit in a measure simply because we were born again, but without the Baptism in the Holy Spirit, we couldn't receive the fullness of His ministry.

You might say we had only the "bare bones" of Christianity during those years. The Holy Spirit was able to get a few things across to us when we read the Bible, but most of them were elementary.

Eventually, Ken's mother and dad took us to a Holy Spirit church service. It seemed pretty wild to me because the only Christian meetings I'd attended were all so quiet you could hear a pin drop. Even so, I figured if Ken's parents liked it, it was probably okay. At the end of the service, the minister asked those who wanted to be filled with the Holy Spirit to come forward. Ken looked at his mother and said, "Is that something I should do?"

She said it was, so he went up for prayer.

I was more hesitant. I wasn't sure the Baptism in the Holy Spirit was a good thing, so I went upstairs, smoked a cigarette, and thought about it for a while. It's just pitiful when we're in the dark, isn't it? There I was, smoking a cigarette, trying to figure out if something plainly written in the Bible is right!

I couldn't make up my mind, so after a while I went back into the meeting and took my seat. Meanwhile, the people who had been praying for Ken decided he should lay hands on me and pray for me. When he did, *he* started speaking in tongues. I received the Holy Ghost the next night. What a difference the Holy Spirit inside us made in our lives!

From that time on, we began to grow spiritually as never before. Our desires changed for the better. The Holy Spirit began to do for us exactly what Jesus said He'd do. He took us to the next level by teaching us the things we needed to know (John 14:26). He showed us truths in the Bible that set us free. He showed us how to live in victory.

In addition to revealing to us truths from the Scriptures, the Holy Spirit also began to lead us in the day-to-day details of our lives. My, how that helped us! We were able to avoid some big mistakes and escape some dangerous traps of the devil by paying attention to the promptings of the Holy Spirit and following His guidance in our hearts.

Sometimes people ask me, "Do I really have to receive the Baptism in the Holy Spirit? I'm not really comfortable with that speaking-in-tongues stuff."

Of course, the answer is no. No one has to be baptized in the

Holy Spirit. God won't force us to receive His gift. But I always assure them that life will be better if they do. Things are so much easier when you have the Teacher and Guide inside you. It's wonderful in times of emergency or danger or despair to sense Him rising up within you, giving you direction. It's such a blessing to know He is with you and in you.

Frankly, I can't imagine trying to live long and finish strong without the Holy Spirit's help. There have never been as many crazy people running loose on the streets as there are now. No place is safe. In today's world, it's not unusual for some deranged person to start shooting people in a school, a store, or even a church.

Not long ago, a relative of Ken's who is a high school coach was shot while in his office. The shooter was the father of one of his students. The man was angry because the coach didn't let his son play on the ball team. By the mercy of God, Ken's relative survived, but if that father had gotten his way, he wouldn't have. He shot him at close range, fully intending to kill him—just because of a ball game!

We live in a sin-ridden, mixed-up world. We need all the help we can get from God if we want to live safe and healthy for 120 years. We not only need His Word, we need the Baptism in the Holy Spirit so we can hear His voice saying, "Don't go there." "Don't do this." "Stay away from that place today." Instructions like those can lengthen our lives.

For Our Own Good

Actually, all the fears and arguments about Christians being in legalistic bondage to the Bible melt away once we understand that everything the Lord tells us to do, both in the Scriptures and by the leading of the Holy Spirit, is meant to help us. The commands God gives are for our own good. When we obey, we please Him because we promote our own well-being and open the door to His nothing-missing, nothing-broken, *shalom* kind of peace. We tap into the wonderful treasure described in Psalm 31:19, which says: "Oh how great is thy goodness, which thou hast laid up for them that fear thee; which thou hast wrought for them that trust in thee before the sons of men!"

God gave us His Word and His Spirit so we can retrain our souls to think as He thinks, act as He acts, and enjoy the goodness He has laid up for us. He gave us His commands to help us learn to avoid sin—not because He wants to deprive us of pleasure or box us in with rules, but so we can have abundant life.

You see, God knows even when we don't that sin will kill us. He never loses sight of the fact that "the wages of sin is death" (Romans 6:23). That's the reason He commands us to stay away from it. That's why He warns us to avoid not only the sins we consider to be big (such as murder), but also the sins we think are small and relatively harmless (not walking in love).

Let's look at worry, for example. God understood long before medical science that it is dangerous, so He told us in the Bible to rid ourselves of it. He assured us in His Word that He would take care of us and commanded us not to stress out and be fearful about the future. Jesus said:

I tell you, *don't worry* about everyday life—whether you have enough food, drink, and clothes. Doesn't life consist of more than food and clothing? Look at the birds. They don't need to plant or harvest or put food in barns because your heavenly Father feeds them. And you are far more valuable to him than they are. Can all your worries add a single moment to your life? Of course not. And why worry about your clothes? Look at the lilies and how they grow. They don't work or make their clothing, yet Solomon in all his glory was not dressed as beautifully as they are. And if God cares so wonderfully for flowers that are here today and gone tomorrow, won't he more surely care for you? You have so little faith! So *don't worry* about having enough food or drink or clothing. Why be like the pagans who are so deeply concerned about these things? Your heavenly Father already knows all your needs, and he will give you all you need from day to day if you live for him and make the Kingdom of God your primary concern. So *don't worry* about tomorrow. (MATTHEW 6:25–34 NLT, ITALICS ADDED)

Three times in that one passage of Scripture, God commanded us not to worry. But He didn't do it just so we'd have another rule to keep. He did it because, as research has recently revealed, worry and stress shorten our lives. They are major causes of disease, premature aging, and early death. Thousands of years ago when the Bible was being written, people didn't realize that stress can cause heart disease and strokes and contributes to cancer and countless other ailments.[2] But God did. So, to help us avoid those things, He gave us instructions such as:

- Humble yourselves therefore under the mighty hand of God, that he may exalt you in due time: Casting all your care upon him; for he careth for you. (1 Peter 5:6–7)

- Don't worry about anything; instead, pray about everything. Tell God what you need, and thank him for all he has done. (Philippians 4:6 NLT)

- Be not afraid, only believe. (Mark 5:36)

Ken and I learned how to obey these commands very early in our Christian lives. We had lots of opportunities, especially in the realm of finances, because we had very little money. There were many times back then when we didn't know how we were going to pay our bills or buy groceries, but instead of worrying about it, we cast the care of it over onto God and trusted Him to take care of us.

Years later, I was very glad we learned to do that because as our ministry grew larger, the bills grew, too. Instead of being utility and rent bills of fifty or one hundred dollars, they became million-dollar television bills. Do you know what we discovered? The same faith in God's promises and obedience to His Word that brought us victory when our needs were small still brought us victory when our needs became greater.

Only God knows how much our lives will be prolonged because we've followed God's instructions about not worrying. Only He knows how many years we might have lost had we disobeyed Him and gotten stressed out over money issues. I have no doubt the pressure of it would have affected our health by now. But thank God, the Word protected us and kept that from happening! It enabled us to have peaceful days even when we were facing financial challenges.

The Word worked—as it always does—for our good.

Even When You Don't Understand

Amazing as it may seem, even commands you find in the Word that you don't fully understand can still bring you blessing and prolong your life, if you'll obey them.

The nation of Israel found that out thousands of years ago under the Old Covenant. God gave them all kinds of instructions in His Word about what foods to eat, for example, and what foods to avoid. He told them when and how to wash themselves when they came in contact with dead bodies and certain diseases. No one understood the reasons for the commands at that time. No one back then knew about germs, food poisoning, or bacteria. As far as the Israelites could tell, God was just demanding about their diet.

They may have even thought He was too strict, that He was depriving them of some great foods. But in reality, He was protecting them. History and medical science have now proven that beyond question. According to *The Maker's Diet* by Dr. Jordan Rubin, the Old Testament nation of Israel stands out among the many primitive cultures studied by anthropologists, health professionals, and nutritional historians:

> This group of people carefully restricted scavengers (unclean meats) from their diet ... and lived a lifestyle that kept them free from illnesses and plagues throughout history—as promised in Exodus 15:26....The Israelites of antiquity followed a diet established by God and were consistently healthier than all of their neighbors....There is abundant historic evidence that reveals that the average Israelite, up

to the end of the last century [19th], was much longer lived than the average Gentile.…It appears that God indeed knew what nourishment to recommend.[3]

Of course, as believers under the New Covenant, we aren't bound by religious law to observe the dietary restrictions God gave to Israel in the Old Testament. Although we can still learn a lot about healthy eating from those guidelines, the New Testament gives us different instructions. It tells us that "every creature of God is good, and nothing is to be refused, if it be received with thanksgiving: for it is sanctified by the word of God and prayer" (1 Timothy 4:4–5).

Does that mean we eat unhealthy food and God will bless us with long life anyway? I don't think so. Now we even have natural information on foods that are healthy and foods that are unhealthy. God knew these things all along. It is smart to eat good, healthy food. I think it definitely helps increase our life span.

As believers, we have been freed from the law of the Old Covenant, but we still have one law we must observe. It is a law that must govern every area of our lives. It is the law of love. Walking in love is healthy.

What does walking in love have to do with our eating habits?

Everything! The New Testament says that love doesn't seek its own. Love doesn't do just what it wants to do without considering what effect its actions will have on others. If we're walking in love, we won't pig out and eat like gluttons. We won't yield to our fleshly lusts and stuff ourselves with worthless, unhealthy foods just because we like the way they taste. That kind of overindulgence will damage our bodies and shorten our lives. (Researchers have found a low incidence of obesity among centenarians—see chapter 3.)

If we love our families, we want to be around long enough to help our children and grandchildren grow up. We want to be strong and healthy so we can be a blessing to our wives or our husbands. We want to have the physical energy and stamina—even into old age—to be of service to the people around us.

Therefore, treating our bodies with wisdom by eating right is a loving thing to do. It's a way of expressing our commitment to the people who need us. It's a way of obeying God's command to love others as we love ourselves (Matthew 22:39). That's why Galatians lists temperance as part of the fruit of the Spirit. The apostle Paul wrote:

> Every man that striveth for the mastery is temperate in all things. Now they do it to obtain a corruptible crown; but we an incorruptible. I therefore so run, not as uncertainly; so fight I, not as one that beateth the air: But I keep under my body, and bring it into subjection: lest that by any means, when I have preached to others, I myself should be a castaway. (1 CORINTHIANS 9:25–27)

The word *castaway* used in that verse makes me think of a person left alone on a desert island, cut off from the blessings of life and unable to be a blessing to others. That's what happens to us when we disregard the Word and yield to the lusts of our flesh. It not only hurts us, it hurts others. It hinders our usefulness in the kingdom of God.

I am reminded of that in a vivid way when I see reports on television about the problem of obesity in America. Some people have eaten so much and grown so big that they can't even get out of bed. They've become completely helpless. What's worse, some of these people have children who have to take care of themselves—and their obese parents.

I'm not judging those people. Maybe they are unsaved and don't know any better. But their situation still reminds us that when God tells us to discipline our flesh and walk in love, it's not because He doesn't want us to have any fun. It's because He wants us to be blessed and to be a blessing to others. He wants us to enjoy good, long, healthy, productive lives.

Obedience Pays ... and Pays ... and Pays

When I think of how the Israelites obeyed God's dietary commands even though they didn't necessarily understand them, I'm reminded of how I felt early in my Christian life when I first heard about tithing. Unlike Ken, I didn't grow up in a home where tithing was practiced, so the idea was new to me and I couldn't see how we could afford to do it. Our total income at the time was only about five hundred dollars per month, and we were always in a financial jam. How could it be in our best interests to give away 10 percent? I figured we needed that money far more than God did.

Even so, I wanted to obey the Word, so I got up my nerve and made the commitment to tithe. The amount wasn't very big back then—just fifty dollars or so—but it was still a *leap* of faith because that fifty dollars could have bought a basket of groceries.

I didn't know then what we know now about how God blesses people financially when they tithe and give to Him. I didn't know tithing would ensure our abundance in the long run. It looked to me as if it would make us poorer. But we said, "Okay, we'll tithe first, and if we end up without enough money for groceries, we'll just have to do without them." No faith, but we were determined to obey God, no matter what the cost.

You can probably guess what happened next. Much to my surprise, the money we had left after we tithed stretched much further. We couldn't figure out how it happened. We just knew we were able to do more with 90 percent of our income than we'd done with 100 percent. Money also began to come in here and there from unexpected sources. God began to add to us financially, and He saw to it that we always had enough.

Even though Ken came from a tithing family, there wasn't a lot of teaching at that time about the financial blessings of God. We didn't have much revelation about verses like Malachi 3:10–11:

> Bring ye all the tithes into the storehouse, that there may be meat in mine house, and prove me now herewith, saith the LORD of hosts, if I will not open you the windows of heaven, and pour you out a blessing, that there shall not be room enough to receive it. And I will rebuke the devourer for your sakes, and he shall not destroy the fruits of your ground; neither shall your vine cast her fruit before the time in the field, saith the LORD of hosts.

We obeyed the Word of God and did what it told us to do, and in the process we found out He wasn't trying to take money away from us. He was showing us how to cooperate with Him so He could give us more of it. We learned a good lesson: even when it looks as if obeying God is going to cost you…in the end, it always pays great dividends.

If we'll do what God commands us to do about our finances and give Him the 10 percent that belongs to Him first, we can rest assured our needs will always be well met. It won't matter if our worldly pension programs dry up. It won't matter if the economy staggers. God will keep us prosperous all the way through old age.

That's not a problem for Him. He isn't broke and never will be. Heaven's economy isn't in a slump. Everything there is going well today and will still be going well there when we're celebrating three-digit birthdays. Even then, God will be well able to bless us financially and meet all our needs.

If you've never tithed before and you're not sure how to do it, I recommend you do more than just scribble out a check and drop it in the offering bucket at church. Take some time to pray and worship God over your tithe. It's precious to Him. It's a way of honoring Him. Let it be important to you. Tithe with purpose—to honor and worship the Lord from your heart.

That's what Ken and I do. We get together at home and come before God with a grateful heart. We take Communion over our tithe and thank God for His blessings. We pray over anything in our family that needs prayer. Then we lay our hands on the tithe, offer it to God, and tell Him how much we appreciate the opportunity to give it to Him. We joyfully thank Him for receiving it.

We release our faith and believe to receive the prosperity He promises us. We speak His Word over our finances and say things like, "God meets our needs according to His riches in glory! He makes all grace abound toward us so that we, always having all sufficiency in all things, have abundance for every good work."

We believe and say those things because we don't want to be like the people the book of Malachi talks about—those whose words were stout against God. They said things like, "It doesn't do any good to tithe. Obeying God doesn't benefit us at all. The wicked are more blessed and prosperous than we are!" It's impossible to walk in the financial blessings of God and make those kinds of statements. They are insulting to Him. That kind of talk casts doubt on God's character. It robs Him of His place in our lives as El Shaddai, the One who blesses, prospers, and takes care of us.

We've been tempted to say such things in our ignorance and make the mistake of comparing our financial condition to that of some ungodly person who appears to be better off than we are. *That guy lives like the devil,* someone might have thought, *and he is making money hand over fist. I'm a tither. I love God. But I'm not half as prosperous as he is.*

When you find your thoughts turning that way, stop and remind yourself that real prosperity is more than just money. Prosperity is doing well, enjoying peace in every area of life, and having communion with God. It doesn't matter how much money a wicked person makes, he will never have those things. "There is no peace for the wicked" (Isaiah 57:21 NLT). So never allow yourself to envy others. It will grieve the heart of God and block His blessings in your life. Unbelief robs you in every area, from healing to finances to peace of mind.

Good Fathers Correct Their Children

"But what if I'm tithing and God still isn't blessing my finances?" you might ask.

Let me give you a tip. If you ever find that something isn't working for you the way the Bible says it should, or if it seems you're not seeing God's promises fulfilled in your life, don't bother pointing the finger at God. He is never the problem. Save yourself the time and trouble of saying, "God, where are You? Why aren't You doing Your job?" Instead, examine your own life—not your spouse's—but yours. See if you're holding to the faith. See if you've been faithful to do what God has commanded you.

That's what Ken and I have learned to do over the years. When we find ourselves in a personal test or trial and the pressure is on, we check up on ourselves. We seek God's guidance in the Word and in prayer. We ask Him to show us where we're missing it. When He does, we make a change and things always turn out all right.

Some people don't like God to show them where they are missing it. They get upset by that. But I don't. I appreciate God's correcting me because it keeps me out of trouble. I believe God is doing me a favor when He shows me something I'm doing wrong because that helps me shut the door on the devil. It enables me to walk in freedom and prosperity.

Actually, I'd be concerned if God didn't correct me. I'd have to wonder if He really loved me because the New Testament says God disciplines those He loves (Hebrews 12:6). His grace is what shows us the difference between right and wrong. It teaches us "that, denying ungodliness and worldly lusts, we should live soberly, righteously, and godly, in this present world" (Titus 2:12). I want that kind of teaching because that's where God's blessing is. That's where health is and where long life is—in righteous, godly living.

When God corrects me, I receive that correction with gratitude. If He says, "Gloria, you were unkind today. You said things you shouldn't have," I repent right away. It's not fun to hear that kind of thing, but I appreciate it anyway. I say, "Thank You, Lord, for that correction. You have done me a real favor today. I can see I've been wrong in that area, so I repent of that and I'm grateful You pointed it out."

If you want to live long and finish strong, I highly recommend you adopt that attitude. When God deals with you and tells you to change your behavior in a certain area, when He tells you to quit saying or doing certain things, obey Him with joy. Remember that He isn't just trying to be hard to get along with. He is endeavoring to get you into a position where He can bless you and help you more fully receive His goodness.

God gives you words of instruction and correction through His written Word, by the voice of His Spirit, and through ministers and other believers because He knows that correction will bring life to you. He does it because He wants you to gain "intelligent discernment, comprehension, and interpretation [of spiritual matters]" (Proverbs 4:1 AMP). He gives you His wisdom because that wisdom will "keep, defend, and protect you...and...guard you" (Proverbs 4:6 AMP).

If you have difficulty receiving God's correction with gladness, consider this. God's wisdom is what makes Him great. He wants you, as His child, to have it because it will make you great, too. That's the way all good fathers are. They want their children to have the benefit of their learning and experience. They want to impart as much of it as they can so their children won't make unnecessary mistakes and suffer needless defeats. Good fathers discipline, teach, and correct their children because they want them to get the most out of life.

Because God is a good Father, He is like that, too. He wants us to benefit from His knowledge so we can enjoy the same kind of abundant life He has. He wants us to live the way He lives so we can be as free as He is. That's why He endeavors to get His thoughts into us and show us how to live in victory. God doesn't want to see us suffer from being stupid.

Aren't you glad He isn't stingy with His wisdom? Aren't you grateful He wants all of His family to have it? Aren't you thankful that He loves us so much that He said:

Hear, O my son, and receive my sayings, and the years of your life shall be many. I have taught you in the way of skillful and godly Wisdom [which is comprehensive insight into the ways and purposes of God]; I have led you in the paths of uprightness. When you walk, your steps shall not be hampered [your path will be clear and open]; and when you run, you shall not stumble. Take firm hold of instruction, do not let go; guard her, for she is your life. Enter not into the path of the wicked, and go not in the way of evil men. Avoid it, do not go on it; turn from it and pass on....My son, attend to my words; consent and submit to my sayings. Let them not depart from your sight; keep them in the center of your heart. For they are life to those who find them, healing and health to all their flesh. Keep and guard your heart with all vigilance and above all that you guard, for out of it flow the springs of life. (PROVERBS 4:10–15, 20–23 AMP)

In the King James Version of the Bible, the last verse in that passage uses the word *diligence* instead of *vigilance*. It tells us to be diligent to fill our hearts with God's Word. *Diligence* is "steady application to business of any kind, constant effort to accomplish that which is undertaken, and perseverance."[4] It takes diligence to read and meditate on God's Word every day. It takes perseverance and steady effort to spend time in prayer and do the things the Bible tells us to do. We have to apply ourselves if we're going to get up early in the morning and have time with God before we go to work.

But if we'll do it, we'll walk in victory. Life will flow out of us so continually that when unexpected trouble comes, we won't even have to search for our Bibles to find out what to do. We'll already know. We'll already be full of the Word and have the faith to believe it will come to pass in our lives.

The reverse is also true. If we're not diligent to keep our hearts full of the Word, when trouble threatens we won't know what to do. We won't know what to say. We'll open our mouths and instead of faith pouring out, we'll find ourselves saying, "Oh, no. I'm not going to make it through this! I'm going to lose everything! I'm going to fail for sure!"

Since we have whatever we say, those aren't the kinds of words we want to be speaking when emergencies arise. So we should determine in advance to be diligent and faithful to seek out and apply God's wisdom. Even though it isn't easy, it's always worth the effort. The Bible leaves no doubt about that. It says:

≈ A faithful man will abound with blessings. (Proverbs 28:20 NKJV)

≈ The LORD preserves the faithful. (Psalm 31:23 NKJV)

❧ You have been faithful over a few things, I will make you ruler over many things. (Matthew 25:23 NKJV)

Daniel (of the lions' den fame) was faithful, and his life proved the truth of those verses. He not only received angelic help in time of danger, he prospered and remained powerful in Babylon, the greatest nation on earth in his day, through the reigns of several kings. In the midst of a most difficult situation, God promoted and increased him in amazing ways.

So be like Daniel. Be found faithful. Keep doing the right thing. Keep honoring God's Word. Don't get off it when things get hard. Don't give up when the devil hammers you and tells you that God doesn't love you and isn't going to help you. Don't give in when he says you might as well surrender to sin.

Be diligent! Stick with God's Word and God will stick with you. Sure, it will take time and dedication to do that, but think of the time you won't have to spend being beaten up, stomped on, and kicked around by the devil. You're going to spend your time one way or another—either on God's path of freedom or in the devil's prison of bondage. It's your choice.

Which will it be?

Living Long in the Fear of the Lord

Most people choose the wrong answer to that question. Even though God has offered life to them, and though He yearns for them to experience His blessings, they waste their opportunities to live long and finish strong by neglecting or disobeying God's Word.

Why do they do it?

Because they lack the one thing the Bible guarantees will keep them on the blessing side of God's two-edged sword. They lack the fear of the Lord. The Bible puts great emphasis on the fear of the Lord:

❧ The fear of the LORD is the beginning of wisdom. (Psalm 111:10)

❧ The fear of the LORD is the beginning of knowledge. (Proverbs 1:7)

❧ The fear of the LORD is to hate evil: pride, and arrogancy, and the evil way. (Proverbs 8:13)

❧ The fear of the LORD prolongeth days. (Proverbs 10:27)

❧ In the fear of the LORD is strong confidence. (Proverbs 14:26)

❧ The fear of the LORD is a fountain of life, to depart from the snares of death. (Proverbs 14:27)

❧ The fear of the LORD tendeth to life: and he that hath it shall abide satisfied; he shall not be visited with evil. (Proverbs 19:23)

❧ By humility and the fear of the LORD are riches, and honour, and life. (Proverbs 22:4)

Fearing the Lord doesn't mean being afraid of Him the way you would be frightened of something bad. It simply means honoring Him enough to find out what His Word says and doing it. When we fear the Lord, we seek to know His commandments. We spend time and effort learning how He wants us to live. In the process, if we realize that something in our lives is displeasing to Him, we don't justify or ignore it; we make a change.

And, as we've already seen, that change always makes our lives work better.

According to the Bible, if we fear the Lord by living in obedience to the light God has already given us and search daily for more light, we won't have to wonder if we're going to make the right decision about our jobs or the investment opportunity we're facing. We won't be at a loss about what to do in times of crisis because God will always teach us how to choose what is best. He will put us right in the middle of His circle of blessing. (What a great place to live!)

He will not only surround us with His goodness, He will extend that goodness to our children as well. They won't have to start out broke, living in a dumpy house and sleeping on a rollaway bed. If we'll raise them in the fear of the Lord, they can start out blessed and then keep on increasing.

If we walk in the fear of the Lord, God will be our closest Friend. He'll make sure we can reach Him at any time of the day or night. When we call Him for help, He'll answer us right away. We won't get His answering machine. His secretary won't say, "I'm sorry, God can't talk to you right now. He's on another line."

God will make Himself known to us when we seek Him. He'll share with us the secrets of His promises. He'll give us revelations of His goodness and show us things in His Word that others don't see—things that will help us live long and strong.

Think all that sounds too good to be true? It's not. Psalm 25:12–14 plainly says:

> ✂ What man is he that feareth the LORD? him shall he teach in the way that he shall choose. His soul shall dwell at ease; and his seed shall inherit the earth. The secret of the LORD is with them that fear him; and he will show them his covenant.

> ✂ Who, then, is the man that fears the LORD? He will instruct him in the way chosen for him. He will spend his days in prosperity, and his descendants will inherit the land. The LORD confides in those who fear him; he makes his covenant known to them. (NIV)

> ✂ Where is the man who fears the LORD? God will teach him how to choose the best. He shall live within God's circle of blessing, and his children shall inherit the earth. Friendship with God is reserved for those who reverence him. With them alone he shares the secrets of his promises. (TLB)

❧ Who are those who fear the LORD? He will show them the path
they should choose. They will live in prosperity, and their
children will inherit the Promised Land. Friendship with the LORD is
reserved for those who fear him. With them he shares the secrets
of his covenant. (NLT)

Ken and I have lived in the light of these verses year after year
for more than four decades now. We've discovered that the more we
learn about God's Word and obey it, the more prosperous, satisfying, and joy-filled our lives become.

And we're not finished yet!

We're still learning more about God's ways. We're still increasing in our obedience to Him. We spend more time with God now
than we ever have, and we don't plan to cut back. Why should we?
As long as we keep growing in Him, our lives keep getting better…
and better…and better.

No matter how old we get (and we plan to get very, very old),
as long as we continue to live in the light of God's Word, as long
as we keep seeking more light, we'll never get bored. There will
always be a new challenge ahead. There will always be another step
of faith to take, another impossible mountain to move, and higher
places to go.

From now to the end of our long, strong lives on earth…and
into eternity, God's blessings will always be increasing, not only in
our lives, but in the lives of all believers everywhere who are wise
enough to walk in the fear of the Lord.

POINTS TO REMEMBER

❧ The Bible isn't just a set of rules we're required to keep. It's a
  divine Guidebook that tells us how to live as we were born to
  live—in total victory.

❧ God commanded us not to worry because worry and stress
  shorten our lives and are major causes of disease, premature
  aging, and early death.

- Even though we have been freed from Old Testament religious laws, there is still one law that must govern every area of our lives. It is the law of love.

- If we'll do what God commands us about our finances and give Him the 10 percent that belongs to Him first, He will keep us prosperous all the way through our old age.

- The fear (or reverence) of the Lord is the one element that will keep us on track when others are going astray.

SCRIPTURE

The fear of the LORD prolongeth days. (Proverbs 10:27)

CONFESSION

Because I am born again in the image of God, I love to obey His commands. I delight to do His will and seek every day to live according to the law of love. I don't worry about anything. Instead, I pray about everything and cast all my cares on the Lord, knowing that He cares for me. I put God first in my finances by tithing on all my income with rejoicing, knowing He will prosper me all the days of my long, strong life.

CHAPTER 8

Spiritual Antioxidants: The Rejuvenating Power of the Fruit of the Spirit

ntioxidants. Over the past few years, they've caused quite a buzz in nutritional circles. Researchers say that in the right quantities they combat everything from cancer to wrinkles. They are valiant defenders that come to us through fruits and vegetables. They help protect us from the toxic world around us by working inside our bodies to neutralize its damaging effects.

I'm in favor of antioxidants. They're great. But do you know what's even greater? The protective power of the fruit of the Spirit: love, joy, peace, patience, kindness, goodness, faithfulness, gentleness, and self-control. Although many Christians don't realize it, those qualities are much more than pleasant character traits. They are spiritual forces that work much like antioxidants. When released in our lives, the fruit of the Spirit renews our youth. It protects us from the effects of this fallen world. It defends us from the attacks of the devil and helps keep us from dying before our time.

Unlike natural antioxidants, the fruit of the Spirit doesn't come to us from the outside. They bubble up within us from the wellspring of our reborn spirits. They flow like a river from our inner man.

"I don't know about that," you might say. "I haven't noticed much patience and self-control bubbling up in me lately."

That may be true, but the fruit of the Spirit is inside you nonetheless. All of us who've been born again have that fruit within us because of our union with Jesus. Forces like love, joy, and peace are the supernatural by-products of His divine life within us.

Whether we realize it or not, we as believers are actually the most alive people on earth. We have residing inside us the very Author and Source of life. Think of it! The Lord Jesus Christ, who is the embodiment of life, has moved into our re-created spirits. He has released within us a fountain of His divine life that will never run dry. During His ministry on earth, Jesus confirmed it again and again (italics added):

> ✨ Whoever drinks of the water that I shall give him will never thirst. But the water that I shall give him will become in him a fountain of water springing up into everlasting *life*. (John 4:14 NKJV)

> ✨ I am the bread of *life*: he that cometh to me shall never hunger; and he that believeth on me shall never thirst. (John 6:35)

> ✨ I am the *living* bread which came down from heaven. If anyone eats of this bread, he will *live* forever; and the bread that I shall give is My flesh, which I shall give for the *life* of the world. . . . Whoever eats My flesh and drinks My blood has eternal *life*. (John 6:51, 54 NKJV)

> ✨ "If anyone thirsts, let him come to Me and drink. He who believes in Me, as the Scripture has said, out of his heart will flow rivers of *living* water." . . . This He spoke concerning the Spirit, whom those believing in Him would receive. (John 7:37–39 NKJV)

> ✨ I am the light of the world. He who follows Me shall not walk in darkness, but have the light of *life*. (John 8:12 NKJV)

⟡ I am the resurrection and the *life*. He who believes in Me, though he may die, he shall *live*. And whoever lives and believes in Me shall never die. (John 11:25–26 NKJV)

⟡ I am the way, the truth, and the *life*. (John 14:6)

⟡ Abide in me, and I in you. As the branch cannot bear fruit of itself, except it abide in the vine; no more can ye, except ye abide in me. (John 15:4)

⟡ If ye abide in me, and my words abide in you, ye shall ask what ye will, and it shall be done unto you. (John 15:7)

According to those Scriptures, wherever Jesus is, there is life, *life*, *LIFE*! And since we as believers have been made one spirit with Him, the same can be said of us. We have within us His own unquenchable, eternal, overcoming life. The New Testament leaves no doubt about it. Verse after verse declares (italics added):

⟡ The law of the Spirit of *life* in Christ Jesus hath made me free from the law of sin and death. (Romans 8:2)

⟡ We are equipped to "reign in *life* by one, Jesus Christ." (Romans 5:17)

⟡ We are called to "walk in newness of *life*" and hold forth to a sin-deadened world the "word of *life*." (Romans 6:4; Philippians 2:16)

⟡ We are given a "crown of *life*." (James 1:12)

⟡ We have passed from death unto *life*. (1 John 3:14)

⟡ He that hath the Son hath *life*. (1 John 5:12)

⟡ We have the "right to the tree of *life*" and the opportunity to "take the water of *life* freely." (Revelation 22:14, 17)

That's a lot of life! It's more than enough to keep us full of youthful vigor and health for at least 120 years, wouldn't you say? In fact, with that much divine life in our spirits, the devil shouldn't be able to kill us at any age. We all ought to be able to live like Moses, in full strength until the Lord Himself tells us we've finished our courses and calls us to heaven.

Most believers today, however, don't do that. They don't live as if they have a wellspring of eternal life springing up within them. They don't throw off the toxic effects of sin, sickness, and defeat the way people who have been supercharged with an endless supply of divine life ought to do. On the contrary, many Christians live anemic existences. When the devil comes to damage or cut short their lives, they fall prey to his devices. They don't have the knowledge or the strength to fight him off.

Why is that?

They don't have enough revelation of the Word working, and they're running short of spiritual antioxidants. They don't have enough of the fruit of the Spirit abounding in their lives. They've been weakened by a lack of love, joy, peace, patience, kindness, goodness, faithfulness, gentleness, and self-control. All of these are mighty and powerful, overcoming forces.

Even More Crucial Than a Healthy Diet

If you think I'm overemphasizing the healthy effects of the fruit of the Spirit, think again. Not only does the truth of the Bible back up those effects, I've found scientific evidence as well. Consider, for example, the recent study revealing that people who do volunteer work had a 19 percent reduction in mortality risk compared to non-volunteers.[1] It's easy to figure out that people who volunteer to help others have qualities such as love, kindness, goodness, patience, and faithfulness operating in their lives. They are clearly fruit-of-the-Spirit kind of people and, according to this study, they live longer than those who aren't.

Dr. Gary Small, author of *The Longevity Bible* and director of the UCLA Center on Aging, also gives evidence of the healthy impact of the fruit of the Spirit—especially the forces of joy and peace. He says:

> Scientific evidence…shows that keeping a positive outlook helps us live longer and healthier. In a recent study, positive and satisfied middle-aged people were twice as likely to survive over 20 years compared to more negative individuals. Optimists have fewer physical and emotional difficulties, experience less pain, enjoy higher energy levels and are generally happier and calmer in their lives. Positive thinking has been found to boost the body's immune system so we can better fight infection.[2]

Not only does the presence of the fruit of the spirit lengthen life, medical researchers have also discovered that the absence of it can cut it short. One study of more than 21,000 nurses concluded that on-the-job stress (which indicates a lack of peace and joy) weakens a woman's health as much as smoking or a sedentary lifestyle.[3]

Those and other longevity statistics I've read are enough to convince me that the fruit of the Spirit is even more important to living long and strong than a healthy diet and a rigorous exercise program. I am fully persuaded that walking in love will do even more to protect our bodies from sickness and disease than a basketful of vegetables. A lifestyle of joy will do more to reverse the effects of aging than an aerobics class—although I wholeheartedly support both.

A man named Jackson John Pollock lived to be 128 and confounded conventional wisdom by smoking Prince Albert tobacco all the way through his old age. When asked what he attributed his longevity to, he answered, "Trust in God and He'll pull you through."[4] Whether Mr. Pollock knew it or not, his smoking wasn't doing him any good, but the peace he experienced because of his faith in God was apparently enough to overcome it. (Think how long he might have lived if he'd given up Prince Albert!)

A friend told me of his relative who lived to be one hundred, despite eating lard every day. That lard should have killed him at a much younger age, but it didn't. The reason? My friend said he was the kindest, gentlest, most loving person you would ever meet.

The stories of people like Mr. Pollock and my friend's lard-eating relative absolutely thrill me because they demonstrate just how effective our spiritual antioxidants can be. They show us that while we should do all we can to be good stewards of our physical bodies, even if we can't eat a nutritionally perfect diet, and even if we can't get to the gym every single day, we can still join the ranks of the centenarians if we'll maintain our supply of the fruit of the Spirit.

There is more than just a handful of anecdotal evidence to support that statement. Today, medical doctors are realizing that a positive mind-set (a fruit of the Spirit) can be as vital to a person's physical body as nutritious food. They are discovering that attitudes and emotions can make—or break—a person's health. In his eye-opening book, *Deadly Emotions*, Dr. Don Colbert makes the straightforward assertion that how you feel emotionally can determine how you feel physically:

> Certain emotions release hormones into the physical body that, in turn, can trigger the development of a host of diseases. Researchers have directly and scientifically linked emotions to hypertension, cardiovascular disease, and diseases related to the immune system. . . . Specifically, research has linked emotions such as depression to an increased risk of developing cancer and heart disease. Emotions such as anxiety and fear have shown a direct tie to heart palpitations, mitral valve prolapse, irritable bowel syndrome, and tension headaches, as well as other diseases.[5]

According to Dr. Colbert, depression, anxiety, and fear aren't the only deadly emotions. Others such as rage, hostility, bitterness, resentment, unforgiveness, and stress can also do damage to our bodies and open the door to premature aging, disease, and early death.[6]

The link between negative emotions and disease might be surprising news to modern scientists, but God has known it all along. Jesus warned us more than two thousand years ago about the deadly effect that fear, for instance, can have on the heart. Describing the terrible things that would take place on the earth at the end of the age, He said there would be "distress of nations, with perplexity, the sea and the waves roaring; *men's hearts failing them from fear* and the expectation of those things which are coming on the earth, for the powers of the heavens will be shaken" (Luke 21:25–26 NKJV, italics added). Long before Jesus issued that warning, the Old Testament declared both the positive and negative physical effects of emotions. Consider these revealing verses:

- A merry heart does good, like medicine, but a broken spirit dries the bones. (Proverbs 17:22 NKJV)

- A relaxed attitude lengthens life; jealousy rots it away. (Proverbs 14:30 NLT)

- A cheerful look brings joy to the heart; good news makes for good health. (Proverbs 15:30 NLT)

- I am dying from grief; my years are shortened by sadness. Misery has drained my strength; I am wasting away from within. (Psalm 31:10 NLT)

- Wrath kills a foolish man, and envy slays a simple one. (Job 5:2 NKJV)

- Cease from anger, and forsake wrath; do not fret—it only causes harm. (Psalm 37:8 NKJV)

The Bible and medical science agree that it's good for your health to be merry, relaxed, cheerful, and optimistic. It's bad for your health to be angry, sorrowful, anxious, envious, and pessimistic.

Stay Connected to the Vine

"But Gloria," you might say, "how can we possibly stay free of deadly emotions in this dangerous, high-pressure age? How can we maintain positive attitudes when negative experiences and circumstances surround us?"

The answer is simple but demanding. We do it by maintaining our fellowship with Jesus. When we cultivate and strengthen our union with Him, by spending time with God in His Word, doing what it says, and fellowshipping with Him in prayer, the positive forces of the fruit of the Spirit will abound in our lives. That's not just my opinion. It's what Jesus taught:

> I am the true vine, and My Father is the vinedresser. Every branch in Me that does not bear fruit He takes away; and every branch that bears fruit He prunes, that it may bear more fruit. You are already clean because of the word which I have spoken to you. Abide in Me, and I in you. As the branch cannot bear fruit of itself, unless it abides in the vine, neither can you, unless you abide in Me. I am the vine, you are the branches. He who abides in Me, and I in him, bears much fruit; for without Me you can do nothing. If anyone does not abide in Me, he is cast out as a branch and is withered; and they gather them and throw *them* into the fire, and they are burned. If you abide in Me, and My words abide in you, you will ask what you desire, and it shall be done for you. By this My Father is glorified, that you bear much fruit; so you will be My disciples. As the Father loved Me, I also have loved you; abide in My love. If you keep My commandments, you will abide in My love, just as I have kept My Father's commandments and abide in His love. These things I have spoken to you, that My joy may remain in you, and that your joy may be full. This is My commandment, that you love one another as I have loved you. (JOHN 15:1–12 NKJV)

Just as natural antioxidants and other valuable nutrients are most potent when they come from fresh foods that have been recently connected to the plant on which they grew, the divine life within us is most potent when we're connected to our spiritual Vine. Our fruit is most robust when our fellowship with Jesus is fresh and we are staying in contact with Him.

When we don't stay in contact with Him, we're like a vine that's been broken off the branch. What happens to such a vine? It withers and is destroyed. It just can't live without the sap and life of the vine coming into it. Even if you put that branch really close to the vine, if it's not connected, if it's not in living contact, it won't be able to bear fruit.

That's why we must be diligent to maintain our fellowship with the Lord. That connection enables us to live from the inside out. It empowers us to walk in the Spirit, bear the fruit of the Spirit, and conquer the deadly emotions and activities of the flesh. Galatians 5:16–23 puts it this way:

> Walk in the Spirit, and you shall not fulfill the lust of the flesh. For the flesh lusts against the Spirit, and the Spirit against the flesh; and these are contrary to one another, so that you do not do the things that you wish....Now the works of the flesh are evident, which are: adultery, fornication, uncleanness, lewdness, idolatry, sorcery, hatred, contentions, jealousies, outbursts of wrath, selfish ambitions, dissensions, heresies, envy, murders, drunkenness, revelries, and the like; of which I tell you beforehand, just as I also told you in time past, that those who practice such things will not inherit the kingdom of God. But the fruit of the Spirit is love, joy, peace, longsuffering, kindness, goodness, faithfulness, gentleness, self-control. (NKJV)

If you look at the nine words used to describe the fruit of the Spirit, then compare them to the nine deadly emotions we listed earlier (rage, grief, hostility, stress, fear, anxiety, bitterness, resentment, and unforgiveness), you'll notice something interesting. The two lists are exact opposites of each other. It's no wonder that when we allow the fruit to flourish in our lives, it counteracts the toxic effects of the deadly emotions. The fruit is divinely designed to protect us from the emotional harm this fallen world inflicts on us. If we will cultivate the fruit, if we will yield to its influence, the fruit will keep us healthy inside and out, literally adding years to our lives.

Think of the physical benefits that can be ours when we allow love to conquer hostility and resentment, joy to vanquish depression, peace to overpower anxiety, and patience, kindness, and gentleness to stop rage in its tracks. Imagine how our bodies will respond as we rid ourselves of the destructive, life-shortening effects of those toxic emotions and replace them with the spiritual antioxidants of God! Not only will we be physically strengthened, our lives will be sweeter in every way. The fruit of the Spirit will deliver to us what Proverbs 3:2 promises: "years of a life [worth living]" (AMP).

Keep Your Heart Healthy with Love

This book isn't meant to be an exhaustive study on the fruit of the Spirit. But no teaching on long, strong living would be complete without a section on love. Listed as the first aspect of the fruit of the Spirit, love is the foundation of everything in the Christian life. It is the one law of the New Covenant. It is the single command we are required to keep because in keeping it, we fulfill all the others.

Most people today don't have any idea what real love is. They assume romantic feelings are love. They confuse lust with love. They talk about loving everything from peanut butter to rock stars. People might say they love their friends or their spouses, but few could tell you exactly what that means.

The Bible, on the other hand, isn't confused about the issue. It gives us a clear description of love:

Love endures long and is patient and kind; love never is envious nor boils over with jealousy, is not boastful or vainglorious, does not display itself haughtily. It is not conceited (arrogant and inflated with pride); it is not rude (unmannerly) and does not act unbecomingly. Love (God's love in us) does not insist on its own rights or its own way, for it is not self-seeking; it is not touchy or fretful or resentful; it takes no account of the evil done to it [it pays no attention to a suffered wrong]. It does not rejoice at injustice and unrighteousness, but rejoices when right and truth prevail. Love bears up under anything and everything that comes, is ever ready to believe the best of every person, its hopes are fadeless under all circumstances, and it endures everything [without weakening]. Love never fails. (1 CORINTHIANS 13:4–8 AMP)

All we have to do is read that definition to realize that if we walk in love, we won't be dogged by hostility and anger. We won't be walking around hating people and holding unforgiveness toward them. Love overpowers those kinds of things and delivers us from them. In the process, it helps protect not only our spiritual hearts but our physical hearts as well.

One recent report revealed that unloving, hostile people (people we might say "have a short fuse" or are "quick-tempered") are at greater risk of heart disease than people who smoke or have high cholesterol. They are nearly five times as likely to die of heart disease than those who are less hostile.[7]

Apparently, if we want our hearts to keep ticking for 120 years, we'd be wise to walk in love!

"But Gloria, that's hard!" you might say. "I don't think I can do it."

Not in your own strength and ability, you can't. But if you'll walk in the Spirit and depend on the help of the Holy Ghost, you'll be well able because as a believer, you are created to love. You have been born again in the image of God Himself, and *God is love*! (1 John 4:8). Because you are a partaker of His divine nature, love comes as naturally to you as it does to God Himself. The love of God is shed abroad in your heart by the Holy Ghost (Romans 5:5). Love is in there. Let it come out!

Walking in love takes practice. It requires great dependency on the

Holy Spirit and consistent fellowship with the Lord, but it's worth the effort because the lifestyle of love has a lot of perks! It will keep you out of strife, for example, and strife makes you age fast. Strife is *dis*-harmony, and *dis*-harmony opens the door to *dis*-ease. You might say it this way: strife causes disharmony in your body.

Getting into strife with anyone—your husband or your wife, your children, your relatives, your friends and coworkers, or anyone else—is just asking for trouble. Wise and obedient people don't do it. The Bible says:

> Who is a wise man and endued with knowledge among you? let him show out of a good conversation his works with meekness of wisdom. But if ye have bitter envying and strife in your hearts, glory not, and lie not against the truth. This wisdom descendeth not from above, but is earthly, sensual, devilish. For where envying and strife is, there is confusion and every evil work. But the wisdom that is from above is first pure, then peaceable, gentle, and easy to be entreated, full of mercy and good fruits, without partiality, and without hypocrisy.
> (JAMES 3:13–17)

Those verses aren't just good spiritual advice, they are good medical counsel, too. Strife and unforgiveness open the door to a host of physical evils—evils that can kill you before you finish your course (Acts 20:24).

If you want to live a long, strong life, you cannot afford to hold on to unforgiveness. You must do what the Bible says: "When ye stand praying, forgive, if ye have ought against any: that your Father also which is in heaven may forgive you your trespasses" (Mark 11:25). It doesn't matter what people have done to you—forgive them! After all, your unforgiveness doesn't hurt them nearly as much as it hurts you. Someone said that holding a grudge is like drinking poison and expecting someone else to die. Don't do it.

If someone has done you wrong, forgive him, bless him, and let him go. When you do that, you'll be set free yourself, not just emotionally but physically. One study proved just how true that is. It showed that participants who received one week of forgiveness training experienced "a statistically significant increase in their feelings of physical vitality and general well-being, and 35 percent of the people in the study said they felt 'less distress.'"[8]

Somewhere in my files, I have a newspaper clipping about a couple of happily married centenarians who found that out for themselves. They lived many years together by partaking daily of the fruits of forgiveness and love. One way they did that was by holding hands every night. When they had a little spat, they would forgive and forget before the sun went down so they could keep their hand-holding tradition in the evening and end that day in love and harmony. (I don't know if they realized it, but that's scriptural. Ephesians 4:26 says, "Let not the sun go down upon your wrath.")

That practice must have helped them maintain their appreciation for each other in a number of ways because even at 106 years old, the husband was still talking about what a fine pair of legs his wife had when they got married!

What a great example that couple sets for the rest of us! If we'll follow in their footsteps and forgive quickly and end every day in harmony with everyone, we'll be well on our way to longevity. There's no question about it: walking in love is good for your health!

The Only Sure Cure for Depression

Another aspect of the fruit of the Spirit essential to long life is joy. Joy follows love on the fruit of the Spirit list, and that's appropriate because if we're not walking in love, somebody will steal our joy before the day is out. Someone can do or say something unkind or irritating to us that makes us mad and our joy will fly right out the window. If we're operating in love, however, we have the power to pay no attention to that suffered wrong. We can just forgive the person and go on our happy way.

Joy is a "very glad feeling of happiness, great pleasure, or delight."[9] For the Christian, joy has a spiritual basis. It isn't dependent on outward conditions or even the ebb and flow of our emotions. Our joy comes from our relationship with the Lord. It bubbles up from within us because our spirits are in contact with God, and in His presence is "fulness of joy" (Psalm 16:11).

For us, joy is an emotion poured into our lives as we abide in the love of God. It is a gift from Jesus Himself, who said, "If ye keep my commandments, ye shall abide in my love; even as I have kept my Father's commandments, and abide in his love. These things have I spoken unto you, that my joy might remain in you, and that your joy might be full" (John 15:10–11).

The joy Jesus gives is desperately needed in our world today. Statistics tell us that depression is on the rise in people of all ages. Increasing numbers of children, teenagers, and adults of all ages and occupations are taking antidepressant medications. It seems sorrow isn't just an occasional emotion that people feel when they experience extraordinary loss anymore. It has become a way of life for many people.

If we want to enjoy Bible longevity, however, we must steer clear of that way of life because it is dangerous. Medical science has linked depression to a number of diseases including heart disease, osteoporosis, and cancer.[10] Scientifically, the verdict is in: prolonged sorrow, grief, and depression will weaken our bodies and shorten our lives.

Joy, on the other hand, will make us stronger. It has a tremendous, positive effect on our health. Consider the following Scriptures:

- **The joy of the LORD is your strength. (Nehemiah 8:10)**

- **A glad heart makes a happy face; a broken heart crushes the spirit. (Proverbs 15:13 NLT)**

- **All the days of the afflicted are evil: but he that is of a merry heart hath a continual feast. (Proverbs 15:15)**

🦋 A merry heart doeth good like a medicine: but a broken spirit drieth the bones. (Proverbs 17:22)

🦋 A cheerful heart is good medicine, but a broken spirit saps a person's strength. (Proverbs 17:22 NLT)

🦋 A happy heart is good medicine and a cheerful mind works healing, but a broken spirit dries up the bones. (Proverbs 17:22 AMP)

🦋 Always be full of joy in the Lord. I say it again—rejoice! (Philippians 4:4 NLT)

Although joy doesn't always lead to laughter, there's no disputing the connection between the two. It's interesting to note that experts have discovered that laughter boosts the immune system, reduces dangerous stress hormones, and lowers blood pressure. One researcher claims that laughter is as good for the body as exercise because it ventilates the lungs, increases circulation, enhances the flow of oxygen, and warms and relaxes the muscles, nerves, and heart.[11]

You may feel today as if you can't laugh. You may be struggling with depression. You may be wondering, *Can I ever be truly joyful?*

Yes, if you're a born-again child of God, you can! Even if you've been through some very bad things in your life, even if you've suffered sorrow and grief, you can throw off negative emotions and rejoice.

The Bible says that Jesus has "borne our griefs, and carried our sorrows" (Isaiah 53:4). When He went to the cross, He took our sadness and depression on Himself. At the same time Jesus bore our sins, He bore our sorrows! He carried them so we wouldn't have to! We've been set free!

Although most Christians don't realize it, grief is an enemy. It's a thief. It comes to steal, kill, and destroy the abundant life that's yours in Christ Jesus. Grief and death go together. Doctors see it all the time. One member of a family will die and then grief sets in on other family members. They'll get depressed and sorrowful. That sadness will begin to press down (that's what *depress* means: "to press down"[12]) the flow of life from their inner man. Before long, they begin to get sick. Sometimes they die early as a result. Grief is a deadly emotion! It's a force the devil uses to destroy people.

As believers, we must resist the spirit of grief and refuse to let it take hold of us. Certainly we'll feel pain and experience sadness when someone we love dies. But when we do, we should stir up our faith and get over on the glory side of it. We should focus on what the Word says.

Ken and I know what that's like because we've had to do it. Two of our relatives whom we loved dearly were killed in car accidents at young ages. We felt sad about that. We miss them. But the Bible says we as believers should "sorrow not, even as others which have no hope" (1 Thessalonians 4:13). Instead of just lying down and groveling in grief, we set our minds on the fact that our loved ones are in heaven. They are in the presence of the Lord! And that is far better than anything we have on the earth.

The very best the earth can offer is nothing compared to the joy of living in heaven. Our loved ones wouldn't want to come back. They're having a far better time there than we're having here. What's more, they wouldn't like it if they knew we were letting the devil lie to us and steal our usefulness to God by keeping us depressed over their departure. They'd want us to snap out of it, rejoice with them, and get on with God's plan for our lives.

I realize that can be tough to do. I've been there! After those car wrecks, I had to resist the sorrowful thoughts and pictures that pressed on my mind. But I refused to yield to them. I said, "No, I'm not entertaining grief in my mind. I'm not giving in to that. My loved ones are in heaven. I have reason to rejoice. Sure, I'll miss them, but I have the comfort of the Holy Spirit and the Word of God to minister truth to my heart. What's more, I have a job to do for Jesus, and I'm not going to let grief move into my house and stop me from getting it done!"

"But I don't know if my loved one was saved or not," you might say.

That's right, you don't know. So just trust God. There are

multiplied millions of people who receive Jesus in the seconds just before their deaths. I remember one man Ken knew who was a real rascal. He had lived a bad life and rejected the Lord for years. But after he died, the Lord showed Ken that he had prayed the sinner's prayer in his last moments and gone to heaven. "Kenneth, I'm working to get people into heaven," He said, "not keeping them out!"

If you have a relative who died and you're not sure of his spiritual condition, trust God with the situation. If you loved that person and prayed for him, believe that God was moving on that person in his last moments, revealing his need for Jesus. Expect to meet that person in heaven when you get there.

Remember, through the plan of redemption Jesus has given us a good report for every bad report the devil can give. Where our unsaved loved ones are concerned, Jesus has declared that He "desires all men to be saved" (1 Timothy 2:4 NKJV). Where our own lives are concerned, Jesus has reported to us that all the promises of God are ours in Him. He has declared to us that "whatsoever is born of God overcometh the world: and this is the victory that overcometh the world, even our faith" (1 John 5:4)!

As we've already seen, "A good report makes the bones healthy" (Proverbs 15:30 NKJV). So, no matter what has happened in our lives, we can trust God, rejoice, and have good health. We can look forward to our future with gladness knowing that it's full of the blessings of God. We can expect to live always gaining ground, going from faith to faith, from glory to glory, and from victory to victory. In tough times when disappointments come and circumstances don't go our way, we can say with the prophet Habakkuk:

> Even though the fig trees have no blossoms, and there are no grapes on the vine; even though the olive crop fails, and the fields lie empty and barren; even though the flocks die in the fields, and the cattle barns are empty, yet I will rejoice in the LORD! I will be joyful in the God of my salvation. The Sovereign LORD is my strength! He will make me as surefooted as a deer and bring me safely over the mountains. (HABAKKUK 3:17–19 NLT)

Of course, we won't just stumble into that kind of joyful attitude by accident. We must pursue it on purpose. We must determine in our hearts to believe God and do what Philippians 4:4 tells us to do: "Rejoice in the Lord always" (NKJV)!

We must say to ourselves, *I will yield to joy. I refuse to let anything I see or feel rob me of it.*

A great man of God, Charles Finney, said many years ago, "Whenever you lack this state [of joy], you may know that you have unbelief."[13] Depression or discouragement is a sign you are doubting God's promises to you in some way. You are abandoning your confidence in His Word. So, when depression starts to slip in on you, open your Bible and stir up your faith. Get God's Word in front of your eyes. Put it in your ears. Don't just read it and say, "I wish that word would come to pass for me." Say, "That's mine, in Jesus' name. I believe I receive it."

If you don't, depression will push you down. It will choke off the flow of God's life within you. The devil will use it to steal from you and destroy you. He is the one behind depression, you know. So when he tries to pawn it off on you, do what the Bible says. Resist him and he will flee from you (James 4:7). Say, "No, devil! I'm not having depression in my life. I'll not live in sorrow and grief. I will rejoice in the Lord!"

Then put that proclamation into action. Stop thinking about yourself (I've never known a depressed person who wasn't consumed with himself) and focus on being a blessing to others. Go out and minister to others in need. Lay hands on the sick and pray for their healing. Share the love of God with them. Give of your money and your time. If you'll do that, depression won't have any place to hide in you.

I'm not naive to the difficulties of depression. I realize that it is a real force, but I'm convinced that if we, as believers, will walk in the Spirit, stay full of the Word, get in God's presence every day, and love others, we don't have to yield to it. We don't have to put up with a sad day. We don't have to endure blue Mondays...or Tuesdays...

or any other kind of blue days. If we'll walk in God's wisdom and bear the fruit of joy, all our ways will be pleasantness and all our paths will be peace (Proverbs 3:17).

How to Stop Stressing Out

The spiritual antioxidant that follows joy is peace. The Wuest commentary describes it as "tranquility of mind based on the consciousness of a right relation to God; denoting absence of strife; a state of untroubled, undisturbed well-being."[14] Today such peace is desperately needed. The lack of it is quite literally killing people. According to one recent report, 75 to 90 percent of all visits to primary-care physicians are a result of the nonstop stress (which is the opposite of peace) that has become the norm in our culture.[15] Chronic or prolonged stress has a definite and negative impact on the human body. It has been shown to:

- Impair immune function and open the door to disease

- Reduce glucose utilization, which plays a role in both diabetes and obesity

- Increase bone loss

- Reduce muscle mass and inhibit skin growth and regeneration, accelerating the aging process

- Increase fat accumulation

- Impair memory and learning and destroy brain cells[16]

Stress is a serious hazard to our health today. That's easy to believe considering the fast-paced lives most of us try to lead. Almost all of us fall into the trap of packing more into our schedules than we should. What's more, our contemporary culture (and the devil himself) is putting continual pressure on us to live up to fleshly, society-driven images of success.

Many women, for example, feel it's not enough for them to stay at home and take care of their families. They feel driven, by either social expectations or financial need, to be successful businesspersons, great mothers, Martha Stewart–type homemakers, and perfect wives—all at the same time.

That wasn't the case fifty or sixty years ago. I believe that's why the longevity reports I've read reveal that of the fifty thousand centenarians alive today, 85 percent are women. The women who are over one hundred today didn't work in the marketplace, for the most part, the way men did.[17] They were mostly stay-at-home mothers. They weren't trying to build a career and raise a family at the same time. Although being a homemaker has its challenges, most of us would agree there's not as much pressure involved in peeling potatoes and cooking beans as there is in dealing with the business world. Perhaps it's because those women didn't experience as much stress as the men did that more of them are still alive today.

Am I saying that to have peace people must quit their jobs and hide from the stresses of the world?

Of course not.

I am saying that in this hectic age, if we want to have peace, we must get it God's way. We have to turn our backs on the wisdom of the world and live according to the wisdom of the Word. Peace won't come to us from the outside, because there's too much junk going on for us to find peace out there. We'll have to grow our own peace from the inside. We must put fellowship with God first in our lives so the peaceful fruit of the Spirit that's inside us can flow out.

"But Gloria," you might say, "I'm so stressed out these days, I'm not sure I have any peace left in my spirit."

Sure you do. Every believer has peace because Jesus has given it to us. He said: "Peace I leave with you, my peace I give unto you: not as the world giveth, give I unto you. Let not your heart be troubled, neither let it be afraid" (John 14:27).

Just as Jesus imparted to us His own joy, through the indwelling of His Holy Spirit He has also put His own peace inside us, and His peace is better than anything the world offers. It's superior to the fragile kind of peace we try to create ourselves by removing stressful things from our lives. Do you know why? Because no matter how hard we try to create a peaceful environment around us, the troubles of this world will always break in on it. When that happens, natural tranquillity flies away...but the supernatural peace Jesus gives us doesn't. His peace triumphs over every kind of trouble. He told us so Himself. He said, "In me ye...have peace. In the world ye shall have tribulation: but be of good cheer; I have overcome the world" (John 16:33).

Always remember, as believers, our peace comes from being joined to Jesus. It is one aspect of the fruit of the Spirit. It comes not from the absence of trouble, but from the presence of God. Therefore we will have peace to the exact measure in which we live in and partake of His love. That's why the more we think about God, and the more we pursue Him, His Word, and His ways, the more of His divine tranquillity we can enjoy. The Bible says it this way:

> Great peace have they which love thy law: and nothing shall offend them. (Psalm 119:165)

> Thou wilt keep him in perfect peace, whose mind is stayed on thee: because he trusteth in thee. (Isaiah 26:3)

> O that thou hadst hearkened to my commandments! then had thy peace been as a river and thy righteousness as the waves of the sea. (Isaiah 48:18)

> If your sinful nature controls your mind, there is death. But if the Holy Spirit controls your mind, there is life and peace. (Romans 8:6 NLT)

✖ Let us therefore follow after the things which make for peace, and things wherewith one may edify another. (Romans 14:19)

✖ Pursue righteousness, faith, love, peace with those who call on the Lord out of a pure heart. (2 Timothy 2:22 NKJV)

✖ Let the peace of God rule in your hearts. (Colossians 3:15)

Notice that the verses above tell us peace is something we must pursue. We can't just wish for it or even just pray for it. We must "follow after the things which make for peace" (Romans 14:19). We must be determined to let it rule in us.

How do we do that?

By renewing our minds with the Word of God. By replacing worried, anxious thoughts with His promises. Just meditating on the wonders of salvation will do a great deal to settle our hearts and minds. Focusing on Jesus and the good things He has done for us through the great plan of redemption, instead of fussing about the bad things other people have done to us, can remove stress and replace it with peace.

It's no coincidence that the message of redemption is actually called "the gospel of peace." One book I read defined *peace* as a binding together of that which has been separated.[18] That's what the gospel has done for us. It has removed the sin from our hearts that once separated us from God and bound us together with Him. It has made us the object of God's mercy and, through the blood of Jesus, granted us deliverance and freedom from all the distresses that are experienced as a result of sin.

If we'll set our minds on that truth, it won't matter what goes on around us. We'll be at peace because we know we're united with God. We know He is going to see us through and take care of us in every situation. We will be confident that if we stand in faith on His Word, the negative conditions around us will eventually change to reflect the truth of that Word. So we won't have to stress out about them. We can do what Philippians 4:4–9 says instead:

Rejoice in the Lord always [delight, gladden yourselves in Him]; again I say, Rejoice! Let all men know and perceive and recognize your unselfishness (your considerateness, your forbearing spirit). The Lord is near [He is coming soon]. Do not fret or have any anxiety about anything, but in every circumstance and in everything, by prayer and petition (definite requests), with thanksgiving, continue to make your wants known to God. And God's peace [shall be yours, that tranquil state of a soul assured of its salvation through Christ, and so fearing nothing from God and being content with its earthly lot of whatever sort that is, that peace] which transcends all understanding shall garrison and mount guard over your hearts and minds in Christ Jesus. For the rest, brethren, whatever is true, whatever is worthy of reverence and is honorable and seemly, whatever is just, whatever is pure, whatever is lovely and lovable, whatever is kind and winsome and gracious, if there is any virtue and excellence, if there is anything worthy of praise, think on and weigh and take account of these things [fix your minds on them]. Practice what you have learned and received and heard and seen in me, and model your way of living on it, and the God of peace (of untroubled, undisturbed well-being) will be with you. (AMP)

If you want to live to age 120, I recommend you read those verses often and practice them daily. Get them in your heart so that when you're under pressure, you can remember and obey them. Determine right now that when you find yourself under pressure, you will cool it! Then, when the steam starts to rise within you, tell yourself to be quiet and relax. (That's right, talk to yourself. Don't wait for somebody else to do it.) Tell yourself to shut up if you're spouting words of anxiety and unbelief. Tell yourself to calm down. Remind yourself of what God says about the situation.

Remind yourself not to fret or have anxiety about anything because "a relaxed attitude lengthens life" (Proverbs 14:30 NLT).

Follow This Prescription

In addition to love, joy, and peace, there are six other manifestations of the fruit of the Spirit: longsuffering (also known as *patience* or *endurance*), gentleness, goodness, faith, meekness, and temperance (or self-control). All of these attributes will help you stay healthy and strong. In fact, they are so powerful that if you have them all working in your life, the devil won't be able to do a thing to hurt you. He doesn't have enough power to overcome the effects of that fruit. He is helpless against it.

I've seen that fact borne out again and again in my own life. I can't count how many times I've overcome the strategies of the devil by yielding to the fruit of the Spirit. I remember one time years ago when he tried to get me into turmoil over an ugly letter somebody wrote to Ken and me. Just as I started to get upset, I remembered that the Bible says, "Rejoice ye in that day, and leap for joy: for, behold, your reward is great in heaven: for in the like manner did their fathers unto the prophets" (Luke 6:23). Do you know what I did? I started to rejoice.

I jumped up from my desk and began to dance and leap for joy in obedience to the Word. I didn't feel like it at first, but within a few seconds the fruit of joy began to flow up from my heart. It felt good! The negative feelings disappeared, and from that day to this I haven't been bothered at all when people unfairly criticize us. The joy and peace of God have made me free from it. I realize now that persecution comes for the Word's sake, and it just goes with the territory. Don't let it disturb you.

Notice I had to put my faith in action to allow the fruit of the Spirit to flow that day. I had to connect with the Holy Spirit and let Him energize the forces in my inner man. He does that, you know. Just as an evil spirit will sometimes energize negative elements in a person's flesh, the Holy Spirit will stir up and bring a transfusion of power and life to your spirit. Yield to Him in a time of pressure and

He will help you maintain victory. Spend time each day praying in the Spirit, building yourself up "on your most holy faith" (Jude 20).

Cultivate your awareness of the fact that the very Spirit of almighty God is living inside you. Remind yourself that "the anointing which you have received from Him abides in you, and you do not need that anyone teach you; but as the same anointing teaches you concerning all things, and is true, and is not a lie, and just as it has taught you, you will abide in Him" (1 John 2:27 NKJV). Determine to stay sensitive to that anointing (or prompting) of the Spirit. Make the decision each day to follow His leading instead of yielding to the pressures of the flesh.

Every morning when you wake up, say, "I am a temple of God. I am a dwelling place of the Holy Spirit. I will allow the fruit of the Spirit to flow out of my innermost being today. I will walk in the Spirit and not fulfill the lusts of the flesh."

During the day, if you do something that's displeasing to God and the Holy Spirit lets you know about it, be tender toward Him and quick to change. Don't hang on to your own will. Submit without hesitation to the will of God—to what He says is right.

When someone wrongs you, let it go immediately. Don't fuss and fume over it and get into strife. Be quick to forgive. Pray for those who use and persecute you, and you can go free!

The healthiest thing you can do for your spirit, your soul, and your body is to follow this prescription: be quick to repent, quick to forgive, and quick to believe God's Word. Do those things, and the fruit of the Spirit will be yours in abundance. You'll stay full of spiritual antioxidants that will rejuvenate you every day of your long, strong life.

POINTS TO REMEMBER

- The protective powers of the fruit of the Spirit work much as natural antioxidants do. They renew our youth, protect us from the effects of this fallen world, and keep us from dying before our time.

❧ We have the fruit of the Spirit within us because of our union with Jesus. It is a supernatural by-product of His divine life within us.

❧ Our fruit is most robust when our fellowship with Jesus is fresh and we are staying in contact with Him.

❧ Medical science has linked depression to diseases such as heart disease, osteoporosis, and cancer. Joy, on the other hand, has a tremendously positive effect on our health.

❧ Stress is the number one hazard to our health today. Stop stressing out and live in the peace that comes from being joined with Jesus.

SCRIPTURE

The fruit of the Spirit is love, joy, peace, longsuffering, gentleness, goodness, faith, meekness, temperance: against such there is no law. (Galatians 5:22–23)

CONFESSION

Because I am united with Jesus, the fruit of the Spirit is within me. I will allow this fruit to flow out of my innermost man today. I will walk in the Spirit and not fulfill the lusts of the flesh. When someone wrongs me, I will quickly forgive and walk in love. When depression comes against me, I will resist it and rejoice in the Lord, refusing to allow anything I see or feel to rob me of my joy. When trouble threatens, I won't stress out. I will rest instead in the peace of God.

CHAPTER 9

God's Healing Promises: Good at Any Age

want My people well!"

These are the words God spoke to my heart many years ago when He told me to teach healing and lay hands on the sick in our meetings. He didn't say, "I want My young people well." He didn't say, "I want all My people under eighty years old well." He didn't even say, "I want all My people well, except those who are so old they must suffer from age-related infirmities."

No, He simply said, "I want My people well!"

I know I heard Him correctly because He expresses the same desire throughout the Bible from beginning to end. In Genesis, when He created the earth and prepared the Garden of Eden for Adam and Eve, He didn't put sickness in it. He made it a good place, a healthy place, because He wanted His people well. In Exodus, though sin had entered the earth and sickness had become rampant by then, He brought His people out of Egypt, healthy. Unlike the actors in the old movie *The Ten Commandments* who portrayed the Hebrews dragging sick folks along on stretchers and helping crippled old people hobble along, the real Israelites—from the youngest to the oldest—marched out of Egyptian captivity in vibrant, good health. God "brought them forth," says Psalm 105:37, "with silver and gold: and there was not one feeble person among their tribes."

Imagine aged grandmothers and grandfathers, white-haired octogenarians and centenarians, whose bodies had once been bowed over by hard work under merciless Egyptian taskmasters. Think of them with heads held high, striding with strong steps alongside their children and grandchildren. Not one of them was feeble—despite their age and the difficulties they had endured.

God meant for His people to stay well, too. He intended for them to leave sickness, disease, and frailty behind them forever in the land of bondage where those problems belonged. So He told them how to do it:

> ✖ If you will listen carefully to the voice of the LORD your God and do what is right in his sight, obeying his commands and laws, then I will not make you suffer the diseases I sent on the Egyptians; for I am the LORD who heals you. (Exodus 15:26 NLT)

> ✖ You must serve only the LORD your God. If you do, I will bless you with food and water, and I will keep you healthy. (Exodus 23:25 NLT)

> ✖ It shall come to pass, if ye hearken to these judgments, and keep, and do them, that the LORD thy God shall keep unto thee the covenant and the mercy which he sware unto thy fathers: And he will love thee, and bless thee. . . . And the LORD will take away from thee all sickness, and will put none of the evil diseases of Egypt, which thou knowest, upon thee. (Deuteronomy 7:12–13, 15)

> ✖ Pay attention, my child, to what I say. Listen carefully. Don't lose sight of my words. Let them penetrate deep within your heart, for they bring life and radiant health to anyone who discovers their meaning. (Proverbs 4:20–22 NLT)

It's regrettable, but the great majority of Israelites didn't obey those instructions. Even those who received them directly from the mouth of Moses cast them aside not long after they heard them and brought sickness on themselves by their disobedience. God's will for them remained unchanged, however. He still longed to heal them, so much that He lamented over their disobedience and said, "O that there were such an heart in them, that they would fear me, and keep all my commandments always, that *it might be well with them*, and with their children for ever!" (Deuteronomy 5:29, italics added).

The Hebrew word translated "well" comes from the root word *yatab*. It speaks of being blessed in every area of life—spirit, soul, and body. It means to make "well, sound, beautiful, happy, successful, right, be accepted, amend, benefit, make better, seem best, make cheerful, be comely, find favor, be glad, goodness, make merry, please, show kindness, and make sweet."[1] There is no doubt that this word describes a sound, healthy mind and body.

Throughout the Bible, God's desire to provide physical health to His people never wavered. Thousands of years after those first wilderness wanderers died out, He was still telling His people to obey His commands, and "thine health shall spring forth speedily.... For I will restore health unto thee" (Isaiah 58:8; Jeremiah 30:17). "Behold, I will bring [Jerusalem] health and cure, and I will cure them, and will reveal unto them the abundance of peace and truth" (Jeremiah 33:6).

Notice God didn't put any expiration date on His healing promises. He didn't say He would give health just to people who hadn't yet celebrated their seventieth birthdays. He didn't say that those who had already lived ninety or one hundred years wouldn't qualify for His cures. No, all the way through the Old Testament, God offered to all His people of every age the promise of radiant health. He desired for even the oldest of His obedient people to be able to say with the psalmist: "Why art thou cast down, O my soul? and why art thou disquieted within me? hope thou in God: for I shall yet praise him, *who is the health of my countenance, and my God*" (Psalm 42:11, italics added).

Jesus Never Asked People Their Age

"But all those healing promises are in the Old Testament," you might say. "Do they really apply to us today?"

Yes, they do! In fact, they apply more fully to us than they did to the Israelites because we have a "better covenant…established upon better promises" (Hebrews 8:6). As believers, we are in Christ and, as we've already seen, all God's promises are yes and amen in Him. God has said to us just as clearly as He said to the Israelites: "I am the LORD that healeth thee" (Exodus 15:26). For us, as for them, His unchanging desire is this: "Beloved, I wish above all things that thou mayest prosper and be in health, even as thy soul prospereth" (3 John 2).

That one, short New Testament verse perfectly captures God's will for all of us who are His children today. It tells us God still wants us to enjoy physical health. He doesn't just want our souls to be strong and blessed. He isn't concerned only about our spiritual well-being. He cares about us, too, spirit, soul, and body. Some have doubted that fact, but according to *Vine's Complete Expository Dictionary of Old and New Testament Words*, 3 John 2 leaves no room for dispute. In that Scripture, the Greek term *hugianiao*, which refers to our health, is not a spiritual word. It simply means "to be healthy, sound, in good health."[2] Its application is so distinctly physical that the English word *hygiene* is derived from it.

Even if we didn't have that verse to rely on, we could still be certain that God's will for us is health and healing. The New Testament practically shouts it from the rooftops in one book after another. All of the Gospels show Jesus demonstrating His heavenly Father's desire to heal. The book of Matthew alone should be enough to convince the greatest skeptic that God delights to heal people as much now as He ever did. Keeping in mind that Jesus came to earth to do the will of His Father, consider the following statements about His ministry:

- His fame went throughout all Syria: and they brought unto him all sick people that were taken with divers diseases and torments, and those which were possessed with devils, and those which were lunatick, and those that had the palsy; and he healed them. (Matthew 4:24)

- They brought unto him many that were possessed with devils: and he cast out the spirits with his word, and healed all that were sick: that it might be fulfilled which was spoken by Esaias the prophet, saying, Himself took our infirmities, and bare our sicknesses. (Matthew 8:16–17)

- Great multitudes followed him, and he healed them all. (Matthew 12:15)

- Then was brought unto him one possessed with a devil, blind, and dumb: and he healed him, insomuch that the blind and dumb both spake and saw. (Matthew 12:22)

- Jesus went forth, and saw a great multitude, and was moved with compassion toward them, and he healed their sick. (Matthew 14:14)

- Great multitudes came unto him, having with them those that were lame, blind, dumb, maimed, and many others, and cast them down at Jesus' feet; and he healed them. (Matthew 15:30)

- Great multitudes followed him; and he healed them there. (Matthew 19:2)

- The blind and the lame came to him in the temple; and he healed them. (Matthew 21:14)

Anyone who might be tempted to think Matthew was in some way overemphasizing Jesus' commitment to heal all the sick who came to

Him needs only to read the Gospel of Luke to put that thought to rest. Luke confirms all Matthew said and even provides additional reports:

- When the sun was setting, all they that had any sick with divers diseases brought them unto him; and he laid his hands on every one of them, and healed them. (Luke 4:40)

- So much the more went there a fame abroad of him: and great multitudes came together to hear, and to be healed by him of their infirmities. (Luke 5:15)

- A great multitude of people out of all Judaea and Jerusalem, and from the sea coast of Tyre and Sidon, which came to hear him, and to be healed of their diseases; and they that were vexed with unclean spirits: and they were healed. And the whole multitude sought to touch him: for there went virtue out of him, and healed them all. (Luke 6:17–19)

- A woman having an issue of blood twelve years, which had spent all her living upon physicians, neither could be healed of any, came behind him, and touched the border of his garment: and immediately her issue of blood stanched. And...she was healed immediately. (Luke 8:43–44, 47)

- The people, when they knew it, followed him: and he received them, and spake unto them of the kingdom of God, and healed them that had need of healing. (Luke 9:11)

- There was a woman which had a spirit of infirmity eighteen years, and was bowed together, and could in no wise lift up herself. And when Jesus saw her, he called her to him, and said unto her, Woman, thou art loosed from thine infirmity. And he laid his hands on her: and immediately she was made straight, and glorified God. (Luke 13:11–13)

❧ There was a certain man before him which had the dropsy. And Jesus ... healed him, and let him go. (Luke 14:2–4)

❧ As he entered into a certain village, there met him ten men that were lepers, which stood afar off: And they lifted up their voices, and said, Jesus, Master, have mercy on us. And when he saw them, he said unto them, Go show yourselves unto the priests. And it came to pass, that, as they went, they were cleansed. (Luke 17:12–14)

The Gospels of Mark and John include similar verses and cite only one occasion when Jesus wasn't able to heal all who came to hear Him. It was in Nazareth. The reason some went away without receiving healing there is no mystery. The Bible explains, "He could there do no mighty work, save that he laid his hands upon a few sick folk, and healed them. And he marvelled because of their unbelief" (Mark 6:5–6).

Do you know what amazes me about that incident? Even when people's unbelief short-circuited the fullness of the divine power flowing through Jesus, He still endeavored to get them healed. No wonder the book of Acts sums up Jesus' entire ministry in this one statement: "God anointed Jesus of Nazareth with the Holy Ghost and with power: who went about doing good, and healing all that were oppressed of the devil; for God was with him" (10:38). Those words are a glorious confirmation that what God said to me so many years ago is undeniable and true—"I want My people well!"

For those believing for Bible longevity, that's especially good news. Who would want to live to be 120 if it meant putting up with years of arthritis or dragging around with what are often referred to as "age-related diseases"? I certainly wouldn't. So the older I get, the more I appreciate Jesus' ministry to the sick and how it demonstrated God's will for our healing. I'm happy that the Bible says when the multitudes came to Him, He healed them all.

Aren't you glad He healed all? Aren't you grateful He didn't ask people their ages before He ministered to them? Isn't it a relief that Jesus didn't say to even one person, "You are too old to receive healing. You just need to go home and die"?

No, praise God, Jesus never once said those words to anyone during His ministry on earth, and He never says them to anyone today. He still heals all who come to Him in faith because He is "Jesus Christ the same yesterday, and to day, and for ever" (Hebrews 13:8). He is still the "same Jesus" (Acts 1:11), and His healing power and promises are good at any age.

Set Free from the Curse

Actually, God's healing power and promises are not just good *at* any age, they are good *in* any age. The healing power of God works as well in the twenty-first century as it worked two thousand years ago. Contrary to what some think, Jesus' healing ministry didn't end when He ascended to heaven. It expanded. He multiplied its effectiveness by commissioning all His disciples (not just the first apostles, but all who would ever believe in Him) to continue it. He said:

> Go ye into all the world, and preach the gospel to every creature. He that believeth and is baptized shall be saved; but he that believeth not shall be damned. *And these signs shall follow them that believe;* in my name shall they cast out devils; they shall speak with new tongues; they shall take up serpents; and if they drink any deadly thing, it shall not hurt them; *they shall lay hands on the sick, and they shall recover.* (Mark 16:15–18, italics added)

Isn't it wonderful? God's desire to heal people is still so great, He included healing in our assignment as believers. He not only wants us to be well ourselves, He wants us to take healing to others. We Christians haven't done the job as well as we should have. Many people today get the idea that God has gone out of the healing business.

In the early days of the church, however, that wasn't the case. The disciples "went forth, and preached every where, the Lord working with them, and confirming the word with signs following" (Mark 16:20). They stayed busy healing the sick just as Jesus did.

The healing ministries of the first apostles are just like the Master's. (That's no surprise. Jesus said that those who believed on Him would do the works He did and even greater works [John 14:12].) God healed so many people through Peter that multitudes brought the sick out into the streets in hopes that Peter's shadow might fall upon them. "A multitude gathered from the surrounding cities to Jerusalem, bringing sick people and those who were tormented by unclean spirits, and they were all healed" (Acts 5:16 NKJV). God worked such extraordinary miracles of healing through the hands of the apostle Paul that "even handkerchiefs or aprons were brought from his body to the sick, and the diseases left them and the evil spirits went out of them" (Acts 19:12 NKJV).

The apostles weren't the only ones who ministered healing. People like Stephen, who was what we'd call a layman or a helper in the church, also "did great wonders and miracles among the people" (Acts 6:8). So did another layman named Philip. When he traveled to Samaria and preached about Jesus, "the people with one accord gave heed unto those things which Philip spake, hearing and seeing the miracles which he did. For unclean spirits, crying with loud voice, came out of many that were possessed with them: and many taken with palsies, and that were lame, were healed. And there was great joy in that city" (Acts 8:6–8).

Through the years, some have tried to relegate such New Testament healings to days gone by. "God just did those kinds of things to help get the church started," they say. "He never promised divine healing to all believers."

If that's true, the writer of the New Testament book of James (who was Jesus' half brother) didn't know it because he presented divine healing as something every member of the church should enjoy. "Is any sick among you?" he wrote. "Let him call for the elders of the church; and let them pray over him, anointing him with oil in the name of the Lord: And the prayer of faith shall save the sick, and the Lord shall raise him up; and if he have committed sins, they shall be forgiven him" (James 5:14–15).

The apostle Peter also taught that healing belonged to every believer. In his epistle to the church he wrote about the sacrifice Jesus made for us on the cross, saying, "By [His] stripes ye were healed" (1 Peter 2:24). The apostle Paul shed even more light on the subject in his letter to the Galatians, where he wrote: "Christ hath redeemed us from the curse of the law, being made a curse for us: for it is written, Cursed is every one that hangeth on a tree: that the blessing of Abraham might come on the Gentiles through Jesus Christ; that we might receive the promise of the Spirit through faith" (3:13–14).

No Bible-believing Christian would question what Paul wrote. We all agree that as born-again believers we are redeemed from the curse and are recipients of God's blessing. The problem is, many Christians today are confused about the difference between a blessing and a curse. Some have the idea, for example, that sickness can be a blessing in disguise. They may even think that God makes His children sick on occasion to help them in some way.

According to the Bible, however, nothing could be further from the truth. The Hebrew word for *blessing* means "to endue with power for success, prosperity, fruitfulness and longevity."[3] Described in detail in Deuteronomy 28:1–14, the blessing includes everything good, and nothing that causes harm. The Bible never mentions sickness as a part of the blessing.

On the contrary, in Deuteronomy 28:6 the Bible declares that all sickness is part of the curse. The last section of Deuteronomy 28 (NLT), which defines the curse in specific terms, includes in it such illnesses as:

- "Wasting disease, fever, and inflammation." (verse 22)

- "Boils[,] ... tumors, scurvy, and the itch." (verse 27)

- "Madness, blindness, and panic." (verse 28)

- "Indescribable plagues . . . intense and without relief, making you miserable and unbearably sick." (verse 59)

- "Every sickness and plague there is, even those not mentioned in this Book of the Law." (verse 61)

For people who are still under the curse, that is a frightening list. But for those who have put their faith in Jesus as Lord and Savior, it is something to shout about. It's a list of all the sicknesses and diseases from which we've been redeemed—and it includes every one that ever has or ever will exist! God set us free from those sicknesses when He sent Jesus to the cross to bear the entire curse so that we wouldn't have to experience any of it. Jesus paid the price to free us from it all. That's what the prophet Isaiah was talking about when he wrote:

> Surely He has borne our griefs (sicknesses, weaknesses, and distresses) and carried our sorrows and pains [of punishment]. . . . He was wounded for our transgressions, He was bruised for our guilt and iniquities; the chastisement [needful to obtain] peace and well-being for us was upon Him, and with the stripes [that wounded] Him we are healed and made whole. All we like sheep have gone astray, we have turned every one to his own way; and the Lord has made to light upon Him the guilt and iniquity of us all. (ISAIAH 53:4–6 AMP)

Don't Take It Anymore!

A few years ago when the movie *The Passion of the Christ* was released, it gave us a glimpse into the magnitude of the price Jesus paid for our redemption. I didn't want to see that movie at first, but in my spirit I was impressed to go. It was difficult for me to watch as the stripes tore Jesus' flesh. Every lash of the whip that struck Him, He bore for me.

Some people complained about the brutality of the movie, but as shocking as it may have seemed, it didn't convey the fullness of Jesus' suffering. It didn't show the spiritual price He paid. It didn't show Him in hell taking our place and punishment there.

Even so, it had a great impact on me. It stirred my faith and my zeal to walk in the fullness of the redemption Jesus bought for me. I believe it increased my determination to stand against sickness and say, "No! I'll not take sickness because Jesus has already borne it for me. I will honor His sacrifice for me by receiving the healing He paid so dearly for me to have!"

Of course, you don't need to see a movie about the Crucifixion to develop that attitude. All you have to do is read the Word. When the truth of it dawns on you, it will set your faith on fire. It will affect you the same way it did one elderly gentleman who attended Healing School some years ago in Milwaukee. I'll never forget that man. He was a small, gray-haired fellow who, under other circumstances, might have been quiet and reserved. But he got so inspired after hearing what the Bible says about healing and being redeemed from the curse he marched forward to give his testimony with a boldness that let us know he meant business.

I don't remember all he said about his healing, but I do remember he let us know in no uncertain terms that he'd not only been healed, he meant to stay that way. He'd realized that because of what Jesus did at Calvary, the devil had no right to put sickness on him, and he began to declare as he walked around, "I'm not going to take it anymore! I'm just not going to take it anymore!"

When he started shouting, it set the whole congregation on fire. We all started shouting with him! We decided *we* weren't going to take it anymore, either. We saw, just as he did, that it doesn't matter how old we are—it doesn't matter if we're 150—we've been redeemed from the curse and we don't have to put up with it anymore. We have a blood-bought right to stay strong and healthy all the days of our lives.

I'm sure that man must have had much the same experience in Healing School as that Ken and I had when we first heard Kenneth E. Hagin preach "by Jesus' stripes we were healed." That message changed our lives forever.

Until then, when sickness would come, we would pray and ask God to heal us, but we weren't sure if He would. We knew He *could* do it because Ken worked for Oral Roberts and he saw all kinds of miracles in his meetings. But we didn't know that our healing was a done deal. We didn't know that we could lay hold of it by faith because it already belonged to us. So when we'd get a fever or other symptoms, our attitude would be *Hmmm...I'm sick. Where are my pajamas? I'm going to bed!*

Once we realized healing was part of the finished work of redemption, however, we began to see sickness in a different way. When it tried to come into our house, we didn't cooperate with it. We didn't say, "Okay, it's the flu season again. I guess we'll get the flu." We learned to align our words with the Bible. We learned to say, "No, flu. You're not coming here." Because we realized that the devil was behind all sickness and he had no right to put it on us, we resisted sickness just as we resisted sin. Sure enough, it would flee from us just as the Bible says.

We learned back then (more than forty-two years ago) that we cannot talk sickness and disease and walk in health. We can't have it both ways. When someone asked, "How are you today?" we didn't say, "Oh, I'm hurting all over. I feel sick as a dog." Sure, there were times when that's what we wanted to say, just like everyone else. When we felt bad, we naturally wanted to tell someone so they could sympathize with our misery. But we were determined not to do it.

We'd discovered for ourselves what many other people who've walked by faith discovered before us. You cannot tell people about your disease and your pains and moan over your troubles without getting in deeper and deeper. Since Satan is the one behind all sickness, pain, and trouble, when we declare that he has succeeded in putting those things on us, we are confessing he is master and has gained the supremacy.

When we talk about our troubles, we magnify the work of the devil and our troubles grow bigger. When we confess our sicknesses, they get a stronger hold on us. Instead of making us feel better, our pleas for sympathy make us feel worse. We get far better results when we give up our confession of Satan's supremacy and declare instead that Jesus has borne our sickness and by His stripes we were healed. That's why we must break the habit of talking about symptoms of sickness to anyone who asks and establish the habit of doing what the Bible says: "Hold fast the profession of our faith without wavering" (Hebrews 10:23).

That's what my friend Dodie Osteen did. (Dodie's son is Joel Osteen.) More than twenty-nine years ago, she was diagnosed with liver cancer and given only a short time to live. Since there was nothing medical science could do to help her, Dodie and her husband, John, left the hospital, went home, and sought the Lord about what to do. He revealed to them that Dodie should put together a list of healing Scriptures and go over it faithfully, reading and confessing each Scripture daily.

After Dodie and John prayed and received her healing, she and her family spoke and acted as if she were healed. In other words, they lived as if the Bible is true. Although the symptoms lingered for a while, Dodie continued to daily read and confess what the Word says about healing. Eventually her health returned.

In October 2009, Dodie turned seventy-six years old, and she looks younger every time I see her. That doesn't surprise me, however, because she still reads and confesses those healing Scriptures daily. She says she'll do it every day for the rest of her life on earth. (You can read the whole story of Dodie's healing in her book, *Healed of Cancer*.)[4]

Some might say that God did a special miracle just for Dodie—but He didn't. Dodie was healed for one simple reason: She obeyed the instructions in Proverbs 4:20–22. She believed the Word and acted on it. She refused to let God's Word depart from her eyes, and she kept it in the center of her heart. As a result, it became health and healing to her flesh, just as the Bible said it would.

The Hebrew word *marpe*, which is translated "healing" in Proverbs 4:22 (AMP), can actually be used to refer to medicine.[5] So you might say that Dodie was healed because she took God's medicine as prescribed. She proved that, when taken according to the directions of the Great Physician, God's Word will cure even the most deadly diseases.

Seize Divine Health

Not only will God's medicine cure you when you're sick, if you keep taking it the way Dodie did, it will keep you in divine health. Healing is good, but divine health is even better. I'd rather be protected from sickness and disease and never suffer from it at all than fall prey to it and then receive healing, wouldn't you? I'm believing to stay well so that I don't have to waste one day living in weakness or pain. Really, that's God's perfect will for us.

He didn't say in Psalm 91 that when pestilence came on us and made us ill, He'd heal us (although if it does, He will). He said no pestilence or plague would even come close to us. He said, "Thou shalt not be afraid for...the pestilence that walketh in darkness.... It shall not come nigh thee.... There shall no evil befall thee, neither shall any plague come nigh thy dwelling" (verses 5–10).

Many years ago, when John G. Lake was ministering in Africa, that promise saved his life in a very literal way. The bubonic plague struck the region and he was exposed to it day after day. He and another minister not only laid hands on and prayed for those who suffered from the disease, they also helped bury the bodies of the dead. Before long, they caught the attention of the medical doctors. "How can you do this without contracting the plague?" they asked.

John Lake decided to go with them into the medical lab and show them. He allowed the doctors to take plague germs, put them under a microscope, and verify that they were alive and moving. Then he allowed them to put the same germs on his hand and look at them under the microscope again. The germs died instantly![6]

What killed them?

The life of God that was in John Lake.

Mr. Lake had such faith in the power of that divine life that even the bubonic plague couldn't kill him. It couldn't even touch him because when it did, God's power flowed from within him and stopped it in its tracks.

We could all develop the kind of plague-and-pestilence-killing faith John Lake had if we would spend enough time in God's Word and obey it. We'd be wise to do it, too, because there are some serious pestilences around these days. We're living in the times Jesus was talking about in Luke 21 when He said, "There will be mighty and violent earthquakes, and in various places famines and pestilences (plagues: malignant and contagious or infectious epidemic diseases which are deadly and devastating)" (verse 11 AMP).

I've decided that rather than believe for healing from those kinds of diseases after I'm sick, I'll believe to avoid them altogether. That's why I'm glad God's health plan is a wellness plan. It's designed to keep us healthy from the top of our heads to the soles of our feet all the time. If we'll live according to that plan, it will keep sickness away from us. It will keep us feeling good, pain-free, worry-free, and walking in divine power.

I love God's health plan. It's fabulous. It beats any plan medical science or the insurance companies have to offer. Their achievements have been helpful, but they are still limited in what they can do. God, on the other hand, is not limited. He can deliver us from diseases and medical conditions that doctors consider incurable. His health plan leaves nothing out. There are no deductibles and no exclusions. Better yet, it's free because Jesus has already paid for it. All it costs us is faith.

To have the kind of faith it takes to get in on God's health plan, however, we can't be lazy. We must exert the effort to do what Proverbs says to do. We must keep the Word of God in front of our eyes and in our ears so that it stays in the midst of our hearts. Our faith can't be strong for healing if we don't feed regularly on the Word. Faith comes by hearing and hearing by the Word of God (Romans 10:17). If we want to stay well, our faith must be strong because Satan will challenge us.

He comes to steal, kill, and destroy. He is always trying to rip off some believer's health. When he comes knocking at our doors, we must be ready for him. We must be "strong in the Lord, and in the power of his might" (Ephesians 6:10). When the devil shows up at our houses with symptoms of sickness, we can't afford to be weak and wimpy from lack of the Word. We must have the spiritual energy and faith to resist him and say, "Get out of here, in the name of Jesus. I'm not listening to your lies. I've been redeemed from sickness, and I refuse to receive it."

I can tell you from experience, that's not always easy. It takes real inner strength because sometimes sickness and pain can seem overwhelming. When our bodies are hurting and feeling weak, we can be tempted to give in to them. "I feel too bad to read the Word," we might say. "I don't have enough energy to go to church or make healing confessions."

If we want to live long and healthy lives, however, we can't lie down and let sickness run over us. We can't just breathe a prayer and beg Jesus to heal us. We must back up our prayers with words and actions of faith. We must follow the example of the woman with the issue of blood who came to Jesus for healing. She is an inspiration to all of us. Mark 5 tells her story:

> A certain woman, which had an issue of blood twelve years, and had suffered many things of many physicians, and had spent all that she had, and was nothing bettered, but rather grew worse, when she had heard of Jesus, came in the press behind, and touched his garment. For she said, If I may touch but his clothes, I shall be whole. And straightway the fountain of her blood was dried up; and she felt in her body that she was healed of that plague. And Jesus, immediately knowing in himself that virtue had gone out of him, turned him about in the press, and said, Who touched my clothes? And his disciples said unto him, Thou seest the multitude thronging thee, and sayest thou, Who touched me? And he looked round about to see her that had done this thing. But the woman fearing and trembling, knowing what was done in her, came and fell down before him,

and told him all the truth. And he said unto her, Daughter, thy faith hath
made thee whole; go in peace, and be whole of thy plague. (VERSES 25–34)

Think about how bad this little woman's situation was. She had
an incurable disease. It had been draining the life from her body for
twelve years, and the doctors could do nothing to help her. What's
more, her condition made her a social outcast in the Jewish culture.
It was against religious law for her to even go out in public. If anyone
ever had an excuse to just lie down and die without exercising any
faith, she did.

But, thank God, in the midst of her hopeless circumstances,
someone told her about Jesus. Someone must have said something
like, "He's healing everybody!" When she heard that good news,
something happened to her inside. Faith sprang up. It wouldn't have
come if she'd heard that Jesus was just healing one in ten thousand.
Faith wouldn't have been born in her heart if she'd heard that He
healed some because it was His will, but others He left sick for reasons nobody understood.

No, those kinds of reports don't give birth to faith. For faith to
arise, we must know that Jesus heals all!

Once the lady heard about Jesus' healing ministry, she didn't lie
on her bed in silence, hoping and praying He would drop in on her.
She opened her mouth and started making a confession of faith.
"She kept saying, If I only touch His garments, I shall be restored
to health" (Mark 5:28 AMP). Although she may not have realized it,
when she made that confession, she was setting the parameters for
her healing. She was activating the spiritual principle Jesus taught
in Mark 11:23: "Whosoever shall say unto this mountain, Be thou
removed, and be thou cast into the sea; and shall not doubt in his
heart, but shall believe that those things which he saith shall come
to pass; he shall have whatsoever he saith."

This lady didn't make her confession a couple of times and then
give up, either. She didn't let her symptoms convince her she was
too sick and tired to keep speaking. She stuck with it. She also acted

on her faith. (It's not just what you know that brings you victory; it's what you do!) She got up and went after Jesus. She sought out the Living Word. It wasn't easy for her. There were multitudes thronging around Him, so she had to push her way through the crowd to reach Him. But she did it.

How did she find the strength? It's a wonder she didn't faint from exhaustion. What kept her going? I'm convinced that God saw her faith and helped her. He gave her the stamina she needed to keep speaking what she believed. He always helps those who believe and act on their faith.

When she got to Jesus, she did exactly what she said she would do. She touched His garment. When she did, what she had been saying came to pass just the way she'd said it would. At that moment, the hemorrhaging stopped and she felt in her body that she was healed. She became a living demonstration that what Jesus said was true: "What things soever ye desire, when ye pray, believe that ye receive them, and ye shall have them" (Mark 11:24).

Not for Wimps

We sometimes miss the power of the statement "believe that ye receive" from Mark 11:24 because the English word *receive* doesn't fully express the meaning of the Greek word *lambano*, from which it is translated. *Lambano* isn't a passive kind of receiving. It doesn't paint the picture of someone dropping a gift into our laps. It refers to taking or seizing something with strength and boldness.[7]

We can't receive (or seize) God's promise of healing with determination and boldness and be wimps at the same time. We can't take what belongs to us in Christ by sitting around moaning, groaning, and feeling sorry for ourselves. We must grab it with the grip of faith the same way the woman with the issue of blood did. We must latch on to it the way a dog latches on to a bone and run with it.

We must refuse to allow symptoms to stop us. We must refuse to give in to the weakness of our bodies, the bad reports of the doctors, and the discouraging words of other people. If we want to lay hold of our healing, we must be adamant about it. We must be courageous enough to believe, confess, and act on our faith until the manifestation comes.

Some Christians ridicule that idea. "Oh, that confession stuff doesn't work!" they say. "You can't get healed just by saying and acting like you're healed."

You can if you're basing your words and actions on the Word of God. I know that from experience. I've lived that way for a long time. Through the years, our family has faced some serious situations. There were times when our lives were threatened by sickness or disease. It didn't happen often because overall we're a blessed and healthy family. But there have been occasions when this matter of believing, confessing, and acting on God's Word for healing was a matter of life and death for us.

Some years ago, for example, our granddaughter Lindsey contracted neisserian meningitis. By the time she arrived at the hospital, she was delirious. The doctors told us that several children had been admitted with the same disease before she arrived and they died. "The next twenty-four hours will tell the story of whether she'll live or die," they said.

How do you think we responded to that news? Did we just sit in the hospital waiting room and play cards or wring our hands and hope God might intervene?

Certainly not! We did what the Bible says. We took our stand on the Word of God and resisted the devil. We rebuked death. We said, "You're not taking one of our own!"

We knew we'd been delivered from the curse of that sickness. We knew it wasn't God's will for Lindsey to die young. The Bible made that clear. So we fought the fight of faith on her behalf. Even Lindsey herself began to make declarations of faith as she drifted in and out of consciousness. She was just a child, but she had the Word of God in her heart, and it started coming out of her mouth.

Today Lindsey is alive and well. She has a ministry call on her life and is going strong because we all stood together on the Word of God and seized her healing.

"But Gloria, my faith for healing isn't that strong," you might say. "I don't have what it takes to stand against the symptoms coming against me right now."

Then get out your Bible and get some more faith. Do what Dodie Osteen did and is still doing today. Put together a list of healing Scriptures, then read and confess them day and night. Get a copy of the Bible on CD and listen to it at night when you go to bed. I've done that many times when I felt symptoms of sickness coming against me. I'd listen to the Bible as I went to sleep and all through the night. Almost every time, I'd wake up in the morning healed.

If the manifestation of healing doesn't come that quickly for you, don't get discouraged. Don't quit. Don't think, *This isn't working for me. God must not love me.*

Those kinds of thoughts come from the devil, and he is a liar. God does love you! He sent Jesus to the cross to deliver you from the curse of sickness. So you can rest assured, He is not withholding healing from you. As we've seen, He is the One who said, "Beloved, I wish above all things that thou mayest prosper and be in health, even as thy soul prospereth" (3 John 2).

According to that verse, our souls must prosper for health to come. We must renew our minds with the truth of God's Word. If the symptoms in our bodies have been talking to us, trying to brainwash us with lies by saying, "You're not healed. You're sick. You're hurting. You'll never receive your healing," we must turn the tables on them. We must go to work washing our minds with what God has said about the situation by doubling up—or tripling or quadrupling up—on our daily dose of the Word. Remember, that's how faith comes!

Also remember, the Word is God's medicine and can do what no natural medicine can do. It's alive and full of power. There's no pill, no natural prescription, no drug—legal or illegal—that can inject life into your body the way the Word can. So make God's Word the biggest thing in your life. Believe it, confess it, and act on it.

Doing so will put the devil on the run. Believing, confessing, and acting on God's Word will send symptoms scurrying in every direction. No matter how young or how old you are, it will make you well and keep you well. God's plan is the most magnificent health plan the world has ever known.

POINTS TO REMEMBER

- Throughout the Bible, God offers to all His people of every age the promise of radiant health.

- When the multitudes came to Jesus, He healed them all. He still heals all who come to Him in faith because He is the same yesterday, today, and forever.

- The Bible declares that sickness is part of the curse. Jesus went to the cross to bear all the curse so we wouldn't have to experience any of it.

- We cannot talk sickness and disease and walk in health at the same time. We must break the habit of talking about sickness and declare instead that by Jesus' stripes we are healed.

- God's health plan is a wellness plan. It's designed to keep us healthy all the time.

SCRIPTURE

The LORD will guide you continually, watering your life when you are dry and keeping you healthy, too. You will be like a well-watered garden, like an everflowing spring. (Isaiah 58:11 NLT)

CONFESSION

There is no expiration date on the Bible's healing promises. God wants me well at every age. Sickness is part of the curse, and Christ has redeemed me from that curse. Therefore I refuse to receive sickness in any form. I declare instead that I am healed by the stripes of Jesus from the top of my head to the soles of my feet. I align myself with the will of God and declare I will live in divine health all the way through my golden years.

CHAPTER 10

The Live-Long Lifestyle of Faith

You can't break the laws of nature and expect to live a long life. You can't jump off a thirty-story building instead of taking the elevator and expect God to somehow prolong your days. Driving to work on the wrong side of the freeway will wreck your hopes for longevity in a very literal way. No matter how much God loves you, no matter how He desires to bless and extend your life, He won't suspend the laws of nature so you can behave anyway you like.

That's a no-brainer, right? Everyone knows it.

What everyone does not know, however, is this: you can't break spiritual laws and expect to live a long life either. You can't live in unbelief, spout negative words, and fail to walk in love without decreasing both the quality and the quantity of your years on earth. Even though you're a born-again child of God and He loves you with an everlasting love, He normally won't go around suspending spiritual laws for you. So if you want to live to a ripe old age, you must learn to cooperate with the law of faith.

That law is the primary operating principle of the spirit realm. It is the supernatural system by which we, as God's people, are divinely designed to live. The Bible says it again and again: "The just shall live by faith" (Habakkuk 2:4; Romans 1:17; Galatians 3:11; Hebrews 10:38).

Living by faith means more than agreeing to a certain set of doctrines. It involves more than being religious and going to church every Sunday. Living by faith means believing God's Word and acting (not just on Sundays but every day) as though it is true.

Hebrews 11:1 explains why it's so vital for us to do that. It's because "faith is the substance of things hoped for, the evidence of things not seen." Faith is what makes God's Word a tangible reality in our lives. It's the supernatural force that turns God's intangible promises into things we can feel and see (and wear and drive and live in). Faith transfers the blessings of God from the spiritual realm into the natural realm.

Some Christians get nervous when they find out they're supposed to live by faith. They think faith is complicated and difficult. But it isn't. Faith is simple. It's just trusting God to do for us exactly what He said He would do in the Bible.

Through the years, some have made fun of Ken and me for our emphasis on faith. They've called us "faith preachers," as if that is some kind of insult. As far as I'm concerned, however, it's a compliment. I'm glad we're faith preachers. I think that's better than being unbelief preachers, especially when you remember that "without faith it is impossible to please him: for he that cometh to God must believe that he is, and that he is a rewarder of them that diligently seek him" (Hebrews 11:6).

To God, faith is a very big deal, and here's why: He wants to bless us, and we can't receive those blessings without it!

Faith is God's divine delivery system. Just as the natural law of gravity ensures that what goes up must come down, the spiritual law of faith ensures that we receive what we believe. If we believe that by His stripes we were healed, disease is banished from our bodies and we enjoy divine health. If we believe God meets our needs according to His riches in glory by Christ Jesus, our bills will be paid and our needs will be met. If we believe God will satisfy us with long life and show us His salvation, longevity and deliverance will be ours.

During His ministry on earth, Jesus revealed the connection between faith and receiving again and again.

- He said to the centurion, "Go thy way; and as thou hast believed, so be it done unto thee." (Matthew 8:13)

- He said to the woman with the issue of blood, "Thy faith hath made thee whole." (Matthew 9:22)

- He said to the blind men who asked for their sight, "According to your faith be it unto you." (Matthew 9:29)

- He said to the Gentile woman who sought help for her demon-possessed daughter, "O woman, great is thy faith: be it unto thee even as thou wilt." (Matthew 15:28)

- He told the apostle John to write to the angel of the church in Smyrna, "Be faithful until death, and I will give you the crown of life." (Revelation 2:10 NKJV)

- He said, "If ye have faith, and doubt not, ye shall not only do this which is done to the fig tree, but also if ye shall say unto this mountain, Be thou removed, and be thou cast into the sea; it shall be done. And all things, whatsoever ye shall ask in prayer, believing, ye shall receive." (Matthew 21:21–22)

Lessons from Abraham and Sarah

People who are content to die young and accept whatever circumstances life brings their way don't have to learn much about the faith life. But those who want to live to one hundred and beyond should make a study of it. If we want to stay safe and healthy for that many years, we'll need to release faith for blessing, healing, and protection. If we want to have enough money to go on shopping sprees in our old age and buy presents for our great-great-grandchildren, we'll need faith for prosperity.

That's why I think every prospective centenarian should study the life of Abraham. According to the Scriptures, he is "the father of all them that believe" (Romans 4:11), and he is an inspiring example for us because He stood in faith many years for something that, in the natural scheme of things, seemed absolutely impossible. He believed at one hundred years of age that he and his barren wife, Sarah, were going to have a son. How did Abraham get the faith he needed to believe such a thing? He believed God,

> who quickeneth the dead, and calleth those things which be not as though they were. Who against hope believed in hope, that he might become the father of many nations, according to that which was spoken, So shall thy seed be. And being not weak in faith, he considered not his own body now dead, when he was about an hundred years old, neither yet the deadness of Sarah's womb: He staggered not at the promise of God through unbelief; but was strong in faith, giving glory to God; and being fully persuaded that, what he had promised, he was able also to perform. (ROMANS 4:17–21)

Notice those verses tell us Abraham didn't consider the natural facts that appeared to contradict God's promise. He didn't look at his wrinkled body and think about how old he was. He didn't look at childless Sarah and figure up how many years she'd been barren.

He fixed his mind, instead, on the fact that God had promised him a son. He focused on that promise day after day, month after month, year after year, until it eventually became the biggest thing in his life—bigger than his hundred-year-old body, bigger than Sarah's barren womb, and bigger than any natural circumstance.

In the process, an amazing thing happened. Abraham's body was changed. As he attended to God's Word and kept it in the center of his heart, the Word did just what Proverbs 4:22 says it will do. It brought fresh life and health to his flesh. It reversed Abraham's biological clock and turned him into a father at an age when father-ing would normally not have been an option.

It took a little longer for Sarah to get with the program. She ini-tially laughed when she heard God say she would have a baby. But somewhere along the line, the seed of God's Word took root in her and faith sprang up. Hebrews 11:11 says: "Because of faith also Sarah herself received physical power to conceive a child, even when she was long past the age for it, because she considered [God] Who had given her the promise to be reliable and trustworthy and true to His word" (AMP).

Sarah's experience should be an encouragement to all of us who struggle at times to believe God's promises. She proved it's possible to move from unbelief to faith by considering God and His Word to be reliable and trustworthy. She showed us that God's Word is a sure cure for doubt.

Here's something else we can learn from Sarah: before the Word can become a reality in our lives, we must hear and believe it for our-selves. That's what Sarah did. Even though Abraham had a promise from God, she didn't just rely on what Abraham said. She received God's Word herself. She considered God to be faithful "Who had given her the promise"!

If we want to be like Sarah, we must do the same thing. We can't stand in faith on someone else's revelation. We must take the time to go to the Scriptures for ourselves and see what God has promised us. We can't believe for healing or long life or prosperity just because our pastor or a television preacher told us we could. That doesn't work.

Think about it this way and you'll see why. Imagine I promised a friend of yours that I'd pay his rent next month. Your friend might call you with great excitement and tell you that he believes I will send him the money. He might be jumping for joy and confess his faith, saying, "I believe Gloria is paying my rent! I believe it and I receive it!"

Well, I'd like Gloria to pay my rent, too, you might think. *So I'm going to make the same confession.* Your confession, however, wouldn't be based on faith, because I didn't promise to pay your rent. You have no grounds to assume that I will do something I didn't promise *you* I'd do.

The same is true with God. You can't believe Him for something if you're not sure He promised to do it for you. To have full faith in His promises, you must go to His Word and receive them for yourself. You must see with your own eyes what He has said to *you*. You must hear, with the ears of your own heart, the voice of the Holy Spirit speaking to you through the words of the Bible, saying, "Thus saith the Lord...to *you*!"

Once you've received God's Word directly from the Bible, you can grow in faith, just as Abraham did. You can stop considering the contrary circumstances around you. You can stop pondering the doctor's bad report, the news articles that say you have to become feeble as you age, or the stories your relatives tell you about the diseases that run in your family. You can consider instead what God has said to you. You can keep your eyes on His Word until you are fully persuaded that what He has promised, He is able to perform!

Say What?

Once you begin to do that, you'll be ready to take the next step Abraham took. You'll be ready to put your faith to work by calling things that be not as though they were.

"But Gloria, that faith confession stuff is strange! Why do I have to do it? Why can't I just believe God in silence?"

Because faith doesn't go to work until it is spoken. It doesn't move from our hearts into our circumstances until it is released through the words of our mouths. Faith is activated when we say what God says about us and our situations. It goes into operation when we speak.

That ought to be good news to us! After all, most of us are very good at talking. We do it a lot because we are designed by God to speak what is in our hearts. We're like those windup dolls that repeat the recording inside them. We open our mouths and out comes whatever we've programmed ourselves with. If we've programmed ourselves with negative junk, we will blab that junk to anyone who will listen. (Junk in...junk out—it's a spiritual law.) If we've programmed ourselves with the Word of God, we'll speak the Word. But one way or another, we're speaking something all the time!

God teaches us to turn our words to our advantage. He intends for us to do what Abraham did and fill our mouths, not with natural reports about our negative circumstances, but with the positive report of the Lord. Every day, many times a day, Abraham called himself "the father of many nations." That's what *Abraham* (which is the name God gave him) means (Genesis 17:5). Every time he said, "My name is Abraham," he spoke his future.

Since he and Sarah had been childless for almost a century, some of Abraham's friends and relatives probably chuckled behind his back about his positive confessions. They probably looked at one another and rolled their eyes when he said, "From now on, I'm not Abram anymore. I am the father of many nations. I am Abraham!"

Right. Whatever, they must have thought.

But praise God, Abraham didn't care about what other people thought. He didn't let his unbelieving relatives and friends rob him of the promise of God. He was determined to have descendants as plentiful as the sands of the sea and stars in the sky (Genesis 22:17). So, he put God's Word in his mouth and said it...and said it...and said it. He called himself what God called him. And because he did, eventually Isaac was born.

If we want to see God's promises born in our lives, we must do the same thing. We call ourselves healed—even when we still look and feel sick. We call ourselves strong—even when, in the natural, we seem weak. We call our youth renewed—even when we see evidence to the contrary. No matter how bad our natural circumstances may seem to be, we must train our mouths to say not what we have, but what we desire to have in our lives.

When we do that, we're acting the way God acts. We are made in His image. We are operating, not according to human wisdom, but according to the wisdom He used to create the earth. We're doing the same thing He did in Genesis 1.

When you read the account of Creation, you'll see that in the beginning, when the earth was without form and void, and darkness was on the face of the deep, God didn't say a word about that dingy, formless mess. He didn't gather all the angels and say, "Look how dark it is! Have you seen how dark the earth is right now?"

No, He called things that were not as though they were. He said, "Let there be light!" Or, as the original Hebrew text reads, "Light be!"[1] And light was.

That's always the way God releases His creative power. He changes things and brings them into line with His will by speaking His Word to them. He calls things not what they are, but what He wants them to be.

"But He can do that," you might say. "He's God!"

Certainly He is…and we're made in His image. We're commanded to "be imitators of God [copy Him and follow His example], as well-beloved children [imitate their father]" (Ephesians 5:1 AMP).

Jesus taught that the words of faith we speak will determine what happens in our lives. He told us, in essence: *If you're not satisfied with what you have, change what you say.*

Because God designed us to live by the power of our words, whether we realize it or not, our words are always working—either for us or against us. What we have in our lives now is a product of what we said in years past. What we are saying today will determine our future. That means if we want to enjoy Bible longevity, we must get our words in line now. We must fill our mouths with confessions of faith that will lengthen and strengthen our lives in the years to come.

We must also rid ourselves of words that will cut our lives short. We must make sure we don't make the mistake one young man made some years ago. I heard his story from a well-known minister who was called to his bedside in the hospital after he had been diagnosed with an inoperable brain tumor. When the minister arrived, the young man was slipping into a coma and doctors didn't give any hope for his recovery.

The minister had seen many people divinely healed and he had a special anointing to pray for this kind of situation, so he was puzzled when the man's condition was not changed by his prayers. *Somehow the door has been shut on me in the spirit and I can't help him*, he thought.

When he talked with the man's relatives, he found out the reason his prayers didn't prevail. They told him that ever since the man was a young boy, he'd said, "I'll never live to see forty years old." By making that confession throughout his life, he had shortened his future with his own words. As a result, when the time of crisis came, not even an anointed minister of God could help him.

Without even realizing it, that man activated, in a negative way, the principle Jesus taught. He spoke words over his life, believed they would come to pass, and sure enough, they did. He died before his fortieth birthday.

Make a Permanent Vocabulary Change

The devil understands far better than most Christians that our words either open the door to him or close the door to him. So he puts tremendous pressure on us to abandon our confession of faith and speak negative, unbelieving words instead. We have all felt—and yielded to—that pressure at times. Despite our intentions to maintain our confession of faith about a situation, we've found ourselves telling every neighbor, relative, or friend our sad story.

Sometimes we want sympathy. Sometimes the devil is pushing us to use our words not only to perpetuate our own trouble, but to lay our burden on others, so it can weigh them down, too. That's the way the devil works. He goads us into spreading his depressing news through our words in order to get control.

It seems our natural tendency is to report the negative things we experience rather than declare the report of the Lord. Especially when it comes to aging, we must beware of such inclinations. If we want to live long and finish strong, we can't afford to sit around with our friends and talk about "our" arthritis, or "our" high blood pressure, or "our" forgetfulness. We can't participate when people get together and talk about the negative aspects of aging. If we preach to others and listen to them preach to us the bad news about age-related infirmities, we'll end up experiencing those infirmities. That's a spiritual law. There's no way around it. We can have what we say.

It's impossible to confess that old age is robbing us of our vitality and have our youth renewed like the eagle's at the same time. It just can't be done! So if we want to end up like Moses, full of health, life, and purpose at 120, we must cultivate the habit of calling ourselves what God calls us. We must say things like, "I am fruitful in my old age. I am full of divine strength and life. My body is healed. My mind is sharp. I'm a living memorial to the goodness of God!"

When you first start speaking words like that about yourself, it may seem strange. Other people may think you are peculiar. Your positive confessions may sound far out, even to many of your Christian friends. They may have been taught that everything is up to God and He does whatever He wants in our lives. Perhaps they've been taught that if He wants us to be healthy and live long, then we will. Or if He wants us to be sick and die young, then we will. They may believe we don't have anything to do with it, that we're just helpless victims.

I don't blame people for such unscriptural thinking because most of them learned it in church. They were brainwashed by religious tradition to believe that we just leave everything up to God and receive whatever happens as His will. But, as we've seen, that's not what the Bible teaches. It tells us that if we want God's will in our lives, we must cooperate with Him.

One of my favorite ministers likes to say it this way: "We can't leave up to God what God has left up to us!" And according to Jesus, God has left it up to us to release our faith with our words. He has given us the responsibility of bringing His promises to pass in our lives by believing His Word in our hearts and speaking it with our mouths.

Because they're uncomfortable with the idea of calling things into being by faith, some people prefer just to pray about them. Praying is good. It's important. But Jesus didn't tell us just to pray about the mountains in our lives. He told us to speak to them. He told us to move them with words of faith. That's where most Christians miss it. If arthritis attacks their bodies, all they do is talk to God about it. "Lord, please heal me of this arthritis," they say. Prayers like that are good as long as we add faith to them and believe we receive healing when we pray. But once we've done that, we should take the next step. We should exercise our faith in God's healing Word by saying, "Arthritis, I rebuke you in Jesus' name. You get off my body. Pain, you leave me. I give you no place in me. Body, I call you healed, strong, and pain-free. You are healed by the stripes of Jesus."

"But I tried saying those things and it didn't work," you might say. "I did it for a whole week, and I felt as old and sickly at the end of the week as I did at the beginning."

That's because it's not just what you say for a little while that comes to pass. It's what you say on a consistent basis. As the Lord told me so many years ago, "In consistency lies the power!" What you say continually is what you are having in your life. Do you speak one way when you're in prayer or in church and another way when you're with your friends? Do you declare you are strong and youthful when you are reading your Bible, then confess to your friends that you're going downhill? If you do, you won't see supernatural progress because your negative words will cancel out your positive words. You'll end up spinning your wheels, getting nowhere fast.

To see results, you must make a permanent vocabulary change. You must determine that from now on, you will speak words that work *for* you instead of against you. That's what Ken and I did back in 1967 when we first learned about the spiritual power of words. We decided to start living by what Jesus says in Mark 11:22–24. We dared to believe and act on His Word that *whosoever* (we figured we qualified!) will speak words of faith can have what he says.

We didn't do it because we were highly spiritual. We did it because we needed a lot of things back then and had no other way to get them. Our greatest problem at that time was financial. Since Jesus said we could have "whatever" we said, we decided to start saying things like, "God meets our needs according to His riches in glory by Christ Jesus. We don't lack any good thing." We also had a lot of debt, so we spoke to it and called that debt "paid."

When we started speaking words of faith over our finances, we were in a desperate situation. As I mentioned earlier, we were not only in debt, we were broke. We had children to support, and Ken was a thirty-year-old freshman at Oral Roberts University, working part-time for about a hundred dollars a month. (We had so little money one year, we ate canned Chinese food for Christmas dinner!)

When you're that broke, you tend to talk broke. When you can't pay your bills and they are piling up in front of you, you tend to think about them all the time. So, until I learned about Mark 11:22–24, that's what I always did. When we fell behind on the payments for our washer and dryer and the finance company threatened to take them away from us, I thought about it nonstop. I had children's clothes to wash! I needed those machines!

Every time we said something negative, our condition of financial lack would become more entrenched in our minds. Our faith in our poverty would grow because poverty was what we were saying. But when we got hold of the revelation that we could change the situation by changing our words, Ken and I determined to get a grip on what we believe in our hearts and say with our mouths.

I found that was not an easy task! I'd spent years saying whatever came into my mind. Like everyone else, when I got mad or sad or fear tried to grip me, I'd open my mouth and let the negative confessions fly. I'd spent my whole life practicing talking my problems. Developing the habit of speaking the end result that I wanted rather than complaining about the woes of our current predicament was a real challenge.

I was desperate, and Ken was, too. So we began to change our words. We resisted the urge to talk about the trouble we were facing. We spoke God's promises instead, day after day—with consistency.

We weren't perfect at it. We still aren't. We miss it sometimes. But the more we practiced and the more we fed on God's Word, the more we developed in it. Within eleven months, all of the debt was gone, and we were beginning to prosper!

We've been prospering and speaking words of faith ever since. For more than forty-two years now, in crisis after crisis, we've found that when the Word is in our hearts and we say it with our mouths, that Word comes to pass in our lives.

Get into the Overflow

Maybe you've tried to change your vocabulary and bring it in line with the promises of God. Maybe you've attempted to speak words of faith on a consistent basis, but the minute you relax, negative confessions pop out of your mouth. If so, don't despair. You can solve the problem. Here's how you put the Word in your heart in greater abundance.

Get your Bible and underline all the Scriptures about longevity, health, and money (or whatever else you're believing for). Take time every day, maybe even several times a day, to read those Scriptures out loud to yourself. Write them on note cards and carry them with you so you can look at them and think about them on and off throughout the day. Read good books about the subject that are packed with the Word of God. Find teaching and preaching CDs that inspire your faith. Listen to them while you're driving to work or download them onto your MP3 player so you can hear them while you're doing housework or working out at the gym. Go to a faith-teaching church every week. Go to believers' conventions.

In other words, stuff yourself with God's Word! Get as much of it into your heart as you can. You'll be amazed at what will happen when you do. You'll get so full that when the devil puts the squeeze on you, the only thing he'll be able to get out of you is the Word. You won't have to struggle to hold back negative confessions anymore. You'll find yourself declaring the Word of God before you even have a chance to think about it.

How can I be so sure? Because Jesus said,

⚹ A good man out of the good treasure of the heart bringeth forth good things: and an evil man out of the evil treasure bringeth forth evil things. . . . *For out of the abundance of the heart the mouth speaketh.* (Matthew 12:35, 34, italics added)

⚹ The mouth speaks out of that which fills the heart. (12:34 NASB)

⚹ Whatever is in your heart determines what you say. (12:34 NLT)

⚹ A man's heart determines his speech. (12:34 TLB)

⚹ Out of the overflow of the heart the mouth speaks. (12:34 NIV)

If you're not full of God's Word, you might be able to confess it for a while, but you won't be able to keep it up. If you'll feast on the Word enough, however, you'll not only get so saturated with it, you'll start to overflow. That's when life really gets exciting. That's when your words of faith take on real power—when they are overflowing from a heart full of God's Word!

Once you get in the overflow, stay there. Maintain it. If you'll do that, the devil will find it impossible to put negative words in your mouth. I received revelation on that many years ago when Ken and I were ministering in Manila, Philippines. I was in our hotel room preparing for a meeting and I looked out the window of my hotel room and saw a fountain gushing with water. As I watched it, I realized it would be impossible to put any trash in the mouth of that fountain. The force of water flowing out would push it away in an instant.

"That's the way it is when you live in the overflow of My Spirit and My Word," the Lord told me. "No matter how hard he tries, the devil can't get any of his trash in you."

I wish it were as easy for us to overflow with the Word as it is to turn on a water fountain. But it's not. That kind of overflow doesn't come in a day. It takes time. So be patient with yourself. When you get under pressure and speak words of unbelief, don't give up. Just repent and get right back on your faith. Overturn your negative confession and replace it with a confession of the Word. Remember this: every test is an open-book test. What an advantage. You can do this!

Say,

> Lord, forgive me for agreeing with the devil for a moment instead of agreeing with Your Word. Forgive me for speaking faithless words. I repent of those words now and break their power over my life. I command them to fall to the ground and I say they will not affect me. I declare that Your Word, Lord, is what will come to pass in my life. I declare that I am healed. I am whole. I am victorious. I am strong in every area of life. I am prosperous I am more than a conqueror in Christ Jesus!

Then get right back with the program. Get busy breaking the habit of speaking words of unbelief, and get into the overflow. Become a fanatic about it. That's what Ken and I did. Sure, some people made fun of us for it. They thought we were silly for being such sticklers about confessing the Word. They accused us of being extremists, and we are guilty as charged. We are extreme when it comes to God's Word. And as a result, we are extremely healed, extremely prosperous, and extremely blessed in every way.

That's why I'm more of a fanatic about the Word of God today than I ever was. It's also why I plan on being an even bigger fanatic about it tomorrow. I don't intend to slow down on my faith walk as I get older; I intend to speed up and enjoy the increase!

Pick Up Your Pace with Praise

If you feel as I do and you're eager to accelerate the development of your faith, there's one more tip you can take from Abraham. Instead of staggering toward the manifestation of God's promises in your life, you can pick up your pace by doing what he did: "He grew strong and was empowered by faith as he gave praise and glory to God" (Romans 4:20 AMP).

There is something powerful about praising God and thanking Him for fulfilling His promises in your life, even when you are still waiting to see them come to pass. It puts a turbocharger on your faith. It pushes you forward more quickly into the place where, like Abraham, you are fully persuaded that what God has promised He is able also to perform.

Praising the Lord is good for you! It stirs up your joy (and as we've already seen, the joy of the Lord is your strength). It puts the devil on the run. It puts your faith into action. No wonder the Bible says:

> Praise ye the LORD. Praise, O ye servants of the LORD, praise the name of the LORD. Blessed be the name of the LORD from this time forth and for evermore. From the rising of the sun unto the going down of the same the LORD's name is to be praised. The LORD is high above all nations, and his glory above the heavens. Who is like unto the LORD our God, who dwelleth on high, who humbleth himself to behold the things that are in heaven, and in the earth! He raiseth up the poor out of the dust, and lifteth the needy out of the dunghill; that he may set him with princes, even with the princes of his people. He maketh the barren woman to keep house, and to be a joyful mother of children. Praise ye the LORD. (PSALM 113)

According to those verses, it's impossible to praise the Lord too much. We could praise Him all day long, from sunrise to sunset forever, and we wouldn't be finished.

Some believers make the mistake of waiting until they feel like praising God to get started. *When things start looking up in my life*, they think, *I'll give God the glory for it*. But Abraham didn't do that. He praised God before his circumstances changed. He gave God glory when he and Sarah were still as barren as they'd ever been. He worshiped and thanked God in faith. As he did, his faith was empowered to such a degree that nothing the devil did could make him stagger at God's promise.

If we'll follow his example, we'll have the same experience. The longer we stand in faith, the stronger our faith will become. That's important because God's promises don't usually come to pass the first instant we believe them. More often than not, we must wait for a while to see them fulfilled. That's why Hebrews 6:12 says it's through "faith and patience" that we "inherit the promises."

So, if you don't see an instant change in your circumstances, just keep praising God. Don't worry about how long it will take for things to turn around. Chances are, you spent years getting yourself in the negative situation you're in right now. If it's not fixed before sunset, don't sweat it. Just stick with your confession of faith, and remember, you have the assurance of God's Word that if you turn your mouth around, your situation will eventually turn around. If you keep sowing the Word into your heart and life (and don't give up), you will reap in due season if you "faint not" (Galatians 6:9). Don't give up! Stay with it. Be strong to believe God while His Word does its work.

Ken and I have done a lot of waiting in faith over the years. Even though we saw our indebtedness disappear in just eleven months, we've waited in faith much longer for other things. Some of those things took years to manifest. We believed God for the ministry airplane we have now, for example—for years. Think of it! We confessed that *Citation X* was ours for a whole decade! God gave us other airplanes while we were waiting for it, so we had transportation. He took care of us. But it took endurance and patience for the *Citation X* to come into our possession. Was it worth it? Absolutely!

Ken and I have learned in our years of walking by faith that patience pays great dividends. Take our word and God's Word on it and don't quit. No matter what comes against you, no matter what the devil and other people might say to discourage you, no matter how many days, weeks, months, or years go by, keep standing and believing God. Don't let go of His promise. Let faith and patience have their full work, and you'll end up seeing that promise fulfilled because God never fails to keep His Word.

"But Gloria, I know somebody who stood in faith and they didn't receive!" you might say.

No, you don't. If you ever see a situation where it looks as if God failed to keep His Word, you can be sure there's something you don't know about that situation. As I heard one minister say, "Never put the righteousness of God up against anybody." People can fail. God never will. So don't ever doubt Him. Don't ever let someone else's experience rob you of your confidence in His Word. Keep your heart and your mouth filled with faith.

If you do that, you'll not only enjoy the benefits of it years down the road by living longer and finishing stronger; you'll experience the instant blessing of being more joyful and full of peace on the inside. Your life will be different right away. Keep the switch of faith turned on, and you will see the manifestation of God's power in your circumstances.

Even if it takes awhile for some of the things you're believing for to come to pass, what does it matter? You're going to spend that time doing something anyway. Think where you'd be if you had spent them in unbelief. You would have bigger troubles and more problems.

If you'll stick with the Word, however, you'll continually improve. You'll just keep being more...and more...and more blessed. So why not choose the path of faith? Spend the rest of your life feeding on God's Word, believing what it says, all the while increasing your capacity for faith. Instead of throwing years away just watching television and wallowing in unbelief, why not invest in your future by spending time reading and meditating on the Scriptures and speaking things that be not as though they were?

I can assure you, if you'll do that, you'll never be sorry. No matter how long it takes to see the changes you're believing for, you'll never regret spending that time cultivating your faith. So go for the overflow! You'll be forever glad you did.

POINTS TO REMEMBER

❧ To live to a ripe old age, you must learn to live by faith—that means believing God's Word and acting (not just on Sundays but every day) as though it is true.

❧ Faith is God's divine delivery system. Just as the natural law of gravity ensures that what goes up must come down, the law of faith ensures that we receive what we believe.

❧ To grow in faith as Abraham did, we must stop considering the contrary circumstances and keep our eyes on God's Word until we are fully persuaded that what He has promised, He is able to perform.

❧ We must train our mouths to say not what we have, but what we desire to have in our lives. We must speak words that work *for* us instead of against us.

❧ Praising God puts a turbocharger on our faith. We can accelerate the manifestation of God's promises in our lives with praise.

SCRIPTURE

Having been justified by faith, we have peace with God through our Lord Jesus Christ, through whom also we have access by faith into this grace in which we stand, and rejoice in hope of the glory of God. (Romans 5:1–2 NKJV)

CONFESSION

I am a person of faith. I believe God's Word and do not doubt. I keep the Word in my heart in abundance and say continually what the Bible says about me. I am full of divine strength and life. My body is healthy. My mind is sharp. I am fruitful at every age. I am a living memorial to the goodness of God!

A Divine Departure

She came forward to give her testimony after a Healing School I taught in the Ukraine. Surrounded by others eager to tell how the Lord had healed them during the service, she was the picture of a Ukrainian grandmother. Her hair tied up in a scarf and a full peasant skirt gathered around her waist, she was a real babushka (or, in Ukrainian, *babulia*)!

Earlier that morning, she had lined up outside the building with a crowd so eager to hear the Word that they broke the glass door panes in their rush to get inside. Like so many of those who streamed in around her, she came expecting to receive from God. She also came hobbling in on legs afflicted with some kind of infirmity.

I don't remember the exact cause of her affliction. But I do remember it was her birthday.

Have you ever wondered what kind of birthday present Jesus would give an elderly grandmother? Some people might think He would give her grace to bear the ailments of old age. They might assume, since her hair was silver-white and her skin weathered, that He would comfort her with the knowledge that her race on earth was almost run and give her the courage to limp across the finish line on feeble legs.

But that's not the kind of birthday present this grandmother was expecting. She, and the bevy of other Ukrainian grandmothers who had trooped with her to the front of the meeting hall, all flush-faced and chattering with excitement, expected much more from Jesus than that. They'd heard the Word of God offered them healing, and it didn't occur to them there might be an age limit on that offer. So they reached out by faith and received the gift Jesus bought and paid for them to have.

Every one of those grandmothers was memorable. When our interpreter, Konstantin, tried to cut their lengthy testimonies short by pulling the microphone away, some of them almost wrestled him over it. They wanted to tell their whole stories! The most unforgettable of all, however, was the lady who had come with the leg problems. Instead of contending with Konstantin for more microphone time, she finished off her testimony with a demonstration of what God had done for her.

She lifted her skirt a few inches above her ankles like a debutante attending a ball. With her eyes sparkling and her face crinkled into one great smile, she danced all the way across the front of the auditorium...and back.

In that moment, she became a living illustration of what God wants for all of His people. He wants us to be living memorials of His goodness throughout our lives. He wants us to finish our course with joy and strength and health. He wants us to dance our way to glory.

It's sad to say, but most believers today can hardly imagine such a thing. They've let the world and the devil so influence their way of thinking, they assume Christians must slip into physical decline during the final years, months, and moments of their lives, just as non-Christians do. They suppose that in order to die, they must let the devil evict them from their bodies by illness or accident.

One dear woman was so certain of it she became alarmed when she heard Ken and me preach about how to receive divine healing by faith. She even wrote us a letter asking us how, if she kept believing

God for healing, she would ever manage to die. Ken and I couldn't help but chuckle over her question. We'd never before encountered someone actually concerned about being unable to die!

I must admit, however, she did raise an interesting point. God has promised health and healing to us all regardless of age, so how does He plan for us to make our departure? What does the Bible say about how we, as born-again believers, should make our final exit from the earth?

Go in Victory

First and foremost, the Scriptures make it clear that the death of the righteous is one of victory and triumph. They confirm again and again that for the believer, it is not a painful end, but a glorious promotion. As we've already seen, even the Old Testament provides us with thrilling examples of saints whose earthly departures make us want to shout, "O death, where is thy sting? O grave, where is thy victory?" (1 Corinthians 15:55). We see:

- Abraham, who fathered babies in his old age (talk about dancing your way to glory!), whose "spirit was released" at 175 years old, so that he "died at a good (ample, full) old age, an old man, satisfied and satiated, and was gathered to his people." (Genesis 25:8 AMP)

- Isaac, whose "spirit departed" at 180 years of age; "he died and was gathered to his people, being an old man, satisfied and satiated with days." (Genesis 35:29 AMP)

- Jacob, who decided at 147 years old that it was time to die, so he called all his sons together, had a little family reunion, and prophesied over everyone, then "gathered up his feet into the bed, and yielded up the ghost, and was gathered unto his people." (Genesis 49:33)

✄ Moses, who at 120 years old was "gathered to [his] people" on the
mountaintop, bright-eyed and full of strength, his body buried by
God Himself. (Deuteronomy 32:48–50; 34:4 –7 AMP)

Notice the Bible doesn't mention anything about those men
being killed by disease. Nor does it say they had accidents that drove
the life from their bodies. It says they released their spirits and were
gathered to their people.

I love how they departed this earth, because they showed us how
to leave—not by demonic eviction, but in divine style! They finished
out their lives, decided they were satisfied, and shrugged off their
physical bodies the way you'd throw off an old coat. They said, "Hey,
I'm out of here!" and swooshed off to join their God-fearing kinfolk
who'd gone on before them.

"But they were the patriarchs!" somebody might say.

That's right. They were Old Covenant saints. They didn't have
the Holy Spirit living inside them as we do in the New Covenant,
yet they were able to believe God for a full life. They stuck around
until they were satisfied, and when they sensed the season had come
for them to depart, they left this earth in peace and victory. Surely,
we, as New Testament believers who have the fullness of redemption
and the power of the indwelling Holy Spirit, should be able to do as
well as they did!

Actually, we ought to do even better. After all, we're living in the
days they were looking forward to. We're living in the time when
Jesus has triumphed over the power of death and over all the power
of the devil and taken from him the keys of death and hell (Revelation 1:18).

Because of what Jesus did on the cross and through His resurrection, death no longer has the power to dominate God's people.
The devil has no authority to harm us in any way. Jesus stripped him
of that power. We have the blood-bought right to stay on earth in
strength, health, and safety until we've lived out our full lives and
God lets us know we're ready to go to heaven.

Until that time comes, we should treat death like a foe to be put under our feet. We should see it the way Jesus sees it: as the last "enemy that shall be destroyed" (1 Corinthians 15:26). We should stand our ground and let the devil know he has no right to force death upon us because, according to the Bible:

- Our Lord and Savior, Jesus Christ, "hath abolished death, and hath brought life and immortality to light through the gospel." (2 Timothy 1:10)

- He went to the cross so that "through death he might destroy him that had the power of death, that is, the devil; and deliver them who through fear of death were all their lifetime subject to bondage." (Hebrews 2:14–15)

- Therefore, "death hath no dominion over him" (Romans 6:9) and because we're in Him, it has no dominion over us either!

When the devil tries to push us out of here before we have finished our race, we must remember those truths. When, in our golden years, we find ourselves battling some kind of physical or circumstantial challenge and Satan pressures us to abandon the fight of faith and surrender to premature death, we must rebuke him and say, "Get out of here, devil. I'm not leaving this planet one day early. I'm staying here and serving the Lord until I'm satisfied and satiated, and the season comes for me to go home. And when I go, I'll go in victory, in health, and in strength. I won't die from disease or discouragement. I'll die by divine departure! I will go on and up with God!"

That's what the apostle Paul did. When he was in prison and the devil tried to kill him, instead of giving in to death, he decided to stay alive. He made up his mind to stay on earth until he finished what God called him to do. Because of the hardships and dangers he was facing, it wasn't an easy choice for Paul to make. "I'm torn between two desires," he wrote in his letter to the Philippians. "Sometimes I want to live, and sometimes I long to go and be with Christ. That would be far better for me, but it is better for you that I live. I am convinced of this, so I will continue with you so that you will grow and experience the joy of your faith" (Philippians 1:23–25 NLT).

If anyone ever had good reason to let the devil talk him into getting weary of life and quitting early, it was the apostle Paul. As we have seen, he endured beatings, stonings, shipwrecks, and continual persecution in his ministry. Who could have blamed him if he'd decided to call it quits?

But thank God, he didn't. He stayed on earth until he completed the assignment Jesus had given him. He lived until he knew the season for his departure had arrived. He set a good example by showing us how to rejoice in difficult circumstances, get through them in victory by the power of God, and keep pressing to fulfill God's will.

In his determination to do everything God wanted him to do before he left, Paul not only completed his own course, he wrote words that have inspired Christians for centuries to complete theirs as well. He challenged us to say, as he did:

> I follow after . . . that I may apprehend that for which also I am apprehended of Christ Jesus. Brethren, I count not myself to have apprehended: but this one thing I do, forgetting those things which are behind, and reaching forth unto those things which are before, I press toward the mark for the prize of the high calling of God in Christ Jesus. (PHILIPPIANS 3:12–14)

What an immeasurable blessing Paul's life and writings have been to believers over the centuries! What benefits the church has reaped from his ministry—all because, instead of giving up and dying too early, he kept living for Jesus through the hard times, resisting discouragement and death at every turn, until he could say:

> I am now ready to be offered, and the time of my departure is at hand. I have fought a good fight, I have finished my course, I have kept the faith: henceforth there is laid up for me a crown of righteousness,

which the Lord, the righteous judge, shall give me at that day:
and not to me only, but unto all them also that love his appearing.
(2 TIMOTHY 4:6–8)

The apostle Peter left us a wonderful example to follow as well. Attending to the work of the ministry into his old age, he, too, anticipated the season of his earthly departure. When he wrote to the believers under his care to give them some final instructions, he said:

Brethren, give diligence to make your calling and election sure: for
if ye do these things, ye shall never fall: for so an entrance shall be
ministered unto you abundantly into the everlasting kingdom of our
Lord and Saviour Jesus Christ. Wherefore I will not be negligent to
put you always in remembrance of these things, though ye know them,
and be established in the present truth. Yea, I think it meet, as long as
I am in this tabernacle, to stir you up by putting you in remembrance;
knowing that shortly I must put off this my tabernacle, even as our
Lord Jesus Christ hath shown me. Moreover I will endeavour that
ye may be able after my decease to have these things always in
remembrance. (2 PETER 1:10–15)

Like the patriarchs who lived thousands of years before them, Peter and Paul knew when their missions on earth had been accomplished. They sensed when it was time to go, and when that time came, they took off in victory! Although history records they both died as martyrs for the sake of the gospel, the Bible affirms they departed when they were ready. It can be said of them, as it was of Jesus: no one took their lives from them. They willingly laid them down.

Most of us won't be called on to die for preaching the gospel, but we can still follow their example. We can stay on earth until we've completed our divine assignments and God is ready for us to go home to heaven. We can refuse to allow death to overtake us by surprise. We can, by faith, live long and finish strong. We can sense when the season of our departure has come and leave the earth right on time, like a person catching a train. Hallelujah!

Death by Divine Kiss

If you think that's unrealistic, think again. Any number of contemporary Christians have died exactly that way. Remember F. F. Bosworth, minister and author of *Christ the Healer*, mentioned in a previous chapter? He's a great example of a believer who left this earth in true biblical style. At age eighty-one, when he sensed his divine mission was complete and his season of departure had come, he announced he would soon be off to glory and invited the whole family to come home for a final reunion.

According to his son Robert, who recorded the details of his death, F. F. Bosworth wasn't sick at the time. Having lived many years in divine health, he prayed specifically that God would help him glorify Jesus in death as in life by dying without sickness, and his prayer had been answered. So he fully enjoyed his last three weeks on earth, sitting in bed, surrounded by his family, who gathered around to talk, laugh, and sing with him.

In "The Ultimate Triumph" (included as an afterword in later editions of *Christ the Healer*), Robert describes the moment his father left that earthly gathering to join another, more glorious one in heaven: "He looked up and saw the heavenly realm." Robert wrote:

> He saw what was invisible to us. He began to greet people and hug people—he was enraptured. Every once in a while he would break off and look around saying, "Oh, it is so beautiful." He did this for several hours. Finally, with a smile on his face, he put his head back and slept. My wife, Stella, was sitting with him when she suddenly realized that he had stopped breathing. There had been no struggle, no pain, no sound, no death rattle. The psalmist had described it correctly—God had simply removed his breath and he was home![1]

Glory to God! I believe such a divine departure is far from being an unusual homegoing but is God's will for all His people. He wants every one of His beloved saints to leave this earth, not with a whimper of defeat, but with a shout of victory. He wants us, like the patriarchs, to die satisfied and full of years and be gathered in glory to the marvelous family reunion that awaits us in heaven. God never intended for us to leave here like nonbelievers, suffering with sickness and clinging in sorrow to this earthly life. He planned for our final hours and moments on this earth to be crowned with His glory, for as Psalm 116:15 says: "Precious in the sight of the LORD is the death of his saints."

The Hebrew word translated "precious" in that verse refers to an item of great worth or value such as a precious gem. It speaks of something that has splendor, honor, and glory. The word can also refer to something rare or difficult to find. One Hebrew commentary chooses that definition as the most appropriate and explains:

> It is difficult for God to remove a devout man from the world, for his fulfillment of God's precepts and his Torah study, [or His study of the Word] are extremely precious.... God must entice the soul of a righteous man away from his body by showing him the precious spiritual reward which awaits in the afterlife. When God draws a pious soul to Himself in this fashion, it is known as *Death by Divine kiss*.[2]

Death by Divine kiss. That's God's desire for us. Not death by demonic eviction. Not death by cancer or calamity. Not death by sickness and sorrow, but a deliberate departure that takes place when God entices us to leave the earth by giving us glimpses of glory and our heavenly reward.

What a glorious way to go! No wonder the Old Testament prophet Balaam cried out, "Let me die the death of the righteous [those who are upright and in right standing with God], and let my last end be like theirs!" (Numbers 23:10 AMP). No wonder the Bible tells us that, as believers, we don't have anything to fear in death.

Death has no sting for us. It has no victory over us. In fact, if we'll stand in faith on God's Word, death won't even be able to touch our bodies until we've taken off for heaven. When it arrives on the scene, it will find that we're already gone, having left behind us nothing but an empty shell!

"Gloria, are you saying that, as believers, we will never actually experience death?"

Yes, that's exactly what I'm saying because that's what Jesus taught. He said, "Whoever continues to live and believes in (has faith in, cleaves to, and relies on) Me shall never [actually] die at all. Do you believe this?" (John 11:26 AMP).

You see, as born-again children of God, we have already done all the dying we're going to do. We died the moment we were born again. In that instant, our old, sinful selves ceased to exist, and our spirits were re-created and made alive with God's own eternal life—never to die again.

Certainly, should Jesus tarry, these mortal flesh-and-blood bodies, these earth suits we're wearing, will die someday. But since they won't die until we're finished with them and our spirits have been released, we won't experience that death. All we'll experience is a divine departure! We'll just leap from the earthly realm into the realm of heaven. And if we'll make that leap in faith the way God intends us to, it will be the most thrilling, joyous, peaceful adventure of our lives.

I have friends and loved ones who have experienced such a departure. One dear minister we know, for instance, passed from earth to heaven a few years ago in a most inspiring fashion. A great man of faith, he lived until he was satisfied (as he always taught we should do) and stayed active in ministry throughout his life.

Those who were with him the morning he died said he was feeling good that day. He'd been through some physical challenges but had recovered from them. When he came to the breakfast table, he was peaceful and enjoying himself. After he finished his meal, he smiled and, in an instant, he was gone.

A woman who prayed for his ministry for many years told his friends and family at the graveside about a vision God gave her of his arrival in heaven. She said she saw a big crowd gathering by a river, preparing to meet him. (He'd been in ministry for more than sixty years, so there were a lot of people who'd been blessed by him and wanted to be a part of his welcoming committee.) "He's coming! He's coming!" they called out.

Just as he arrived, the group parted and made way for Jesus, who was accompanied by an entourage of the minister's family members. Mother, brothers, sisters—everyone was there. It was just like an earthly family reunion—only better. After greetings and hugs were exchanged all around, Jesus took him by the arm and they began to walk together.

People who don't know the Lord might think such a vision is imaginary. They might argue that heaven is just a fairy tale. But they'd be mistaken.

Heaven is a very real place. Jesus assured us of it. He said, "In my Father's house are many mansions: if it were not so, I would have told you. I go to prepare a place for you. And if I go and prepare a place for you, I will come again, and receive you unto myself; that where I am, there ye may be also" (John 14:2–3).

Going to heaven will be great fun! Our arrival will be a delightful event, and once we get there, we'll have forever to enjoy it. Life in heaven won't be boring either. It will be fabulous. We'll love coming home to our mansions and experiencing all the beautiful things God has for us there.

We'll love having the freedom to zip around without the encumbrances of our mortal bodies. If we want to go somewhere far away in heaven, we can be there in an instant. We won't even have to take any luggage! We'll be clothed in garments of light that won't need to be changed, cleaned, or pressed. They'll just glow and look dazzling all the time.

Some people who've had visions of heaven say it's such a happy, beautiful place that even the flowers sing there. I hear the colors are more beautiful than anything we have on earth. And the believers' meetings there will be, shall we say, out of this world! They'll be full of joy and glory and celebration—and Jesus Himself will be the main speaker.

I don't know about you, but I've been in some great believers' meetings here on earth. I've heard some splendid songs and some stirring messages. But those meetings were just a warm-up for the heavenly meetings to come!

Fighters Live Longer

As great as heaven is, however, you shouldn't plan to go there a moment too soon. You shouldn't fly out of here with your angels until you've lived out a long, strong life and fulfilled your divine purpose on earth. Before you start making your heavenly travel plans, you should make sure the season for your departure has arrived.

How can you do that?

You can start by asking yourself if you're satisfied. As we've already seen, the Bible says of the righteous man, "With long life will I satisfy him, and show him my salvation" (Psalm 91:16). To be fully satisfied means to have the desires of your heart fully gratified and to be made content.

You should also ask the Lord if He is satisfied. After all, we don't live just to please ourselves. We live to please God. We're here to carry out His will. So before we decide to take off for heaven, we should ask, "Lord, are You ready for me to go? Have I done everything You intended for me to do? Have I fulfilled Your plan for my life?"

When you've lived out a full, long life, and you and God are both satisfied, then—and only then—it will be time for you to take off. But even when that time comes, make up your mind you won't go sick. If the devil has put some kind of infirmity on you, get healed first, then head for heaven.

That's what E. W. Kenyon did. A marvelous minister of faith and redemption realities, he set an example for us, not just by how he lived, but also by how he died. E. W. Kenyon's divine departure is especially inspiring because in his latter years he faced some fierce battles with sickness and injury. Unwilling to surrender to the devil at any age, he fought the good fight of faith and won those battles. He served the Lord in the earth until, in his eighties, he decided he'd finished his race and went home to heaven.

Instead of slipping downhill to death in his old age, E. W. Kenyon's last years were among his strongest and healthiest. After winning a victory over infirmity at seventy, he wrote:

> When I awaken in the morning [at the age of 71] I am as fresh as a boy. I haven't an ache or a pain. I awaken at four or five in the morning, ready for a long day of grueling work. And at night I am still fresh.
>
> I have passed the seventieth milestone, and I am as vigorous today as ever in my life.
>
> And I believe you can be as healthy as I am.
>
> I have been given up for dead twice; I have heard the nurse count me out, saying, "He is dying," but I have refused to die, refused to stay sick.
>
> I refused to be sick; I have refused to be laid aside.[3]

You can tell from those words that E. W. Kenyon was a fighter—and fighters live longer! When death comes knocking on their doors prematurely, they answer it with the spirit of faith and put it on the run. They say what the Word of God says:

> ✕ I shall not die, but live, and declare the works of the LORD. (Psalm 118:17)

> ✕ [God] ransoms me from death and surrounds me with love and tender mercies. (Psalm 103:4 NLT)

> ✕ [He has] delivered my life from death, my eyes from tears, and my feet from stumbling and falling. I will walk before the Lord in the land of the living. (Psalm 116:8–9 AMP)

> ✕ The Lord will keep [me] from all evil; He will keep [my] life. The Lord will keep [my] going out and [my] coming in from this time forth and forevermore. (Psalm 121:7–8 AMP)

Make up your mind that you'll be a fighter. Settle it in your heart that you won't leave this earth until you and God are *both* satisfied.

Make a quality decision, right now, that no matter how fierce the devil's opposition may be, you will live out the full number of your days.

Keith Moore, a good friend of ours who pastors a church in Branson, Missouri, tells a story about his father that reveals just how much difference such a decision can make. Some years ago, before Keith started his church, his dad suffered a severe heart attack and began to die. As he slipped toward heaven, he got so close to the other side, he could actually see into the realm of the spirit. But before he stepped out of his body into that realm, he asked a crucial question.

"Lord, it's not time for me to go yet, is it?"

"No," the Lord answered, "it's not."

At that moment, Keith's father decided he wasn't going to yield to death. He began to resist it. He refused to leave the earth before it was time and, as a result, he lived and recovered. A few years later, he stood in Keith's new church, enjoying the beautiful sanctuary and watching the people flood in to worship the Lord. "I'm so glad I didn't miss this," he said.

Of course, Keith's father isn't the only one who's had that experience. There are any number of saints who could testify about how they faced death and refused to give in to it. I heard one well-known Christian gospel singer give just such a testimony not long ago. He told about a time when, as a relatively young man, he faced a medical catastrophe. His aorta burst and by all medical accounts, he should have died instantly. But he didn't.

Somehow he made it to the hospital alive, and his family (all of whom are believers) gathered there to pray. As he began to slip toward death, he felt a great sense of peace. Then he saw two angels and heard a conversation that changed everything.

"Aren't you the one who's supposed to take him?" said one angel.

"I will if he wants to go," the second answered.

When the singer heard those words, he decided he didn't want to go to heaven yet. He decided to stay on earth and finish his course. As a result, he lived eight more years and said, "I'm ready to go!" He lived out the life God planned for him to live. He's probably saying the same thing Keith's father said: "I'm so glad I didn't miss this."

My friend, let's follow these wonderful examples and start developing our faith for Bible longevity. Let's feed on what the Word says about it until no demon in hell can talk us out of it. Let's learn to abide in the secret place of the Most High, filling our lives with the spiritual antioxidants of the fruit of the Spirit and partaking daily of God's tree of life.

Let's live long and finish strong to the glory of God so that, should Jesus tarry, when we're 100...or 115...or 120 years old, we can look around at everything God has done for us and through us, smile real big, and say: "I'm so glad I didn't miss this!"

Points to Remember

- The Bible makes it clear that the death of the righteous is one of victory and triumph. It is not a painful end but a glorious promotion.

- We can live long and strong until we've completed our divine assignment and we sense the season of our departure has come. Then we can leave the earth right on time, like a person catching a train.

- God's desire for us is not death by demonic eviction—by cancer, calamity, sickness, or sorrow—but a deliberate departure that takes place when God entices us to leave the earth by giving us glimpses of glory and our heavenly reward.

- As born-again children of God, we have already done all the dying we're going to do. When we leave this earth, all we'll experience is a divine departure.

- When the time comes to take off, make up your mind that you won't go sick. If the devil has put infirmity on you, get healed first and then head for heaven when you and your Lord Jesus are ready!

SCRIPTURE

Precious (important and no light matter) in the sight of the Lord is the death of His saints (His loving ones). (Psalm 116:15 AMP)

Precious in the sight of the LORD is the death of his saints. (Psalm 116:15)

Precious in the sight of Hashem is the death of His devout ones. (Psalm 116:15)[4]

Abraham gave up the ghost, and died in a good old age, an old man, and full of years; and was gathered to his people. (Genesis 25:8)

CONFESSION

I will not leave this planet one day early! I will stay here and serve the Lord until I've finished all that God has called me to do. I will live until I'm fully satisfied and I sense the season has come for me to go home to heaven. When I go, I'll go in victory, in health, and in strength. I won't die from disease or discouragement. My body will die by divine departure. I will receive my glorious promotion and go on and up with God!

Afterword

Long Life, Strong Life: Otis "Dad" Clark Has Weathered a Century of Storms

When Kenneth Copeland acknowledged 105-year-old Otis Clark, who was seated on the front row during a morning session of the 2008 Southwest Believers' Convention in Fort Worth, Texas, those sitting close enough to get a good look at the man stared in surprise.

"Did Brother Copeland say 105?" someone whispered. "Surely not! There's no way that man is 105 years old!"

The astonishment was understandable.

Photo credit: Michael Augustat.

With his radiant smile, broad shoulders, and upright posture resembling that of a man two-thirds his age, Otis "Dad" Clark defies every stereotype attached to aging. He is a centenarian who has not only survived, but thrived—a living testimony to the truth of Psalm 92:13–14: "Those who are planted in the house of the LORD shall flourish in the courts of our God. They shall still bear fruit in old age; they shall be fresh and flourishing" (NKJV).

Born on February 13, 1903, in Indian Territory now known as Meridian, Oklahoma, this sturdy, vibrant, oak of a man, who is affectionately known by most as "Dad Clark," has weathered storms that might have toppled others—storms that include the Tulsa race riot of 1921, a devastating event in history that shattered his family when he was eighteen years old. His stepfather was killed and their home reduced to a smoldering pile of rubble.

Yet, somehow, the memories of this tragic event and other occurrences in his life have not stolen the sparkle from Dad Clark's eyes.

How has he done it? How has Otis Clark overcome such adversity and defeated all natural odds to live such a long life and remain so strong?

"There are several things," says Dad Clark, now 106 years of age.

One is having a solid relationship with God.

"If you're going to live long, get on God's side and stay there," says a confident Dad Clark. "No matter how many times you mess up, repent and stay on the winning side."

Another is forgiveness—something that not only has been a major key Dad Clark has used to unlock the door to living a long, productive Christian life, but one that has enabled him to preach the gospel for more than eighty years and see many come to know the Lord.

"Once I got on God's side, I forgave all those people," Dad Clark said. "I had to because I'd been forgiven."

Dad Clark said the realization of who he is in Christ, and the authority he has as a born-again believer, has been of great help to him.

"Most Christians don't have a revelation of what it means to be an heir with Jesus," says Dad Clark. "So instead of acting like royalty—a child of God—they act like they're nobody. That's the most important revelation a believer can get, because it'll change everything."

As someone who has walked in that revelation for many years

now, Dad Clark offers one simple piece of advice to believers who want to do the same: "Get rid of the fuss!"

"Proverbs 14:30 says, 'A heart at peace gives life to the body,'" Dad Clark says (NIV). "If you're going to live in peace you've got to get rid of fussing and frustration. Get rid of worry, because worry is nothing more than dwelling on negative things. It's important to speak only positive words about yourself and everyone else, but don't stop there. Go even further and refuse to have negative thoughts, negative emotions, or negative attitudes. Being negative will give you anxiety and stress and will raise your blood pressure. It'll make you sick.

"When you really *know* you're an heir to the kingdom of God, you know you're on the winning side so it doesn't matter how bad things might look, eventually everything will work out right. If you *know* you're an heir, what could you possibly worry about? When you get that revelation, you'll have a smile on your face and be optimistic too."

Dad Clark also attributes his longevity to living by spiritual principles and proper nutrition.

"The first and most important thing is to spend time every day with your Divine Creator," he says. "I believe in humbling myself before God by lying prostrate on the floor or kneeling to pray. You'll be refreshed in His presence....I also spend time meditating on God's Word every day, and that brings health to your body. And praying for other folks will bring God's blessings on you."

Dad Clark's philosophy regarding eating is simple: "The most important thing about food is to pray and thank God for it, and eat in moderation.

"Romans 14:2 says, 'One man's faith allows him to eat everything, but another man, whose faith is weak, eats only vegetables' [NIV]. I believe that meat makes men strong, so my faith allows me to eat meat, especially beef. I still enjoy cooking my own breakfast of steak and eggs or bacon and eggs. I like to make a pot of beef stew with garlic cloves, tomatoes, and potatoes.

"Another thing is that digestion starts in the mouth and a good rule is to chew each bite of food twenty-two times," Dad Clark adds.

Photo credit: Michael Augustat.

"I go quite a bit beyond that and chew my food thirty to forty times per bite. I use a toothpick after every meal and I still have all my teeth."

In addition to practicing good eating habits, Dad Clark stays active by doing such things as working in his yard and exercising in the pool.

"I take walks and always stop to smell the flowers," says Dad Clark. "The doctor says I have the heart of a thirty-five-year-old man. I can still thread a needle and mend my own clothes. I also enjoy soaking for a long time in a hot bath. I take one or two hot baths a day."

Despite his age, Dad Clark says he finds no reason to act as if he is 106.

"Most people get more set in their ways the older they get, but I refuse to do that. When I was ninety-seven, I had some business to take care of in Seattle so I drove from Atlanta to Seattle and back—alone. When I was ninety-eight, I drove to San Francisco and back. I'm always ready to try something new, and one way I do it is by following young folk around.... Don't tell me I can't do something, because with God *all* things are possible! My goodness, just believe the Bible."

And no one is trying to tell Dad Clark what he cannot do.

Today, at 106, he still preaches (he preached in Zimbabwe, Africa, in 2006 and 2007), exercises daily, spends time working in his yard, and even makes it a point to dress up in a suit and tie every day.

"I've lived through the Tulsa race riot, the pandemic flu of 1918, the Great Depression, and both world wars," Dad Clark says. "Now the economy is shaking again, but there's nothing to fear if you're on God's side, because God's side *always* wins."

—Adapted from Melanie Hemry, "Long Life, Strong Life,"
Believer's Voice of Victory, August 2009, 12–15;
Dr. Gwen Williams and Star Williams, *His Story, History, and His Secret: Life Through the Eyes of 105 Year Old Otis Grandville Clark.* © 2008. Used by permission.

Live Long, Finish Strong
Scriptures

The LORD said, My spirit shall not always strive with man, for that he also is flesh: yet his days shall be an hundred and twenty years. (Genesis 6:3)

Thou shalt go to thy fathers in peace; thou shalt be buried in a good old age. (Genesis 15:15)

Abraham was old, well advanced in age; and the LORD had blessed Abraham in all things.... This is the sum of the years of Abraham's life which he lived: one hundred and seventy-five years. Then Abraham breathed his last and died in a good old age, an old man and full of years, and was gathered to his people. (Genesis 24:1; 25:7–8 NKJV)

The days of Isaac were one hundred and eighty years. So Isaac breathed his last and died, and was gathered to his people, being old and full of days. (Genesis 35:28–29 NKJV)

The whole age of Jacob was an hundred forty and seven years.... And when Jacob had made an end of commanding his sons, he gathered up his feet into the bed, and yielded up the ghost, and was gathered unto his people. (Genesis 47:28; 49:33)

If thou wilt diligently hearken to the voice of the LORD thy God, and wilt do that which is right in his sight, and wilt give ear to his commandments, and keep all his statutes, I will put none of these diseases upon thee, which I have brought upon the Egyptians: for I am the LORD that healeth thee. (Exodus 15:26)

Ye shall serve the LORD your God, and he shall bless thy bread, and thy water; and I will take sickness away from the midst of thee. There shall nothing cast their young, nor be barren, in thy land: the number of thy days I will fulfil. (Exodus 23:25–26)

Remember this and keep it firmly in mind: The LORD is God both in heaven and on earth, and there is no other god! If you obey all the laws and commands that I will give you today, all will be well with you and your children. Then you will enjoy a long life in the land the LORD your God is giving you for all time. (Deuteronomy 4:39–40 NLT)

These are all the commands, laws, and regulations that the LORD your God told me to teach you so you may obey them in the land you are about to enter and occupy, and so you and your children and grandchildren might fear the LORD your God as long as you live. If you obey all his laws and commands, you will enjoy a long life. (Deuteronomy 6:1–2 NLT)

The LORD commanded us to do all these statutes, to fear the LORD our God, for our good always, that he might preserve us alive, as it is at this day. (Deuteronomy 6:24)

Lay up these my words in your heart and in your soul, and bind them for a sign upon your hand, that they may be as frontlets between your eyes. And ye shall teach them your children, speaking of them when thou sittest in thine house, and when thou walkest by the way, when thou liest down, and when thou risest up. And thou shalt write them upon the door posts of thine house, and upon thy gates: That your days may be multiplied, and the days of your children, in the land which the LORD sware unto your fathers to give them, as the days of heaven upon the earth. (Deuteronomy 11:18–21)

Observe and hear all these words which I command thee, that it may go well with thee, and with thy children after thee for ever, when thou doest that which is good and right in the sight of the LORD thy God. (Deuteronomy 12:28)

I call heaven and earth to record this day against you, that I have set before you life and death, blessing and cursing: therefore choose life, that both thou and thy seed may live: That thou mayest love the LORD thy God, and that thou mayest obey his voice, and that thou mayest cleave unto him: for he is thy life, and the length of thy days. (Deuteronomy 30:19–20)

Moses was an hundred and twenty years old when he died: his eye was not dim, nor his natural force abated. (Deuteronomy 34:7)

The LORD has kept me alive, as He said, these forty-five years, ever since the LORD spoke this word to Moses while Israel wandered in the wilderness; and now, here I am this day, eighty-five years old. As yet I am as strong this day as on the day that Moses sent me; just as my strength was then, so now is my strength for war, both for going out and for coming in. (Joshua 14:10–11 NKJV)

The joy of the LORD is your strength. (Nehemiah 8:10)

Thou shalt come to thy grave in a full age, like as a shock of corn cometh in his season. (Job 5:26)

Job [lived] an hundred and forty years, and saw his sons, and his sons' sons, even four generations. So Job died, being old and full of days. (Job 42:16–17)

Why art thou cast down, O my soul? and why art thou disquieted within me? hope thou in God: for I shall yet praise him, who is the health of my countenance, and my God. (Psalm 42:11)

My flesh and my heart faileth: but God is the strength of my heart, and my portion for ever. (Psalm 73:26)

Because he hath set his love upon me, therefore will I deliver him: I will set him on high, because he hath known my name. He shall call upon me, and I will answer him: I will be with him in trouble; I will deliver him, and honour him. With long life will I satisfy him, and show him my salvation. (Psalm 91:14–16)

The [uncompromisingly] righteous shall flourish like the palm tree [be long-lived, stately, upright, useful, and fruitful]; they shall grow like a cedar in Lebanon [majestic, stable, durable, and incorruptible]. Planted in the house of the Lord, they shall flourish in the courts of our God. [Growing in grace] they shall still bring forth fruit in old age; they shall be full of sap [of spiritual vitality] and [rich in the] verdure [of trust, love, and contentment]. (Psalm 92:12–14 AMP)

Bless the LORD, O my soul, and forget not all his benefits: who forgiveth all thine iniquities; who healeth all thy diseases; who redeemeth thy life from destruction; who crowneth thee with lovingkindness and tender mercies; who satisfieth thy mouth with good things; so that thy youth is renewed like the eagle's. (Psalm 103:2–5)

He brought them forth also with silver and gold: and there was not one feeble person among their tribes. (Psalm 105:37)

The right hand of the Lord is exalted: the right hand of the Lord doeth valiantly. I shall not die, but live, and declare the works of the Lord. (Psalm 118:16–17)

My son, forget not my law or teaching, but let your heart keep my commandments; for length of days and years of a life [worth living] and tranquility [inward and outward and continuing through old age till death], these shall they add to you. (Proverbs 3:1–2 AMP)

Happy is the man that findeth wisdom, and the man that getteth understanding. For the merchandise of it is better than the merchandise of silver, and the gain thereof than fine gold. She is more precious than rubies: and all the things thou canst desire are not to be compared unto her. Length of days is in her right hand; and in her left hand riches and honour. (Proverbs 3:13–16)

Hear, O my son, and receive my sayings; and the years of thy life shall be many. I have taught thee in the way of wisdom; I have led thee in right paths. (Proverbs 4:10–11)

My son, attend to my words; incline thine ear unto my sayings. Let them not depart from thine eyes; keep them in the midst of thine heart. For they are life unto those that find them, and health to all their flesh. Keep thy heart with all diligence; for out of it are the issues of life. (Proverbs 4:20–23)

The fear of the Lord prolongeth days: but the years of the wicked shall be shortened. (Proverbs 10:27)

There is that speaketh like the piercings of a sword: but the tongue of the wise is health. (Proverbs 12:18)

The fear of the Lord is a fountain of life, to depart from the snares of death. (Proverbs 14:27)

A relaxed attitude lengthens life; jealousy rots it away. (Proverbs 14:30 NLT)

A wholesome tongue is a tree of life: but perverseness therein is a breach in the spirit. (Proverbs 15:4)

A cheerful look brings joy to the heart; good news makes for good health. (Proverbs 15:30 NLT)

A merry heart doeth good like a medicine: but a broken spirit drieth the bones. (Proverbs 17:22)

Death and life are in the power of the tongue: and they that love it shall eat the fruit thereof. (Proverbs 18:21)

Fear of the LORD gives life, security, and protection from harm. (Proverbs 19:23 NLT)

True humility and fear of the LORD lead to riches, honor, and long life. (Proverbs 22:4 NLT)

Be not over much wicked, neither be thou foolish: why shouldest thou die before thy time? (Ecclesiastes 7:17)

Have you not known? Have you not heard? The everlasting God, the Lord, the Creator of the ends of the earth, does not faint or grow weary; there is no searching of His understanding. He gives power to the faint and weary, and to Him who has no might He increases strength [causing it to multiply and making it to abound]. Even youths shall faint and be weary, and [selected] young men shall feebly stumble and fall exhausted; but those who wait for the Lord [who expect, look for, and hope in Him] shall change and renew their strength and power; they shall lift their wings and mount up [close to God] as eagles [mount up to the sun]; they shall run and not be weary, they shall walk and not faint or become tired. (Isaiah 40:28–31 AMP)

Even to your old age I am he; and even to hoar hairs will I carry you: I have made, and I will bear; even I will carry, and will deliver you. (Isaiah 46:4)

He has borne our griefs (sicknesses, weaknesses, and distresses) and carried our sorrows and pains [of punishment], yet we [ignorantly] considered Him stricken, smitten, and afflicted by God [as if with leprosy]. But He was wounded for our transgressions, He was bruised for our guilt and iniquities; the chastisement [needful to obtain] peace and well-being for us was upon Him, and with the stripes [that wounded] Him we are healed and made whole. (Isaiah 53:4–5 AMP)

When the even was come, they brought unto him many that were possessed with devils: and he cast out the spirits with his word, and healed all that were sick: that it might be fulfilled which was spoken by Esaias the prophet, saying, Himself took our infirmities, and bare our sicknesses. (Matthew 8:16–17)

Jesus...withdrew himself from thence: and great multitudes followed him, and he healed them all. (Matthew 12:15)

Jesus...saith unto them, Have faith in God. For verily I say unto you, That whosoever shall say unto this mountain, Be thou removed, and be thou cast into the sea; and shall not doubt in his heart, but shall believe that those things which he saith shall come to pass; he shall have whatsoever he saith. Therefore I say unto you, What things soever ye desire, when ye pray, believe that ye receive them, and ye shall have them. (Mark 11:22–24)

[Jesus] came down with them, and stood in the plain, and the company of his disciples, and a great multitude of people out of all Judaea and Jerusalem, and from the sea coast of Tyre and Sidon, which came to hear him, and to be healed of their diseases; and they that were vexed with unclean spirits: and they were healed. And the whole multitude sought to touch him: for there went virtue out of him, and healed them all. (Luke 6:17–19)

The people, when they knew it, followed him: and he received them, and spake unto them of the kingdom of God, and healed them that had need of healing. (Luke 9:11)

I assure you, most solemnly I tell you, the person whose ears are open to My words [who listens to My message] and believes and trusts in and clings to and relies on Him Who sent Me has (possesses now) eternal life. And he does not come into judgment [does not incur sentence of judgment, will not come under condemnation], but he has already passed over out of death into life. (John 5:24 AMP)

God anointed Jesus of Nazareth with the Holy Ghost and with power: who went about doing good, and healing all that were oppressed of the devil; for God was with him. (Acts 10:38)

If by one man's offence death reigned by one; much more they which receive abundance of grace and of the gift of righteousness shall reign in life by one, Jesus Christ. (Romans 5:17)

The law of the Spirit of life in Christ Jesus hath made me free from the law of sin and death. (Romans 8:2)

If the Spirit of him that raised up Jesus from the dead dwell in you, he that raised up Christ from the dead shall also quicken your mortal bodies by his Spirit that dwelleth in you. (Romans 8:11)

Then cometh the end, when he shall have delivered up the kingdom to God, even the Father; when he shall have put down all rule and all authority and power. For he must reign, till he hath put all enemies under his feet. The last enemy that shall be destroyed is death. (1 Corinthians 15:24–26)

Christ hath redeemed us from the curse of the law, being made a curse for us: for it is written, Cursed is every one that hangeth on a tree: that the blessing of Abraham might come on the Gentiles through Jesus Christ; that we might receive the promise of the Spirit through faith. (Galatians 3:13–14)

Honour thy father and mother; which is the first commandment with promise; that it may be well with thee, and thou mayest live long on the earth. (Ephesians 6:2–3)

Is now made manifest by the appearing of our Saviour Jesus Christ, who hath abolished death, and hath brought life and immortality to light through the gospel. (2 Timothy 1:10)

He that will love life, and see good days, let him refrain his tongue from evil, and his lips that they speak no guile. (1 Peter 3:10)

He that hath the Son hath life; and he that hath not the Son of God hath not life. (1 John 5:12)

Beloved, I wish above all things that thou mayest prosper and be in health, even as thy soul prospereth. (3 John 2)

Blessed are they that do his commandments, that they may have right to the tree of life, and may enter in through the gates into the city....And let him that is athirst come. And whosoever will, let him take the water of life freely. (Revelation 22:14, 17)

Prayer for Salvation and Baptism in the Holy Spirit

Heavenly Father, I come to You in the name of Jesus. Your Word says, "Whosoever shall call on the name of the Lord shall be saved" (Acts 2:21). I am calling on You. I pray and ask Jesus to come into my heart and be Lord over my life according to Romans 10:9–10:

"If thou shalt confess with thy mouth the Lord Jesus, and shalt believe in thine heart that God hath raised him from the dead, thou shalt be saved. For with the heart man believeth unto righteousness; and with the mouth confession is made unto salvation." I do that now. I confess that Jesus is Lord, and I believe in my heart that God raised Him from the dead.

I am now reborn! I am a Christian—a child of Almighty God! I am saved! You also said in Your Word, "If ye then, being evil, know how to give good gifts unto your children: *how much more* shall your heavenly Father give the Holy Spirit to them that ask him?" (Luke 11:13, italics added). I'm also asking You to fill me with the Holy Spirit. Holy Spirit, rise up within me as I praise God. I fully expect to speak with other tongues as You give me the utterance (Acts 2:4). In Jesus' name, amen!

Begin to praise God for filling you with the Holy Spirit. Speak those words and syllables you receive—not in your own language, but the language given to you by the Holy Spirit. You have to use your own voice. God will not force you to speak. Don't be concerned with how it sounds. It is a heavenly language!

Continue with the blessing God has given you and pray in the Spirit every day.

You are a born-again, Spirit-filled believer. You'll never be the same!

Find a good church that boldly preaches God's Word and obeys it. Become a part of a church family who will love and care for you as you love and care for them.

We need to be connected to each other. It increases our strength in God. It's God's plan for us.

Make it a habit to watch the *Believer's Voice of Victory* television broadcast and become a doer of the Word, who is blessed in his doing (James 1:22–25).

Notes

Chapter 1: How Old Is Old?

1. U.S. Department of Health and Human Services, National Center for Health Statistics, "Deaths: Final data for 2005."
2. Ibid.
3. Alfred Jones, *Dictionary of Old Testament Proper Names* (Grand Rapids: Kregel Publications, 1990).
4. Nosson Scherman, *The Chumash*, vol. 1, *Bereishis/Genesis* (Brooklyn: Mesorah Publications, 1995), 5.
5. *Webster's New Twentieth Century Dictionary*, 2nd edition (The World Publishing Company, 1964).
6. See http://shalom.askdefine.com.

Chapter 2: Set Your Sights on 120 (or More!)

1. *Tehillim, A New Translation with a Commentary Anthologized from Talmudic, Midrashic and Rabbinic Sources* (Brooklyn: Mesorah Publications, 1977), 1127.
2. F. F. Bosworth, *Christ the Healer* (Grand Rapids: Revell, 1997), 40.
3. *Tehillim*, 1127.
4. *The Amplified Bible, Old Testament* (Grand Rapids: Zondervan, 1965, 1987).
5. Scherman, *The Chumash*, 31, 33.
6. Ibid., 27.

Chapter 3: If They Did It, Why Can't We?

1. See http://www.supercentenarian.com.
2. See information concerning the New England Centenarian Study conducted by the Boston University School of Medicine at http://www.bumc.bu.edu/centenarian/.
3. See http://www.nytimes.com/1997/08/05/world/jeanne-calment-worlds-elder-dies-at-122.html; http://www.wowzone.com/calment.htm; http://growingbolder.com/articles/health/aging/she-defines-human-lifespan-4636.html.
4. Ginnie Netherton, " 'Granny' May Be Oldest Person in State," *Tulsa World*, October 23, 1994.
5. "We Salute Rev. Lawrence Benjamin Scott," *Secure Retirement* magazine, January/February 1995.
6. Adam Clarke, *The Holy Bible, with a Commentary and Critical Notes: The Old Testament*, vol. 3, *Job to Solomon's Song* (New York: Abingdon, circa 1825), 506–7.
7. Clarke, *The Holy Bible*, 506.
8. Ibid.
9. Ibid.
10. Ibid.
11. Ibid., 507.
12. L. A. Johnson, "Detroit Woman, 112, Beats Back Burglar," *Detroit Free Press*, August 6, 1994.
13. Facts in the story about Johnny Miller are from Julie Boatman, "Pilots: Johnny Miller," *AOPA Pilot*, vol. 46, no. 12, December 2003, www.aopa.org; and Johnny Miller, "The Miller Maintenance Plan," *American Bonanza Society*, December 2006.
14. *Webster's Collegiate Dictionary*, 11th ed. (Springfield, MA: 2006).
15. *Webster's New Twentieth Century Dictionary*.

Chapter 4: Putting the Gold Back in the Golden Years

1. *Webster's New Twentieth Century Dictionary*.
2. Ibid.
3. *Tehillim, A New Translation with a Commentary Anthologized from Talmudic, Midrashic and Rabbinic Sources* (Brooklyn: Mesorah Publications, 1977), 1409.
4. Ibid.

5. Robert Young, *Young's Analytical Concordance to the Bible* (Peabody, MA: Hendrickson Publishers, 1984).

Chapter 5: Protecting Your Fountain of Youth

1. F. F. Bosworth, *Christ the Healer* (Grand Rapids: Revell, 1997), 245.
2. Young, *Young's Analytical Concordance*.
3. E. W. Bullinger, *The Companion Bible* (Grand Rapids: Kregel, 1999), 7–8.
4. Taylor Gandossy, "TV Viewing at 'All-Time High,' Neilsen Says": http://www.cnn.com/2009/SHOWBIZ/TV/02/24/us.video.neilsen.

Chapter 6: One Sure Way to Shorten Your Life

1. E. W. Bullinger, *The Companion Bible* (Grand Rapids: Kregel, 1990), 812.
2. Norman Williams and George Otis, *Terror at Tenerife* (Van Nuys, CA: Bible Voice, 1977).

Chapter 7: The Ultimate Guide to Longevity

1. Kenneth S. Wuest, *The New Testament: An Expanded Translation* (Grand Rapids: Eerdmans Publishing Company, 1961).
2. Rob Stein, "Scientists Think Emotional Strain Increases Wear on Healthy Bodies," *Washington Post*, 29 November 2004.
3. Jordan Rubin, *The Maker's Diet* (New York: Berkley, 2004), 34.
4. *Webster's New Twentieth Century Dictionary*.

Chapter 8: Spiritual Antioxidants: The Rejuvenating Power of the Fruit of the Spirit

1. See http://www.psychosomatic.org/media_ctr/press/annual/2005/30.html.
2. Gary Small, *The Longevity Bible* (New York: Hyperion, 2007), esp. chapter 1.
3. Prevention.com. "10 Steps to the Body You Want" by Pamela M. Peeke, MD, MPH. ©Rodale, Inc., 2005.
4. See http://findarticles.com/p/articles/ml_m1355/isn26_v88ao_17623288.
5. Don Colbert, *Deadly Emotions: Understand the Mind-Body-Spirit Connection That Can Heal or Destroy You* (Nashville: Thomas Nelson, 2003), xii.

6. Ibid.

7. Ibid., 40–41.

8. Ibid., 169–70.

9. *Webster's New Twentieth Century Dictionary*.

10. Small, *The Longevity Bible*; and also see http://www.psychologytoday.com/articles/pto-20031202-000001.html; http://abcnews.go.com/Health/DepressionRiskFactors/story?id=4355916; http://www.4therapy.com/consumer/life_topics/ article/7151/110/Depression%2C+Bone+Mass%2C+and+Osteoporosis.

11. Colbert, *Deadly Emotions*, 182–83.

12. *Webster's Collegiate Dictionary*.

13. Charles Finney, "Joy in God," sermon from *Oberlin Evangelist*, September 27, 1843.

14. Kenneth S. Wuest, *Wuest's Word Studies: From the Greek New Testament, for the English Reader* (Grand Rapids: Eerdmans, 1979).

15. Colbert, *Deadly Emotions*, 6.

16. Ibid., 17.

17. See www.thecentenarian.co.uk.

18. Kenneth Samuel Wuest, *Word Studies in the Green New Testament, for the English Reader* (Grand Rapids: Eerdmans Publishing Company, 1980).

Chapter 9: God's Healing Promises: Good at Any Age

1. James Strong, *Strong's Exhaustive Concordance of the Bible* (Nashville: Thomas Nelson, 1984), H 3190.

2. W. E. Vine, Merril F. Unger, and William White Jr., *Vine's Complete Expository Dictionary of Old and New Testament Words* (Nashville: Thomas Nelson, 1985), 295.

3. Young, *Young's Analytical Concordance*.

4. Dodie Osteen, *Healed of Cancer* (Houston: Lakewood Church Publications, 1986, 2003), 9.

5. Young, *Young's Analytical Concordance*.

6. Harold J. Chadwick, *How to Be Filled with Spiritual Power* (Alachua, FL: Bridge-Logos Publications, 2006).

7. Young, *Young's Analytical Concordance*.

Chapter 10: The Live-Long Lifestyle of Faith

1. See www.torah.com.

Chapter 11: A Divine Departure

1. Robert V. Bosworth, *Christ the Healer: The Ultimate Triumph* (Grand Rapids: Revell, 2000), 246–47.
2. *The Artscroll Tanach Series: Tehillim/Psalms* (New York: Mesorah Publications, 2002), 1393.
3. Joe McIntyre, *E. W. Kenyon and His Message of Faith: The True Story* (Orlando, FL: Creation House, 1997), 171.
4. *Tehillim, A New Translation.*